Volume

KT-212-677

SAGE ANNUAL REVIEWS OF COMMUNICATION RESEARCH

Nonverbal Interaction

JOHN M. WIEMANN
and
RANDALL P. HARRISON
Editors

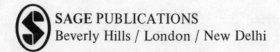

SAGE PUBLICATIONS
Beverly Hills / London / New Delhi

For information address:

SAGE Publications, Inc.
275 South Beverly Drive
Beverly Hills, California 90212

SAGE Publications India Pvt. Ltd.
C-236 Defence Colony
New Delhi 110 024, India

SAGE Publications Ltd
28 Banner Street
London EC1Y 8QE, England

Printed in the United States of America

Library of Congress Cataloging in Publication Data

Main entry under title:

Nonverbal interaction.

(Sage annual reviews of communication research ;
v. 11)
1. Nonverbal communication.   I. Wiemann, John M.
II. Harrison, Randall, 1929-   . III. Series.
P99.5.N64   1982   001.56   82-20539
ISBN 0-8039-1930-1
ISBN 0-8039-1931-X (pbk.)

FIRST PRINTING

NONVERBAL INTERACTION

SAGE ANNUAL REVIEWS OF COMMUNICATION RESEARCH

To Mary and Betty

CONTENTS

INTRODUCTION
Non-Language Aspects of Social Interaction

John M. Wiemann and Randall P. Harrison

NONVERBAL COMMUNICATION appears to be swift and subtle. A similar observation might be made about the domain of nonverbal research; it is fast-growing and increasingly complex. In fact, the increase in the literature has been so dramatic that most authors feel obliged to take note of it—as we do here. One explanation for the growth is the variety of topics that have come to be considered relevant aspects of nonverbal behavior: Anything that might be informative and is not spoken language has been treated by one author or another as nonverbal communication. In this volume we take a more narrow view and focus on the non-language, gestural aspects of face-to-face interaction.

The importance of informal, social interaction in the conduct of our daily lives is beyond dispute. However, the "nonverbal" domain has received little systematic attention. While it would be presumptuous to think that any single volume could redress this situation, we do hope that this collection calls attention to the pervasive role *movement* plays in structuring and defining our relationships. Non-language messages generated by movement, unlike their language counterparts, are unique in that they convey responsiveness on a moment-by-moment basis to the others present in face-to-face interaction. They are the vehicles by which people influence and acknowledge influence attempts.

By limiting our concern to social communication, we omit coverage of such "nonverbal" phenomena as architecture, pictures, music, interior decorating, dress, and the like. Message modalities such as these may be communicative in some fashion. They are frequently crucial in "setting the stage" for relational messages. But they are of a different genre from messages produced by movement of the body (including the vocal apparatus).

The apparently all-inclusive label, *nonverbal communication,* has been something of a hindrance to scholars. First, it seems to have led us to lump all non-language behaviors and artifacts with potential message value into one amorphous category. This "non" category has then been juxtaposed with the verbal (language) category.

As we have indicated, important distinctions should be made among phenomena typically grouped under the rubric "nonverbal communication." Furthermore, as Kendon argues in Chapter 1, there is a close ontological relationship between language and gesture. This relationship may have been obscured by social scientists allotting primacy to verbal behavior in the communication system. Kendon's essay calls into question the subordinate status of gesture vis-à-vis language.

The complexity of the contribution of nonverbal behavior to people's definition of their relationships is clearly illustrated by Knapp (Chapter 6). When we think of social relationships, we tend to focus on their affiliative aspects. Knapp takes a comprehensive look at a particular type of social relationship, one that is proceeding toward intimacy. He proposes a framework for viewing changes in nonverbal behavior as intimacy in the relationship changes. His analysis goes beyond the typical consideration of behavior of strangers in initial interactions, and the model he proposes provides for a global evaluation of relationships as they develop or decay.

Close examination of single modalities provides compelling evidence of the centrality of moment-to-moment behaviors in our evaluation of our relationships. Heslin and Alper's review of the literature on touch (Chapter 2) illustrates how the changing relational context influences the "meaning" assigned to various types of touch. It also provides good examples of three major methodologies that have been used to examine nonverbal messages: judge studies, laboratory experiments, and field observation.

Burgoon's exploration of the use of interpersonal space (Chapter 3) underscores the analogic and ambiguous nature of our behavior. Taking the violation of cultural expectations as her theoretical frame, she demonstrates how various contextual features interact with proximity to give meaning to behavior.

A major issue in this perspective on nonverbal communication in relationships is how people use behaviors to accomplish their interpersonal goals. Both Cappella (Chapter 4) and Duncan (Chapter 5) address this issue. Cappella discusses involvement as a transient state of a person in interaction which is given overt expression (as opposed to, for example, a personality- or communicator-style trait). Involvement can lead to influence of the other and thus be seen as strategic. Mutual involvement seems to lead to attraction and other positive relational outcomes as well as mutual influence.

The relationship of conversational structure to interaction strategy is directly addressed by Duncan. He argues that it is structure that imparts meaning to individual differences in conversation. Duncan's emphasis is on the value of structural research, its rationale and methodological issues.

Buck (Chapter 7) and O'Sullivan (Chapter 8) are also concerned with individual differences and methodological issues. "Nonverbal receiving ability" is treated as a social skill by Buck. He reviews instrumentation for assessing this ability and finds little relationship among extant measures. After discussing the probable reasons for this apparent disarray, Buck proposes a conceptualization of receiving ability that gives an important role to innate factors in the human perceptual system.

O'Sullivan suggests a basic theoretical model for assessing measuring instruments for nonverbal communication research. She provides an historical perspective on the difficult task of developing adequate measures and suggests criteria against which instrumentation can be judged.

Finally, we provide an overview and summary of the broader issues of nonverbal research—which, for those new to this area, might be an appropriate starting point. Given the current status of nonverbal communication scholarship, as reflected in this volume, we offer some thoughts about the future of theory, research, and practice.

Chapter 1

GESTURE AND SPEECH
How They Interact

Adam Kendon

THE WORD "GESTURE" in this chapter will be taken to mean any visible bodily action by which meaning is given voluntary expression. "Gesture" is to be considered separate from emotional expression; it also does not include those various minor tics, mannerisms, or "nervous movements" which, though informative to the eye of another, are not treated in interaction as part of the individual's intended "official" or "given" expression. Practical actions will also not be considered as gestures, even if, as is sometimes the case, such actions have an expressive purpose. Only if a person is seen to pantomime a practical action will this be considered a part of gesture.

Gesture includes such obvious movements as thumbing the nose, beckoning, or waving; it includes such spontaneous pantomime as a person may use when at a loss for words; and it includes the arm wavings and head waggings of vigorous talk. An exact definition is not possible. For the most part, participants in social interaction have little difficulty in distinguishing actions that are intentional and communicative from those that are not (Kendon, 1978), but borderline examples can easily be found.

Sometimes these may be deliberately created. Morris et al. (1979) report several examples of gestures that are considered so offensive they have been made illegal. As a result, versions of them have evolved that have

AUTHOR'S NOTE: This chapter was written while I was in receipt of a National Science Foundation grant, BNS 8024173. I would also like to acknowledge a grant from the Henry R. Luce Foundation to Connecticut College, which has made my presence at that institution possible. It may be noted that in the interests of space, I have been as conservative as possible in citations. Where I had a choice, I have cited reviews that contain good bibliographies of further work, rather than citing separately the many original studies that have here been considered.

an appearance of not being properly "gestural." For example, in Malta, the gesture known as the "Italian salute" has been modified so that it can be mistaken for a mere rubbing of the arm: The left arm is held straight, with the hand clenched in a fist, while the right hand gently rubs the inside of the left elbow.

Examples such as this make it clear that participants are readily able to recognize the features an action must have for it to appear deliberate and communicative. To the extent that an action is regarded as having these features it may be regarded as gestural. It is a matter for a future investigation, however, to establish just what those features are.

Most people consider gesture to be part of an individual's effort at utterance. They may serve as communicative acts on their own, or, in association with speech, they are said to emphasize, illustrate, lend dramatic impact to whatever a person may be trying to say. However, gesture has properties very different from those of speech. In particular, it employs space as well as time in the creation of expressive forms, whereas speech can use only time. We find, therefore, that the way information may be preserved in speech, as compared to gesture, tends to be very different.

In spoken utterance, the elements by which meanings are conveyed are concatenated in temporal sequence, and the way such sequences are organized depends not so much upon what meaning is being conveyed as it does upon rules of syntax. Whether one is describing action, referring to the visible appearances of things, or giving an account of spatial relationships, in spoken language the lexical elements have to be related to one another by rules that govern either their form or their sequential order or both. These rules impose a structure on spoken utterance that conforms it to the rules of the language system, in the first instance, and only indirectly, if at all, to any aspect of the structure of what is being referred to. In contrast, in gesture, motions can be employed that have a direct relationship, in their form, to action sequences. Pictorial diagrams may be produced; spatial relationships can be directly portrayed; and parts of the body, or even the whole body (though rarely) can be moved around as if they were actual objects. This means that there are possibilities available for expression through gesture of a different order from those available through spoken utterance.

In view of such differences, the close relationship between gesture and speech appears remarkable. How can it be that a person can employ two such very different modes of representation, often simultaneously? What implications does this have for our understanding of the nature of mental representation, the processes of speech production, our concept of language, and the management of referential communication?

In what follows, after a brief consideration of classifications of gesture, I review descriptive studies of how gesticulation relates to speech. I then look at certain neurologically oriented studies and consider work on the development of gesturing in children. This, I argue, establishes the *separate* character of speech and gesture at the same time as it shows how they are *functionally* united. After a brief discussion of the significance of gesticulation for theories of mental representation and the role it may play in facilitating speech production, I examine its communicative functions. Here it is indeed appropriate to speak of gesture as a partner of speech, for we shall see how various are the ways in which it may make its contribution to the overall enterprise of the utterance. Gesture that functions communicatively in a fully autonomous way is discussed, and, in a concluding section, I comment on differences and similarities between gesticulation, autonomous gesture, and sign languages.

VARIETIES OF GESTURE

Gesture, as defined above, encompasses a wide range of phenomena. Most who have written on the subject have proposed classifications of gesture. A review of these studies shows that, despite differences in terminology, there is much underlying agreement.

Classifications of two sorts have been offered: *semiotic* classifications, which arrange gestures according to the ways they achieve their meanings, and *functional* classifications, concerned mainly with the way gestures relate to speech. It will be noted that quite often, in these classifications, these principles are not clearly distinguished.

All semiotic classifications recognize distinctions between gestures that realize their meaning through *pointing*, gestures that *characterize* or *depict* their meaning in some way, and gestures in which a connection with the referent is purely conventional. The latter are sometimes called *symbolic*. Wundt (1921/1973) offered a detailed classification along these lines. More recently, Mandel (1977) has developed a detailed analysis of "iconic devices" for American Sign Language, and Kendon (1980c) has further developed this analysis in a discussion of a sign language from Papua New Guinea and of autonomous gestures in speech communities (Kendon, 1981).

Classifications of a more functional sort have been offered by Kaulfers (1931), Efron (1941/1972), Barakat (1969), Freedman (1972), Ekman (1977), Wiener et al. (1972), and McNeill and Levy (1982). Kaulfers (1931) is the only one among the foregoing who distinguishes a class of gestures of interactional management—gestures of greeting, request, demand, refusal, and the like—setting them apart from gestures that play a role in discourse. This distinction is useful and probably sound. There is reason to think that gestures of this sort have a different developmental history from those that are concerned with discourse (Bruner, 1978; Bates, 1979).

Of the other authors listed, we find that Efron (1941/1972), Barakat (1969), Ekman (1977), and Wiener et al. (1972) all recognize a class of gestures that function as complete utterances in themselves, independently of speech, and show a high degree of formalization. Various terms have been proposed: "semiotic gestures" (Barakat), "symbolic or emblematic gestures" (Efron), "emblems" (Ekman), "formal pantomimic gestures" (Wiener et al.). Here we prefer to use the term *autonomous gestures* for this class.

In regard to speech-related gestures, Efron (and Ekman, following Efron; see, especially, Ekman, 1977), Freedman (1972), Wiener et al. (1972), and McNeill and Levy (1982) all recognize a distinction between those that appear to represent some aspect of the content of what is being said and those that have a more abstract relationship. Thus, McNeill and Levy distinguish "iconic" gestures from "beats." Freedman distinguishes "motor primacy" movements, which, when they occur with coherent speech, he refers to as "representational." These movements are contrasted with "speech primacy" movements, which are not representational and which, like McNeill and Levy's "beats," are subordinated to the rhythm of the speech. Efron refers to gestures that provide a pictorial representation of content as "physiographic." He terms "ideographic" those gestures that are "logical" or "discursive" in meaning and that portray the course of the ideational process itself (Efron 1941/1972: 96). These gestures include movements that are clearly the same as "beats" or "speech primacy movements." But they also include other movement patterns to which McNeill and Levy would probably refer as "metaphoric" and which Wiener et al. would call "semantic modifying and relational gestures." These gestures, Wiener et al. note, usually accompany speech and have a much more abstract meaning than those they term "pantomimic gestures"—which are clearly similar to Efron's "physiographic" gestures or McNeill and Levy's "iconic" gestures.

In the present essay, we shall use the term *gesticulation* to refer to all gesturing that occurs in intimate association with speech. We propose this as a purely descriptive term that makes no judgment about how such gesturing relates to the speech with which it is associated (as Ekman's widely used term "illustrators" or Freedman's term "object-focused movements" clearly do). The way gesticulation relates to speech, as our review has just shown, is clearly a complex matter. It seems too early to settle on any particular terminology to describe it.

DESCRIPTIVE STUDIES OF GESTICULATION

It is a common observation that, when a person speaks, muscular systems besides those of the lips, tongue, and jaws often become active. There are movements of the face and eyes, of the head, arms, and hands, and sometimes of the torso and legs which even to a casual observer, are seen as integrated with the flow of speech. Detailed analyses of films of speakers by Condon (summarized in Condon, 1976) have shown that there is a rhythmic coordination or synchrony between the smallest discriminable phrases of movement and those of speech, even below the level of the syllable. Perhaps we should not find this surprising, for the individual speaker is a single organism. A *lack* of coordination would be much more remarkable, and indeed Condon suggests that where this is observed, as it sometimes is, marked pathology is indicated. Condon's findings imply that a similar integration of action would be found if we were to analyze, in a similar way, the flow of movement in someone engaged in activities other than speaking, although to my knowledge this has not been done.

For Condon (1976), the flow of movement is organized into a succession of phrases that are themselves incorporated into phrases of movement at higher and higher levels of integration. At these higher levels of integration, however, there is much differentiation in the way the various parts of the body are involved. For example, one may observe the sweep of an arm or the turn of a head occurring over an entire phrase, while movements in the face or the fingers are coordinated with smaller units of speech.

Just which patterns of movement are regarded by others as gesticulations has never been systematically examined. It would appear, however, that some degree of body-part differentiation is required and that the phrases of movement must have a level of integration at least equivalent to that of a phrase of several words before being picked out in this manner. Movements that are regarded as gesticular phrases occur most frequently in the hands and arms and in the head and face. Hand and arm gesticulation has been most fully investigated, and the studies discussed in most detail below are all concerned with this. However, much more attention should be paid to the participation of the head and face. The few studies that have dealt with head and face gesticulation are mentioned first.

Ekman (1979) has described some examples of facial gesturing during talk and has proposed some criteria by which such actions may be distinguished from facial affect displays. Birdwhistell (1970) describes face and head actions as serving as kinesic markers of linguistic stress and pronominal and deictic words. The involvement of the head in gesticulation has also been noted by Efron (1941/1972), and the patterning of head and eye movements with speech has been described by Scheflen (1964) and Kendon (1972).

Gesticulation in the forelimbs can be observed to be organized in phrases of movement, and these phrases of movement can often be observed to be of some complexity, incorporating smaller phrases of movement within them (Kendon, 1980a). A unit of gesticulation, which may be called a Gesture Unit, is composed of an excursion of the forelimb from a position of rest into free space in front of the speaker and back again to a position of rest. During the course of such an excursion, one or more Gesture Phrases may be observed to occur. A Gesture Phrase is distinguished by a nucleus of movement, termed the *stroke,* in which the gesticulating limb performs some definite pattern of movement, set apart within the overall flow by having distinct dynamic and spatial qualities. Ordinary observers identify the stroke as "the gesture" and see the movement that precedes it and succeeds it as serving only to move the gesticulatory limb to a position suitable for performing the stroke or away to the rest position again (Kendon, 1978).

The flow of gesticulatory activity may thus be partitioned into its respective Gesture Units, and these Gesture Units may then be further analyzed for the one or more Gesture Phrases they may contain. The boundaries of such units may be plotted out on a time-based chart and matched to the concurrent flow of speech. If this is done it is found that the hierarchy of phrases of gesticulation fits rather closely with the hierarchy of phrases of speech (Kendon, 1972, 1980a). Thus, if the flow of speech is segmented into its Tone Units (phonologically defined syllabic groupings so called by Crystal and Davy [1979] comprising a single intonation tune), it is usually found that there is a Gesture Phrase to correspond to each Tone Unit. Furthermore, it is found that, corresponding to the higher-level groupings into which Tone Units can be shown to be organized, there are higher-level organizations of gesticulation. For example, in one analysis (Kendon, 1972), for each new Gesture Unit, the speaker embarked upon a new grouping of Tone Units that constituted a Locution—a grouping approximating a complete sentence—while for each Tone Unit within the Locution a distinct Gesture Phrase could be found.

A Tone Unit is the equivalent of the speech unit known as the "phonemic clause." This is probably the lowest-level unit in terms of which speech production is planned (Boomer, 1978). These units match rather closely units of speech that package one unit of meaning or idea. Occasionally it is found, however, that one such idea unit takes more than one Tone Unit for its expression. Rarely one finds more than one idea unit within a single Tone Unit. In these cases, if gesticulation is going on, it is found that Gesture Phrases match the ideas rather than the phonological phrases. This observation, along with certain other observations on how Gesture Phrases may continue to completion even though their corresponding Tone Units have been disrupted (and, furthermore, that Gesture

Phrases are often begun, and sometimes completed, in advance of the Tone Units to which they are related), suggests that the successive phrases of gesticulation are separate but parallel encodings of *units of meaning.* That is to say, at the same time as the speaker packages meanings into phrases of speech, he or she is also packaging meanings into phrases of gesture. Gesture Phrases and Tone Units tend to match because they are being produced under the guidance of a single conceptual unit. However, gesticulation and speech are separately generated; indeed, as we shall later see, they may serve in the representation of different *aspects* of the single conceptual unit by which they are being guided.

Observations that accord well with this conclusion have been reported independently by McNeill (1979) and Schegloff (n.d.). McNeill (1979) reports an extensive analysis of the occurrence of phrases of gesticulation in the speech of two mathematicians engaged in a technical discussion. He categorized gestures (defined in a way quite similar to the notion of Gesture Phrase) in terms of the kinds of relationship they exhibited with the conceptual structure of the concurrent speech. He found a close fit between the occurrence of a gesture and the occurrence of a speech unit expressing whole concepts or relationships between concepts. In further analyses McNeill shows that the "peak" of the gesture (which corresponds to the *stroke* of the Gesture Phrase) coincides with the conceptual focal point of the speech unit.

McNeill (forthcoming) suggests that each new unit of gesture, at least if it is of the sort that can be considered representational (and not formless and fully subordinated to the speech rhythm) appears with each new unit of meaning. Each such gesture, he suggests, is a manifestation of what, in the current conceptual representation of the discourse, is regarded by the speaker as the most important new meaning. It may be noted that a very similar suggestion has also been made by Delis et al. (1979), on the basis of a study of gesturing in aphasic patients as well as in normals.

In other work, in which people have been observed as they retell the story of an animated cartoon they have just watched, McNeill and Levy (1982) confirm these findings, but they suggest that gesticulations that can be regarded as representations of meaning ("iconic" and also "metaphoric" gestures, in their terms) are distributed differently in relation to what is being said than are the more formless, purely rhythmic gesticulations they term "beats." They find that iconic gestures are, in narrative discourse at least, associated with those speech segments that serve to present the successive stages of the story. Beats, on the other hand, co-occur with extranarrational speech units in which background is explained, the characters' motives are commented on, and the like. McNeill and Levy suggest that with iconic gestures speakers provide representations of their conceptual models of the events they are describing. Beats, on the other hand, mark out units of discourse organization.

A study by Marcos (1979) also shows that it may be important to consider representational gestures as having a separate significance. Marcos compared rates of gesticulation in subjects when observed speaking their native language and when speaking a second language. He found many more nonrepresentational gestures during second-language speaking but no difference in the rate of representational gesturing. As Barrosso (quoted in Freedman, 1977) has suggested, the problem facing someone speaking a language with which he or she is not familiar is not that of deciding what to say so much as that of finding the words and phrases with which to say it. The higher rate of rhythmical, nonrepresentational gestures observed during second-language speaking, then, may be attributed to the smaller word groupings into which second-language speaking is organized. In second-language speaking there are more units of speech execution, and therefore more gestural markers of such units will be observed.

In addition, more detailed analysis is needed before we can gain a clearer picture of the importance of the distinction between beats and iconic gestures. My own observations suggest that this distinction may not be a categorical one. A Gesture Unit may begin, with its first Gesture Phrase, as a clearly representational gesture, and subsequent Gesture Phrases may then be enacted in which the hand form and arm position of the iconic Gesture Phrase are retained, but the movement patterns become merely rhythmical. It is as if, at the outset, the content of the discourse to follow is given gestural representation, features of which are then held as a "frame" for the speech that follows, the successive units of which are then marked motorically with "beats."

It can be seen from the foregoing that gesticulation is organized as part of the same overall unit of action by which speech is also organized. Gesticulation, however, is not dependent upon speech. Rather, it is as if gesture and speech are available as two separate modes of representation and are coordinate because both are being guided by the same overall aim. That aim is to produce a pattern of action that will accomplish the representation of a meaning. It appears that this is done in organized units. In speech these are identified as Tone Units or phonemic clauses. It is in association with these that iconic gesturing is organized. Gesture is also organized in relation to the patterns of action involved in the actual execution of such speech units. As the successive units of the spoken utterance are accomplished, we may see motoric action marking them off in the form of beats. We have suggested that such beats are often fused with iconic gesturing and might perhaps be thought of as arising from the entrainment of iconic gesturing to the rhythms of speech production.

NEUROLOGICAL BASES OF GESTURE

Gesture and speech, then, are separate representational systems that are produced together because they are under joint control. Work from a neurological perspective lends additional support to this view.

Kimura (1976) and Feyereisen (1977) have reported that gesticulation in right-handed individuals tends to be produced mainly by the right hand, while no hand preference is shown for nongesticulatory movements or for movements of the hands made during activities other than speech. This finding suggests that gesticulation and speech are under the governance of the same parts of the brain. Kimura's finding that left-handers (who are known not to be as fully lateralized for speech control as right-handers are) tend to be bilateral in their gesticulations reinforces this conclusion.

Sousa-Poza et al. (1979) and McNeill and Levy (1982) report that such hand preference in gesticulation applies mainly to representational or iconic gesticulations. Beats or other nonrepresentational gestures tend not to be lateralized. This suggests that it is the program governing the organization of representational units—whether these be gestured or spoken—that is mediated by the same centers of control in the brain.

Further light is shed on the neurological control of gesture and its relationship to speech by studies of people with brain damage. Clinical neurologists have long recognized that patients suffering from brain damage that impairs speech (left-hemisphere damage in most cases) also show impairment in their ability to use gesture. This has usually been attributed to apraxia and considered somewhat separate from aphasia, although there is a minority opinion of long standing that gestural impairment in aphasia has the same fundamental origin as the aphasia itself—that it stems from an impairment in the capacity to make use of symbols (Duffy and Liles, 1979). Recently, systematic studies of the gestural capacities of aphasics have been reported.

Cicone et al. (1979) report a study of four aphasic patients, with two controls for comparison, in which the character of their gesticulation and its relationship to speech was studied as it could be observed in informal interviews. To date, this is the only study of its kind. Of the four patients observed, two had been diagnosed as having lesions in the anterior (pre-Rolandic) region of the brain. They exhibited the sparse, agrammatic but intelligible speech of the Broca's aphasic. The other two exhibited fluent but grammatically and semantically incoherent speech. They were diagnosed as Wernicke's aphasics, probably suffering from posterior temporal lobe lesions. Cicone et al. report that the character of the gesticulations of these patients closely matched the character of their speech. Thus, for the Broca's aphasics "output in both modalities is relatively sparse, simple and punctate," but it is "generally informative and clearly intelligible." For the other two patients the gesturing is reported as "frequent, relatively complex, often elaborated" but generally unclear and confusing, like their speech (Cicone et al., 1979: 332). It should be mentioned that Alajouanine and Lhermitte (1974) report summaries of clinical experience that are fully in accord with Cicone et al.'s findings.

Cicone et al. discuss several possible explanations of their findings and conclude that the best explanation is that gesture and speech are separate, but both under the control of a single "central organizer"–a conclusion exactly in accord with the view put forward here.

All of the other studies of gesture in aphasia have examined patients in formal test situations for their abilities to recognize and/or to employ pantomimes and, in some studies, standardized symbolic gestures as well. All of the studies reported so far show a good correlation between degree of aphasia and degree of impairment in gestural abilities. Goodglass and Kaplan (1963), whose investigation was the first of these systematic studies, concluded that the gestural impairment they found could best be understood as a consequence of apraxia. Their interpretation has been criticized on various grounds by Duffy et al. (1975) and by Pickett (1974). These authors offer further data and conclude that gestural impairment in aphasia is best accounted for by an impairment of symbolic capacities rather than in terms of apraxia. Duffy and Duffy (1981) provide three additional studies that strengthen this conclusion. Other support is provided by Gainotti and Lemmo (1976), who show how gestural impairment in aphasia is strongly correlated with impairment in ability to recognize word meanings.

Several other studies have reported, however, that such a capacity to perceive symbolic meaning may sometimes be impaired only for the aural modality. In these cases, patients have been able to benefit from training in the use of gesture systems derived from American Indian sign language (Amerind, devised by Skelly, 1979) or from American Sign Language. Several investigators have reported that patients who can benefit in this way can also read. Peterson and Kirshner (1981), who review these studies, suggest, accordingly (as does Varney, 1978), that symbolic abilities may to some extent be modality-specific. Although it is clear that they are closely related neurologically, visual symbolic abilities do show some degree of separateness from aural symbolic abilities. This is just what we would expect to find if gesture and speech are separate representational modalities, yet both recruited to the service of the same aim.

DEVELOPMENTAL STUDIES

Studies of the development of gesticulation in infants and children are few in number. From what has been done so far, it appears that the child's capacity to make use of gesture expands in close association with growth in his or her capacity for spoken language. However, the way children use gesture appears to be different from the way it is used by adults. It seems that adults use gesture in relation to speech in a much more precise and specialized way. It appears that, with age, there is an increasing degree of coordination between the two modalities.

Most of the work on gesture in children has been done with the very young. Several different researchers (see Bullowa, 1979, for good examples) have shown that an active *interaction* between mother and child is established at an extremely early age. Reciprocated rhythmic exchanges of expressive action and vocalization are entered into in the first few months, and the child is soon thereafter able to initiate requests by using quite well-formalized gestures. Detailed studies of how such gestures become established have been provided by Lock (1980) and Clark (1978). Several investigators, among whom Bruner (1978, for example) is especially conspicuous, have maintained that many structural features of language, such as the understanding of the difference between subject and object and the nature of predication, are first established for the child through social interaction. Participation in turn-taking, in the giving and receiving of objects, and so on, in the view of Bruner and others, provides the child with expectation structures that are at the foundation of grammatical organization.

It is becoming apparent, however, as the social interaction of the very young with their mothers is studied longitudinally, that the gestured actions which provide the first evidence of the child's ability to engage in language-like communication, far from being replaced as the capacity for speech emerges, expand and elaborate. Thus, Bates (1979: 112) concludes from her longitudinal study of 24 children between the ages of 9 and 14 months that her findings "do not support a model of communicative development in which preverbal communication is replaced by language." Language and gesture, she writes, "are related via some common base involving both communication and reference." As this common base develops, the capacity for both gesture and speech develops. A similar conclusion is reached by Wilkinson and Rembold (1981: 184) in their longitudinal study of somewhat older children: "As children become more aware of grammar and more facile at expressing it verbally, they also become more skilled in expressing grammar gesturally."

Studies of gesture in older children have, for the most part, concentrated on providing evidence about changes in the child's capacities for symbolization (see Barten, 1979, for a recent summary). However, there are four studies that look at the way gesture is employed in relation to speech and how it changes between early childhood, middle childhood, and the end of adolescence.

Freedman (1977) observed the gesticular behavior of children between the ages of 4 and 14 as they provided definitions of common words. It was found, in the first place, that more gesturing occurred in older children but that there was a relative decline with age in the frequency with which representational gestures were employed. In the second place, however, it was found that there was a change with age in the way representational gestures were related to speech. The 4-year-olds performed these gestures well before they had attempted any speech. The 10-year-olds' elaborate representational gestures were observed throughout the verbalization, as if, in Freedman's (1977: 121) words, "the child surrounded himself with a visual, perceptual and imagistic aspect of his message." Among the 14-year-olds, representational gestures occurred selectively, usually in relation to a single word, with which they were highly coordinated.

McNeill (forthcoming) compared the occurrence of iconic gestures in adults with those observed in children as they narrated a story of a cartoon they had just watched. He finds that children under 8 years of age, as compared to adults, tend to enact whole scenes, and they relate their gestures to their words in a way suggesting that the gestures are being organized independently of the speech. In the adult, in contrast, iconic gestures are more precisely coordinated with speech units of semantic expression. It is as if there is a convergence of expressive functions, speech and gesture working together in a more cooperative fashion. McNeill also observes how the enactment of iconic gesture in adults is confined to the hands, whereas the child will often employ the whole body. Furthermore, when depicting a whole event, the child is likely to depict the event as if he or she is the center of it. The adult depicts the event in gesture as if a witness to it. Iconic gestures thus become, McNeill suggests, more symbolic in character. They come to serve as signs of actions and events rather than reenactments of them.

Jancovic et al. (1975) also asked children of various ages (4-18) to tell the story of a cartoon they had just seen. They report an increase in the use of gesticulation with age. However, they also report a relative decline in what they term "pantomimic gesturing," but a progressive increase in gestures they refer to as "semantic modifiers" and "relationals." This seems to indicate a shift with age in the way gestures relate to speech: Gestures come to be coordinated more precisely with the semantic units of speech in the older speakers and function less as autonomous representations.

Evans and Rubin (1979) had children between the ages of 5 and 10 years explain, to an adult listener, the rules of a simple game they had been taught. They found that among the youngest children gestures played an important supplementary role. The youngest children's explanations were perfectly intelligible to others, provided the gestures they used were taken into account. The older children's explanations were verbally more autonomous. The gestures they used were described as more frequently "supplementary" or "redundant" rather than as "substitutive," as they were with the youngest groups.

Taken together, these four studies are consistent with one another in several ways. All agree in noting an increase in gesticulation with age. All of them indicate, however, that there are important changes in the kinds of gesticulation that occur and in the way these gesticulations are related to speech. There appears to be a shift away from elaborate enactments or pantomimes, which serve instead of speech, toward a more precise coordination, as if gesture is coming to be used more selectively. Gesture is used much less to depict whole scenes. It is brought in only at certain points along the way. There is also an increasing use of abstract, discourse-marking gesture; iconic gesture becomes more symbolic and more restricted in the aspects of meaning it is called upon to display.

FUNCTIONS OF GESTICULATION

By looking at descriptions of gesticular organization and how it is related to concurrent speech, by examining the little evidence available on the neurological control of gesture, and by considering the few available studies of how gesticulation develops in children, we have argued that the view that gesture and speech are separate representational modes, yet coordinate because employed in the same enterprise, is well supported. By phrasing it the way we do, we imply that gesticulation, like speech, is organized under the guidance of a plan of action. The plan of action in question is to produce a pattern of behavior that serves for others as a *representation* of meaning. This is done by making use of systems of articulated units that, to speak broadly, have reference to concepts. With speech we are dealing with a highly coded system. That is to say, the units and patterned organizations of speech are produced under the guidance of an elaborate system of rules, shared by members of the same speech community by which meanings are related to the units of the code. With gesticulation it seems otherwise. Although it is generally acknowledged that there are gestural units that are highly coded, the kind of gesturing with which we have been dealing so far seems not to be. There are certainly differences between social groups in the forms of gesticulation, but detailed studies of such differences are very rare. The best such study is still that by Efron (1941/1972), yet it is evident that only quite exceptionally is gesticulation organized in a manner that is in any way analogous to a linguistic system. Gesticulation, relatively speaking, is uncoded. It is our position that the uncoded nature of gesticulation is related to the functions it serves in the utterance. Its role in the utterance is generally different from the role played by speech. The question of what this role may be remains; at this point we have very little systematic understanding of it. From the evidence available it is clear that the role of gesticulation in the utterance is quite complex and varied. It serves to complement the communicative work of speech, and it does so in a wide variety of ways.

PSYCHOLOGICAL FUNCTIONS

Before considering the role of gesticulation in the utterance from a communication viewpoint, I should mention its psychological significance. This has been emphasized in particular by McNeill and by Freedman. McNeill (forthcoming) has made it clear that his main interest in gesture arises because gesture provides, as he has put it, "a second channel of observation onto the speaker's mental representations during speech." He views iconic gestures as motoric representations of the conceptual models of the content of discourse, and he suggests that, in gesturing, one may observe enactments of the action schemata of the sensorimotor ideas or semiotic extensions of such ideas that are expressed in speech (McNeill, 1979).

From this point of view it will be seen that the study of iconic gesticulation will have implications for theories of mental representation. Gesture, insofar as it is iconic, represents meaning in a way quite different from speech—as we have already pointed out. McNeill and Levy (1982), for instance, in their analyses of how the forms of gestures relate to the semantic features of verbs they accompany, show that far more than just the action of the verb is represented. They show how, in the gesture, the speaker is representing a complete situation, of which the action referred to in the verb is a part. That speakers are able to do this at the *outset* of a speech unit—often, as my own (Kendon 1980a) and Schegloff's (n.d.) observations have shown, well in advance—clearly suggests that the unit of meaning must be stored in a form that is not organized along lines suggested by spoken language structures. If the format in which all ideas are stored, whether visual or not, is, as some have supposed (see Pylyshyn, 1973), the same as that used for storing verbal information, we would not expect to observe iconic gestures occurring at the initial position of speech units. Nor would we expect such gestures to provide a kind of "micro-cosmic" representation of the whole situation that is to be described. Rather, we might expect such gestures to follow verbal outputs, and this they have never been observed to do. It seems possible that the study of representation in gesticulation could well contribute the sort of critical evidence for theories of mental representation that Anderson (1978), in his review of the problem, has suggested is not available and cannot be obtained by the current techniques of experimental psychology.

Freedman, like McNeill, believes that representational gesturing makes manifest in concrete, motoric form, the imagery that is to be given representation in speech. He argues in addition, however, that representational gesticulation plays a facilitating role in the process whereby content is transformed into spoken form. He has proposed that representational gestures assist in this process because they help to keep available, in the form of concrete representations, the material that is to be encoded in verbal form. He suggests that the representation gesture "acts to cement/ the image's/ connection to the symbol, and it is this connecting process which seems to be the central psychological function of this activity. Through confirmation of the image, and through the work of connecting the image to the world, object focused activity [i.e., gesticulation] ensures the continuity of representing" (Freedman 1977: 113).

COMMUNICATIVE FUNCTIONS

Although it is widely supposed that gesticulation plays a role in communication, some have questioned this assumption. It has been pointed out, for example, that people sometimes gesture when they are talking on the telephone. It is suggested that this shows gesture to be an "automatic" by-product of speaking and not in any way functional for the listener. Furthermore, it is pointed out, telephone conversations are perfectly satisfactory, and people can talk very well together in the dark. Even when they can see each other, gesturing may appear infrequently. Gesticulation, therefore, even if it does play some communicative role, does so, at best, in a minor way. The approaches of such investigators like McNeill and Freedman, already discussed, should fully exhaust any interest gesticulation may have for us.

As will be clear, we do not accept such a view. Indeed, to the contrary, we believe that gesticulation arises as an integral part of an individual's *communicative* effort and that, furthermore, it has a direct role to play in this process. Gesticulation, we maintain, is communicatively important by no means only because it may be a kind of index of a speaker's psychological state. It is important principally because it is employed, along with speech, in the fashioning of an effective utterance unit. Curiously, we find there is very little systematic work by which this view can be supported. Investigations to date provide but hints and snatches of the communicative roles of gesticulation. A thorough exploration of these remains an important task for future work.

One or two studies have compared the rate with which people gesticulate when talking to someone they cannot see and when talking to someone they can see. Cohen and Harrison (1973) had people give routing directions to others, either over a telephone or face-to-face. They found people produced more directional gestures in the face-to-face situation. In another study, Cohen (1977) compared the gesticulations of subjects as they gave directions, not only face-to-face and over a telephone, but also as they practiced giving directions into a tape recorder. He found that directional gestures were used most frequently in the face-to-face situation, regardless of whether the subject had practiced beforehand. Subjects also used directional gestures when giving directions over the telephone. However, over the three practice sessions, directional gestures declined almost to nothing.

It is clear that in these studies, at least, whether or not a person produces gesticulations is influenced by whether the speaker thinks they will be available for a recipient. Evidently, however, if another is present but cannot be seen, some gestural production will be engaged in. It is as if the subject's habits of employing gesticulation are evoked by the give and take that the telephone allows. When the subject believes no one can hear him, as in the practice sessions, he does not use gestures.

A study by Graham and Heywood (1976) may now be mentioned. They compared the speech of subjects who were engaged in a task of describing geometrical shapes to recipients under conditions in which they were allowed to use gesture and under conditions in which they were not. They showed that in the condition in which gestures were not permitted there was no disruption of speech (as some would have expected), but there was a change in the way the descriptions were accomplished. When no gesturing was permitted, there was a significant increase in the use of phrases or words describing spatial relations and a decrease in the number of demonstratives used. Speakers paused more when they did not use gestures, but they otherwise were fluent.

This study draws attention to the complementary relationship between gesture and speech. It shows that, for the task of describing geometrical shapes, at least, gesture is neither an automatic by-product of speech nor is it used redundantly. It suggests that utterers are able to apportion different aspects of the task of the utterance between the instruments of expression that are available.

We may take it, then, that from the speaker's point of view, gesticulation is part of the communicative effort. What of recipients? What communicative value do gestures have for them? This question has been examined experimentally by Berger and Popelka (1971), Graham and Argyle (1975), Walker and Nazmi (1979), and Riseborough (1981). Observational studies of value include Sherzer (1973), Birdwhistell (1970), and Slama-Cazacu (1976). It will be obvious that many more studies are needed.

Berger and Popelka (1971) presented twenty sentences to subjects whose instructions were to write down what they heard. In one condition the sentences were uttered with an accompanying gesture that fitted the meaning of the sentence; in the other condition no gesture was employed. The sentences were short and the gestures chosen to accompanying them were autonomous gestures selected from a list that, in a separate study, had been found to be similarly understood in a sample of twenty students drawn from the same population as the subjects. Berger and Popelka found that accuracy in writing down the spoken sentences was greater when they were uttered with an accompanying gesture than when they were not. It is clear that here the gesture assisted in accurate reception of the sentences, although the experiment leaves it open as to how it did so. It might have been interesting to see if it would have made a difference if the accompanying gesture *did not* fit the meaning of the sentence.

Graham and Argyle (1975) established a situation in which subjects were required to make drawings of complex geometrical shapes that were described to them by senders who either were or were not allowed to use gestures as they did so. The likeness to the originals of the recipients' drawings, as judged by a panel of independent judges, was a measure of the effectiveness of the communication. It was found that recipients made more accurate drawings when the senders used gestures and that this effect was most marked when the figures being described were complex and could not be described with a simple label.

Riseborough (1981) has reported three studies. She showed that subjects were better able to identify objects from descriptions if these descriptions were accompanied by "physiographic gestures." She further showed that subjects, in two recall tasks, could recall word lists more accurately and could recall a story more accurately if appropriate "physiographic" gestures were employed. She also showed that where the sound channel was obstructed by white noise, physiographic gestures made an increased contribution to comprehension.

Other studies that bear on the communicative functions of gesticulation are observational or anecdotal. Birdwhistell (1970) has presented several detailed studies of how movement concurrent with speech is patterned in relation to it, and he describes how contrastive movement patterns differentially mark stress in speech and also how they mark pronominals and deictic particles. He provides a highly interesting summary of these observations which suggests that the *direction* of movement of a moving body part marking a pronominal or deictic particle is systematically related to the meaning of the particle. Thus, in association with "this," "here," "now," "I," and "we" the body part moves toward the speaker. In association with "that," "there," "then," "you," and "they" the body part moves away from the speaker. He also says that the form of the movement differs according to whether the word being marked kinesically is plural or singular. Some of these regularities were observed in British speakers analyzed by Kendon (1972).

As to the communicative role of such patterned movements, Birdwhistell makes two suggestions. He suggests, in one place, that such movements are of communicative value because, in paralleling speech in this way, they contribute to the redundancy of the uttered message. The availability of the same message in more than one channel allows for communication to take place in a wider range of circumstances and among people more variously equipped with capacities to send and receive than would otherwise be the case (Birdwhistell 1970: 107-108). He also suggests, however, that certain kinesic actions may be functionally *equivalent* to linguistic items. Thus, he says, "both the kinesic and the linguistic markers may be alloforms, that is, structural variants of each other" (Birdwhistell, 1970: 127).

Sherzer (1973) has illustrated this last point in some detail in his study of lip pointing among the Cuna Indians of Panama. In this study he shows how lip pointing can be used in conjunction with spoken utterance in a wide variety of ways. He argues, however, that in analyzing the functions of lip pointing, this has to be done in conjunction with an analysis of the discourse structure of Cuna speech events. Thus, he shows how a gestural element must be considered as fully integrated with spoken linguistic elements in the Cuna linguistic system.

The view that gestural elements may serve at the same level of functioning as spoken elements within a discourse has also been urged by Slama-Cazacu (1976). She has pointed out how kinesic elements, whether of the face or of the hands, can be inserted into utterances in such a way that they can replace elements that might otherwise have been spoken. She refers to this phenomenon as "mixed syntax" and gives a series of examples. She argues that kinesic elements can achieve, with words, a synthesis into a single code, "structured *sui generis* and comprising verbal and [kinesic] elements mutually modified and fused in *linguistically* analyzable units" (Slama-Cazacu, 1976: 225).

The observations of Sherzer and Slama-Cazacu are of particular interest because they show how gestures may function on the same level as speech. That is to say, they are not serving as alternative representations of concepts; they are being inserted in *speech* sequences as functionally equivalent with the verbal components of such sequences.

It will be clear from the foregoing that gesticulation does indeed play a part in the utterance from a communicational point of view. Much more observation and analysis is needed, however. In another paper (Kendon, 1980e) I have argued from a series of examples, collected from everyday situations I have happened to witness, that the range of communicative functions for gesture is considerable. I provide examples of gesture substituting for speech when speech cannot be heard momentarily. I also provide examples that show gesture being used as a substitute for speech when others are talking, which suggests how gesture has properties that allow it to be employed for "subordinate" or "side" exchanges without threatening the participant status of those using it in this way. Furthermore examples are provided showing the use of gesture in the disambiguation of potentially ambiguous words; its use as a device for completing a sentence which, if spoken, might prove too embarrassing for the speaker; and its use as a device to convey aspects of meaning that the words being employed convey only partially. In these examples it is possible to show how the speaker appears to be dividing the task of conveying meaning between the two expressive modalities in such a way as to achieve either economy of expression or a particular effect on the recipient.

From a consideration of such examples, it would appear that many people show considerable skill in the deployment of gesture and speech. In several cases it is possible to suggest how speakers adapt their utterance from moment to moment as the structure of the communication situation changes. Such carefully controlled "recipient design" of utterances has been suggested from analyses by Goodwin (1981). By taking into consideration gesture as well, it is often possible to show that gesticulation is likewise deployed skillfully, in conjunction with speech—indeed, as its partner—in the task of achieving the aim of the utterance.

One further observation may now be added. There is some evidence to suggest that there are cultural differences in the amount of gesticulation employed and also differences in the kind of gesticulation employed. Efron (1941/1972) showed, in a study that remains to this day without equal, that people from Southern Italy make extensive use of pictorial or iconic gestures as they talk, whereas people from Eastern European Jewish communities make very little use of such gestures but employ ideographic gestures to a great extent. This raises the possibility that Italians rely on the gesturing of others for a kind of information different from that of East European Jewish people.

Graham and Argyle (1975), in the experiment already mentioned, compared the change in performance of recipients between the absence and presence of gesture, for British university students and for students from Milan in Italy. It was found that the Italians improved, on the whole, very much more than the British did, when gestures were available for them. In a variation on this experiment, Walker and Nazmi (1979) showed that Italian housewives (immigrants living in Australia) were able to recall descriptions of geometrical figures that were accompanied by gestures far better than were housewives of British descent, although there was less difference between the two groups when they were permitted to draw the figures being described to them while the description was still in progress.

These two experiments appear to confirm that Italians are likely to rely on gestures for pictorial information in a way that other cultural groups may not. It would be most interesting to explore the information that ideographic gestures may make available and the use that may be made of it. A comparison of the East European Jews with the Southern Italians of Efron's sample, for instance, might show how each group benefits from gesticulation, but in different ways.

As we said at the beginning of this section, detailed evidence for how gesticulation functions communicatively is scanty. We believe that the few studies available do support the rather strong position we take here but much more work needs to be done. One of the problems that arises for work on this question is that the functions of gesture are very diverse. Furthermore, people are highly skilled in adapting themselves to variations in the communication situation. This makes it difficult to devise experiments to show the communicative values of gesturing, since, as Graham and Heyward's (1976) study suggests, speakers will adjust their expressive resources to meet whatever contingencies they may face. The best approach, at least at this stage, is probably the careful collection of observations on gestural usage. Especially valuable would be observations made from recorded occasions. In this way a detailed account of the circumstances of gestural usage could be compiled and a systematic analysis of its functions could begin.

THE EMERGENCE OF GESTURAL AUTONOMY

Gesticulation, as we have seen, is complementary to speech. It does not serve communicatively in its absence. Even where a gestural form may serve in place of a spoken element within an utterance, as in the "mixed syntax" examples of Slama-Cazacu (1976) mentioned above, the context of meaning already established by the spoken part of the utterance is essential for its comprehension. However, gesture can function independently of speech. In speech-using communities it is found that there are a number of gestural forms that serve as complete utterances by themselves. In circumstances in which use of speech is highly restricted or impossible (for whatever reason), gesture is often found to replace it, becoming organized into gesture systems and sign languages. A detailed discussion of the issues raised by the phenomena of gestural autonomy, especially those raised by sign languages proper, is not possible in this chapter. Here I must be content with some references to contemporary work and a few comments on the circumstances in which gestural autonomy arises. In the final section I shall offer a few remarks on the differences between the way autonomous gestural forms and gesticulations relate to the meanings they convey.

Gestures that, in speech communities, function as complete utterances we shall here call *autonomous gestures.*[1] They include many forms that are highly standardized and explicitly recognized in the community that uses them, and often have names or phrases by which they are glossed. A number of lists of such autonomous gestures have been published for various language and cultural groups.[2]

The methods that have been followed in compiling these various lists and the criteria that have been used in deciding what should be included, not surprisingly, are various and usually not stated explicitly. Ekman and his colleagues (Johnson et al., 1975) have proposed an explicit definition of autonomous gestures that they call *emblems,* and they suggest a procedure by which inventories of them may be acquired. So far, the only list published using these procedures is that by Sparhawk (1978) for Iran. Another useful discussion of methodology in the study of autonomous gestures has been provided by Poyatos (1975).

Besides the work of Ekman and Sparhawk, recent studies of autonomous gestures are surprisingly few. Morris et al. (1979) have published a systematic study of variations in usage throughout Western Europe for twenty gestural forms. Taylor (1956) has provided an extremely detailed study of the history of the "Shanghai gesture" (thumbing the nose). Rickford and Rickford (1976) give an account of two gestures widely used in black communities throughout the Caribbean, Central America, and the United States and trace their origins in Africa. Kirk and Burton (1976) examine the way two adjacent East African groups describe and gloss a number of gestural forms. Calbris (1980, 1981) has published a detailed study of the recognizability of common French autonomous gestures. A critical review of the work of Morris et al. (1979), in which many of the issues involved in the study of autonomous gestures are given detailed discussion, may be found in Kendon (1981).

Autonomous gestures deserve much further investigation. First, systematic cross-cultural comparative studies are badly needed. In particular, cultures should be compared for the extent to which use is made in them of autonomous gestures. As is evident from Morris et al.'s (1979) study, as well as from other sources, the cultures of the Mediterranean appear to be far richer in autonomous gestural forms than are the cultures of Northern Europe. As I suggested above, this raises the interesting question of how these cultures differ in the uses made of gesture in interaction and the differences in the sorts of information gesture is relied upon to provide. It would be a most useful beginning if a survey of autonomous gestural forms were to be undertaken, using a standard procedure of the sort suggested by Ekman and paying careful attention to the social and cultural groupings to which the samples of informants belong. Such a survey would be especially valuable if it were conducted in several different adjacent cultural areas, for then we might gain information about the spread of such forms and the extent to which they vary from one language group to another. Morris et al. (1979) do take some steps in this direction. However, in addition to comparing samples of people from different cultures in their understanding of a small set of autonomous gestures, as was done in this study, a comparison of the size and nature of autonomous gestural repertoires in these cultures should also be made.

A comparison of autonomous gestural forms that are available in existing published lists could also be made. Although such lists have been compiled by quite different methods and vary in the reliance that may be placed upon them, such comparisons could yield interesting results. For example, Creider (1977) has offered a comparison between the autonomous gestures he describes for four linguistically different groups in Kenya and the autonomous gestures described by Saitz and Cervenka (1972) for Colombia and the United States. He finds that although the four Kenyan groups share almost all of the gestures described for any one of them, there are thirteen gestures that are the same between Kenya and North America and eighteen that are the same between Kenya and Colombia.

This implies, first, that the forms of autonomous gestures are mainly *different* from one culture area to another. However, it appears that a culture area that shares gestural forms may be much broader than an area that shares a spoken language. This is also apparent from the study of gestures in Europe by Morris et al. (1979). This seems to show that autonomous gestures are not gestural labels for spoken forms, but rather mark meaning units independently of speech. Creider's comparison also shows that there may be some kinds of gestures that are worldwide or, at least, so widespread as to suggest that they are not the product of cultural processes alone. In his sample, the gestures found in common between East Africa and North America include the shoulder shrug for "don't know"; the headshake for negation and the headnod for affirmation; a flat hand with palm against the cheek, head tilted to one side, for "sleep"; and gestures for "halt" and "sit down," among others.

Further comparisons among many more groups are needed, but it looks as if a group of gestures that are not specific to any culture may be found. It would be very interesting to know what this group of gestures includes. It probably would include gestures that refer to bodily functions, feelings and emotions, and personal activities (like sleeping) that are engaged in by everyone. It should be added that their universality is not evidence of their innateness, necessarily. For many of them, similar forms may arise because of the limited number of ways to which something may be referred gesturally. For discussion of this issue, see Ekman (1977, 1979).

Another kind of comparison that would be worth undertaking would be one in which the meanings of autonomous gestures are compared, regardless of their form. In one preliminary comparative study of this sort (Kendon, 1981) in which gesture lists from Colombia, the United States, East Africa, Southern Italy, France, and Iran are compared, I found that three main types of gesture predominate. The most frequent are those gestures concerned with interpersonal control—that is, gestures of salutation, command, request, insult, threat, and protection. Also frequent are gestures that serve to comment upon another or upon another's actions. Gestures that have a performative function also occur in all lists examined, that is, gestures whose very enactment constitutes an actual accomplishment of an act, such as the swearing of an oath or the making of a promise. On the other hand, gestures that are glossed as if they could serve simply as nouns or verbs—those that could be considered merely as labels for objects or actions—appear to be extremely rare. Indeed, they are found to be entirely absent from three of the lists examined, and they make up only 6% of two of the others.

This comparison suggests, then, that autonomous gestures in speech-using communities may be quite restricted in the range of communicative functions they are called upon to fulfill. This raises the interesting question of why it should be only these functions that are selected. A consideration of the properties of the gestural medium as compared to the spoken medium may point the way to an answer. For example, gesture may be able to accomplish the expression of a single unit of meaning more rapidly than speech. It may be that gesture requires less than speech does in the way of focused attention on the part of a recipient for it to be grasped intelligibly. Furthermore, it may be employed over distances much greater than those over which articulate speech may be used. Gesture may also have a particular kind of impact on a recipient because, so often, it is highly reminiscent of actual physical action. From considerations of this sort it is seen that gesture has properties that predispose it for certain kinds of communicative functions. If it is to be used on its own, where speech is otherwise available, it will tend to specialize in these functions. However, further light will be thrown on this matter only if careful studies of the uses of autonomous gestures are made. A number of detailed communication ethnographies are needed that would pay close attention to the circumstances in which autonomous gestures are used in daily interaction. This might enable us to understand better how such gestures come about and why they tend to be specialized for the particular range of functions they appear to have.

We suggest, then, that in the communicative functions for which autonomous gestures may be specialized, we again may see how gesture serves to complement speech. Where there is no other medium of expression available, however, gesture can be organized to meet any communicative function that may be required. Thus, where speech is impossible— whether for technical reasons, reasons of social taboo or custom, because spoken languages are too sharply divergent, or for physiological reasons— we may observe the emergence of *gesture systems* and also *sign languages*.

Limited gesture systems emerge where only a restricted range of utterances is required. A particularly well-described example is that of the system of gestures used by hitch-hikers and motorists in Poland (Ciolek, 1973). Other such systems include those used by grain merchants, umpires, and flight mechanics (see West, 1960). Properties of one such system used in radio studios have been systematically described by Crystal and Craig (1978).

In the sawmills of British Columbia, such a gesture system has undergone elaboration to allow for much more than the communication requirements of the tasks of the sawmill (Meissner and Philpott, 1975). In this case we see the transition from a gesture system to a *sign language*. A sign language is a gesture system in which there are no longer any restrictions on domain of function and in which the number of items in the repertoire is large and capable of expansion. Such sign languages as have been studied in detail show, to varying degrees, evidence of formational systematicity and syntactic organization. In well-developed cases, such as that of American Sign Language, these features show a high degree of parallelism with spoken language structures.

Sign languages have arisen in three main circumstances. First, they have arisen as *alternates* to spoken languages, where social custom or taboo prevents the use of speech. This has occurred among the Australian Aborigines (for a collection of reports, see the volume edited by Umiker-Sebeok and Sebeok, 1978), among the married women of Armenia, who may not speak in the presence of their affines (see West, 1960, for some account and references) and in the monasteries of the various Trappist orders (Barakat, 1975, provides a recent modern account). Second, sign languages have arisen in at least one circumstance in which diverse languages have come into contact suddenly. In the Great Plains of North America, sign language use spread among the Indians as a *lingua franca* at a time when rapid expansion of certain tribes led to sudden and extensive contacts between people with very different languages (Taylor, 1975). Third, sign languages arise when speech is impossible for physiological reasons, that is to say, because of deafness. It seems that deaf individuals will spontaneously employ gestures, and if there are others who can reciprocate, quite elaborate systems will develop. If a community of sign users persist, such systems may become very elaborate and highly systematized.

Deaf sign languages, or *primary* sign languages, as they may be called, have received much attention lately, as already noted. They are of particular interest because, unlike the alternate sign languages mentioned, they have been developed by people without any access to a spoken language that might serve as a model, whereas, for some alternate sign languages, at least—for instance, those evolved in Australia—there is evidence that the spoken language of the community in which they have developed guides at least some aspects of their structure. For true primary sign languages this cannot be the case. An analysis of primary sign language structure, therefore, should throw light upon the question of what features languages have regardless of the medium in which they are expressed. Most of the recent work done on primary sign languages has been done on American Sign Language. A good review, including an excellent bibliography, is Stokoe's (1980). Other national sign languages are also beginning to receive descriptions (see Stokoe, 1980, for references). Some local sign languages, showing much less systematization, have also been described. Washabaugh et al.

(1978) describe such a sign language from Providence Island, and Kendon (1980b, 1980c, 1980d) describes one from the highland Enga Province in Papua New Guinea. Kuschel (1973) describes a sign language that was invented by a single deaf man on Rennell Island (British Solomons). Goldin-Meadow (Feldman et al., 1978) has described the emergence of gestural communication in very young deaf children who had not been exposed to sign language of any sort. This shows that such communicative usage of gesture can begin at a very early age. Goldin-Meadow's findings also strongly suggest that in certain respects the organization of such gestural utterance is governed by internal factors rather than by processes of learning from others.

CONCLUSION:
GESTICULATION, AUTONOMOUS GESTURE, AND SIGN LANGUAGE

It is the argument of this essay that the gestural modality is as fundamental as the verbal modality as an instrument for the representation of meaning. That is, I maintain that the employment of gesture is not dependent upon the employment of verbal language. Gesture is separate, in principle equal, joined with speech only because it is used simultaneously for the same overall purpose. The development of gesture, like the development of language, waits upon the development of a general capacity for symbolic representation.

Where verbal language is available and is used, gesture is employed in cooperation with it. It serves to complement it in various ways. I have stressed the variety of ways gesticulation may relate to speech and have argued that this means it is best considered as a partner in a common enterprise rather than as a subordinate by-product of speech or as a vestige of more primitive forms of expression. Where verbal language is not used, gesture may take over, to varying degrees, the communicative tasks it would otherwise fulfill. It is to be noted, however, that as it does so, gestural forms change their character. When gesture becomes autonomous it becomes established in stable, standardized forms. Such standardized forms tend to become systematically related to one another in the sense that they preserve features that serve to contrast them with other gestures in the system, regardless of whether those features relate in form to the referents of the gestures. This is well illustrated in the discussion of Persian autonomous gestures by Sparhawk (1978), in which she shows the extent to which a "cheirological" ("phonological") analysis may be applicable. Where such formal standardization occurs, referents also become standardized. A given autonomous gestural form comes to be stabilized in what it is used to refer to. Once this occurs, the way is open for the referents of gestures to become more general and, in consequence, more abstract. Whereas, in gesticulation, gesture may be deployed in a pantomime and represent a whole situation as a single picture, when standardized autonomous gestural forms are used this does not happen. Rather, a single unit of meaning is referenced.

Autonomous gestures are employed by users of speech in various circumstances, but they are employed typically for the purpose of making a single utterance. Where gesture alone is available for referential discourse, before such discourse can be engaged in, extended repertoires of standardized forms must be established. Meaning becomes highly segmented and any specific complex of meaning can only be represented by combinations of gestural forms. The systematization of gestural forms and the corresponding systematization of modes of combination of such forms in strings within utterances lead to structural features analogous to phonology and syntax in spoken languages. Thus we have the establishment of sign languages.

There is every reason to suppose that languages as open and as functionally generalized as any spoken language, may be fashioned in the gestural medium. The sign languages of large, stable, deaf communities, such as may be found in the United States, provide examples of this. The emergence of such languages takes considerable time and also requires the persistence of a community of users, probably for at least as long as two generations, if not longer. However, such systems, it seems clear, emerge by a process of evolution from forms that are much closer to the pantomimes that may sometimes be seen in gesticulation. The process involves a stabilization of forms, their systematic interrelationship, and the progressive segmentation of units of reference with a consequent development of generality and abstractness of such units. The processes by which this evolution is brought about are to be sought in the processes of social interaction. It is the use of such gestural expressions by communities of users for referential exchanges in multiple contexts that leads to these changes.

The expressive devices of a language fashioned in the gestural medium may very well be different from those found in a spoken language because the possibilities of the gestural medium are so very different. Recent work on American Sign Language has demonstrated several ways this may come about. Most notable is the way so-called markers and classifiers are employed. Here we see how space may be used to create expressive forms that relate to meaning units in ways that are quite different from those found in a spoken language. In an example given in Stokoe (1980), for instance, it is shown how, in American Sign Language, by the use of the vehicle classifier, a signer may explain a car journey in a single complex action.

Such examples show how the forms of expression in a language may be closely dependent upon the medium of expression employed. They caution us against erecting any theory of language in general which relies only on what we know of language in one modality alone. A truly general theory of language must look beyond the structures provided by spoken forms alone. We urge, however, that a comparison of sign languages and spoken languages is not sufficient. Close consideration should also be given to the way the two modalities are used in combination, as we may see in the phenomenon of gesticulation and autonomous gesture discussed in the present chapter. Such a consideration must lead us to a theory of language that sees the particular forms in which it may be manifested (its *delological* forms, to use a term proposed by Teodorrson, 1980) as the product of the circumstances in which the effort of utterance is made. The elaboration of language in its various forms is thus to be seen as a product of the conditions of human interaction, and its forms are to be accounted for in terms of an understanding of the uses that are made of it. In this view, it is the act of utterance that comes first. The tools of utterance are fashioned in the process by which the act is made effective as a representation of meaning available to a community of persons.

NOTES

1. *Autonomous gestures* have been termed *emblems* by Ekman, and this usage has been widely followed in recent years. I prefer the term here proposed, however, because it is purely descriptive. Unlike the term "emblem," it implies nothing about the semiotic character of such gestures. Furthermore, the word "emblem" has a well-established use in common parlance, and it seems inappropriate to make a technical term out of it (Efron's "emblematic gesture" would have been better). In addition, by referring to such gestures as "autonomous" the possibility that some gestures may be more autonomous than others is admitted. The term "emblem" is categorical. Terms that suggest the positioning of phenomena along dimensions of variation are, in general, to be preferred.

2. Some of the more recent lists include those of Barakat (1973) for Arabic cultures, Creider (1977) for four language groups in Kenya, Munari (1963) and Efron

(1941/1972) for Italy, Saitz and Cervenka (1972) for Colombia and the United States, Green (1968) and Kaulfers (1931) for Spain and Spanish speakers, and Sparhawk (1978) for Iran. There are also a number of older works. West (1960) provides an excellent annotated bibliography of many of these. See also Hayes (1957).

REFERENCES

Alajouanine, T., and Lhermitte, F. Nonverbal communication in aphasia. In A. De Reuck and M. O'Connor (Eds.), *Disorders of language*. London: J. & A. Churchill Ltd., 1974.

Anderson, J. R. Arguments concerning representations for mental imagery. *Psychological Review*, 1978, *85*, 249-277.

Barakat, R. A. Gesture systems. *Keystone Folklore Quarterly*, 1969, *14*, 105-121.

Barakat, R. Arabic gestures. *Journal of Popular Culture*, 1973, *6*, 749-792.

Barakat, R. *Cistercian sign language*. Kalamazoo, MI: Cistercian Publications, 1975.

Barten, S. S. Development of gesture. In N. R. Smith and M. Franklin (Eds.), *Symbolic functioning in childhood*. Hillsdale, NJ: Lawrence Erlbaum, 1979.

Bates, E. *The emergence of symbols*. New York: Academic Press, 1979.

Berger, K. W., and Popelka, G. R. Extra-facial gestures in relation to speech reading. *Journal of Communication Disorders*, 1971, *3*, 302-308.

Birdwhistell, R. L. *Kinesics and context*. Philadelphia: University of Pennsylvania Press, 1970.

Boomer, D. S. The phonemic clause: Speech unit in human communication. In A. W. Siegman and S. Feldstein (Eds.), *Nonverbal behavior and communication*. Hillsdale, NJ: Lawrence Erlbaum, 1978.

Bruner, J. S. Learning how to do things with words. In J. S. Bruner and A. Garton (Eds.), *Human growth and development*. Oxford: Clarendon Press, 1978.

Bullowa, M. (Ed.). *Before speech*. Cambridge: Cambridge University Press, 1979.

Calbris, G. Etude des expressions mimiques conventionelles françaises dans le cadre d'une communication nonverbale. *Semiotica*, 1980, *29*, 245-346.

Calbris, G. Etude des expressions mimiques conventionnelles francaises dans le cadre d'une communication nonverbale testées sur des Hongrois. *Semiotica*, 1981, *35*, 125-156.

Cicone, M., Wapner, W., Foldi, N., Zurif, E., and Gardner, H. The relation between gesture and language in aphasic communication. *Brain and Language*, 1979, *8*, 324-349.

Ciolek, T. M. Materialy do "alchemic gestow." *Ethnografia Polska*, 1973, *17*, 59-79.

Clark, R. A. The transition from action to gesture. In A. Lock (Ed.), *Action, gesture and symbol: The emergence of language*. London: Academic Press, 1978.

Cohen, A. A. The communicative functions of hand illustrators. *Journal of Communication*, 1977, *27*, 54-63.

Cohen, A. A., and Harrison, R. P. Intentionality in the use of hand illustrators in face-to-face communication situations. *Journal of Personality and Social Psychology*, 1973, *28*, 276-279.

Condon, W. S. An analysis of behavioral organization. *Sign Language Studies*, 1976, *13*, 285-318.

Creider, C. Towards a description of East African gestures. *Sign Language Studies,* 1977, *14,* 1-20.

Crystal, D., and Craig, E. Contrived sign languages. In I. M. Schlesinger and L. Namir (Eds.), *Sign language of the deaf: Psychological, linguistic and sociological perspectives.* New York: Academic Press, 1978.

Crystal, D., and Davy, D. *Investigating English style.* Bloomington: Indiana University Press, 1969.

Delis, D., Foldi, N. S., Hamby, S., Gardner, H., and Zurif, E. A. note on temporal relations between language and gestures. *Brain and Language,* 1979, *8,* 350-354.

Duffy, R. J., and Duffy, J. R. Three studies of deficits in pantomimic expression and pantomimic recognition in aphasia." *Journal of Speech and Hearing Research,* 1981, *46,* 70-84.

Duffy, R. J., Duffy, J. R., and Pearson, K. Pantomimic recognition in aphasics. *Journal of Speech and Hearing Research,* 1975, *18,* 115-132.

Duffy, R. J., and Liles, B. Z. A translation of Finkelnburg's [1870] lecture on aphasia as "asymbolia" with commentary. *Journal of Speech and Hearing Disorders,* 1979, *44,* 156-168.

Efron, D. *Gesture and environment.* New York: Kings Crown Press, 1941. (Republished as *Gesture, race and culture.* The Hague: Mouton, 1972.)

Ekman, P. Biological and cultural contributions to bodily and facial movement. In John Blacking (Ed.), *The anthropology of the body.* London: Academic Press, 1977.

Ekman, P. About brows. In M. Von Cranach, K. Foppa, W. Lepenier, and D. Ploog (Eds.), *Human ethology: Claims and limits of a new discipline.* Cambridge: Cambridge University Press, 1979.

Evans, M. A., and Rubin, K. H. Hand gestures as a communicative mode in school aged children. *Journal of Genetic Psychology,* 1979, *135,* 189-196.

Feldman, H., Goldin-Meadow, S., and Gleitman, L. Beyond Herodotus: The creation of language by linguistically deprived deaf children. In A. Lock (Ed.), *Action, gesture, and symbol.* London: Academic Press, 1978.

Feyereisen, P. [Hand preference for the different types of movement accompanying speech.] *Journal de Psychologie Normale et Pathologique,* 1977, *74,* 451-470. (Original in French.)

Franklin, M. B. Nonverbal representation in young children: A cognitive perspective. *Young Children,* 1973, *11,* 33-53.

Freedman, N. The analysis of movement behavior during clinical interviews. In A. Siegman and B. Pope (Eds.), *Studies in dyadic communication.* Elmsford, NY: Pergamon Press, 1972.

Freedman, N. Hands, words and mind: On the structuralization of body movements during discourse and the capacity for verbal representation. In N. Freedman and S. Grand (Eds.), *Communicative structures and psychic structures: A psychoanalytic approach.* New York: Plenum Press, 1977.

Gainotti, G., and Lemmo, M. Comprehension of symbolic gestures in aphasia. *Brain and Language,* 1976, *3,* 451-460.

Goodglass, H., and Kaplan, E. Disturbance of gesture and pantomime in aphasia. *Brain,* 1963, *86,* 703-702.

Goodwin, C. *Conversational organization.* New York: Academic Press, 1981.

Graham, J. A., and Argyle, M. A cross cultural study of the communication of extra verbal meaning by gestures. *International Journal of Psychology,* 1975, *10,* 56-67.

Graham, J. A., and Heywood, S. The effects of elimination of hand gestures and of verbal codability on speech performance. *European Journal of Social Psychology,* 1976, *5,* 189-195.

Green, J. R. *A gesture inventory for teaching Spanish.* New York: Clinton Books, 1968.

Hayes, F. C. Gestures: A working bibliography. *Southern Folklore Quarterly,* 1957, *21,* 218-317.

Hewes, G. W. Primate communication and the gestural origins of language. *Current Anthropology,* 1973, *14,* 5-24.

Hockett, C. F. In search of Jove's brow. *American Speech,* 1978, *53,* 243-313.

Jancovic, M. A., Devoe, S., and Wiener, M. Age related changes in hand and arm movements as non-verbal communication: Some conceptualizations and an empirical exploration. *Child Development,* 1975, *46,* 922-928.

Johnson, H. G., Ekman, P., and Friesen, W. V. Communicative body movements: American emblems. *Semiotica,* 1975, *15,* 335-353.

Kaulfers, W. V. Curiosities of colloquial gesture. Hispanica, 1931, *14,* 249-264.

Kendon, A. Some relationships between body motion and speech: An analysis of an example. In A. Seigman (Ed.), *Studies in dyadic communication.* New York: Pergamon Press, 1972.

Kendon, A. Gesticulation, speech, and the gesture theory of language origins. *Sign Language Studies,* 1975, *9,* 349-373.

Kendon, A. Differential perception and attentional frame: Two problems for investigation. *Semiotica,* 1978, *24,* 305-315.

Kendon, A. Gesticulation and speech: Two aspects of the process of utterance. In M. R. Key (Ed.) *Nonverbal communication and language.* The Hague: Mouton, 1980. (a)

Kendon, A. A description of a deaf-mute sign language from the Enga Province of Papua New Guinea with some comparative discussion. Part I: The formational properties of Enga signs. *Semiotica,* 1980, *31,* 1-34. (b)

Kendon, A. A description of a deaf-mute sign language from the Enga Province of Papua New Guinea with some comparative discussion. Part II: The semiotic functioning of Enga signs. *Semiotica,* 1980, *32,* 81-117. (c)

Kendon, A. A description of a deaf-mute sign language from the Enga Province of Papua New Guinea with some comparative discussion. Part III: Aspects of utterance construction. *Semiotica,* 1980, *32,* 245-313. (d)

Kendon, A. *Some uses of gesture.* Paper delivered to the New England Child Language Association, New London, Connecticut, 1980. (e)

Kendon, A. Geography of gesture. *Semiotica,* 1981, *37,* 129-163.

Kendon, A. The study of gesture: Some observations on its history. *Recherches Semiotiques/Semiotic Inquiry,* forthcoming.

Kimura, D. The neural basis of language *qua* gesture. In H. Whitaker and H. A. Whitaker (Eds.), *Studies in neurolinguistics* (Vol. 2). New York: Academic Press, 1976.

Kirk, L., and Burton, M. Physical versus semantic classification of nonverbal forms: A cross cultural experiment. *Semiotica,* 1976, *17,* 315-338.

Kuschel, R. The silent inventor. *Sign Language Studies,* 1973, *3,* 1-26.

Lock, A. *The guided reinvention of language.* London: Academic Press, 1980.

Mandel, M. Iconic devices in American Sign Language. In L. A. Friedman (Ed.) *On the other hand: New perspectives in American Sign Language.* New York: Academic Press, 1977.

Marcos, L. R. Nonverbal behavior and thought processing. *Archives of General*

Psychiatry, 1979, *36,* 940-943.

McNeill, D. *The conceptual basis of language.* Hillsdale, NJ: Lawrence Erlbaum, 1979.

McNeill, D. Iconic gestures of children and adults. In A. Kendon and T. Blakely (Eds.) *Approaches to gesture.* Special issue of *Semiotica,* forthcoming.

McNeill, D., and Levy, E. Conceptual representations in language activity and gesture. In R. J. Jarvella and W. Klein (Eds.), *Speech, place and action: Studies in deixis and related topics.* Chichester: John Wiley, 1982.

Meissner, M., and Philpott, S. B. The sign language of sawmill workers of British Columbia. *Sign Language Studies,* 1975, *9,* 291-347.

Morris, D., Collett, P., Marsh, P., and O'Shaughnessy, M. *Gestures: Their origins and distribution.* New York: Stein & Day, 1979.

Munari, B. *Supplemento al Dizionario Italiano.* Milan: Muggiani, 1963.

Peterson, L. N., and Kirshner, H. S. Gestural impairment and gestural ability in aphasia: A review. *Brain and Language,* 1981, *14,* 333-348.

Pickett, L. An assessment of gestural and pantomimic deficit in aphasic patients. *Acta Symbolica,* 1974, *5,* 69-86.

Poyatos, F. Gesture inventories: Fieldwork methodology and problems. *Semiotica,* 1975, *13,* 199-227.

Pylyshyn, Z. W. What the mind's eye tells the mind's brain: A critique of mental imagery. *Psychological Bulletin,* 1973, *80,* 1-24.

Rickford, J. R., and Rickford, A. E. Cut-eye and Suck-teeth: African gestures in New World guise. *Journal of American Folklore,* 1976, *89,* 294-309.

Riseborough, M. G. Physiographic gestures as decoding facilitators: Three experiments exploring a neglected facet of communication. *Journal of Nonverbal Behavior,* 1981, *5,* 172-183.

Saitz, R. L., and Cervenka, E. J. *Handbook of gestures: Colombia and the United States.* The Hague: Mouton, 1972.

Scheflen, A. E. The significance of posture in communication systems. *Psychiatry,* 1964, *27,* 316-331.

Schegloff, E. A. *Iconic gestures, locational gestures and speech production.* Unpublished manuscript, Department of Sociology, University of California, Los Angeles, n.d.

Sherzer, J. Verbal and nonverbal deixis: The pointed lip gesture among the San Blas Cuna. *Language and Society,* 1973, *2,* 117-131.

Skelly, M. *Amerind gestural code based on universal American Indian hand talk.* New York: Elsevier, 1979.

Slama-Cazacu, T. Nonverbal components in message sequence: "mixed syntax." In W. C. McCormack and S. A. Wurm (Eds.), *Language and man: Anthropological issues.* The Hague: Mouton, 1976.

Sousa-Poza, J. F., Rohrberg, R., and Mercure, A. Effects of type of information (abstract-concrete) and field dependence on asymmetry of hand movements during speech. *Perceptual and Motor Skills,* 1979, *48,* 1323-1330.

Sparhawk, C. M. Contrastive identificational features of Persian gesture. *Semiotica,* 1978, *24,* 49-86.

Stokoe, W. C. Sign language structure. *Annual Review of Anthropology,* 1980, *9,* 365-390.

Taylor, A. The Shanghai gesture. *Folklore Fellows Communications,* 1956, No. 166, 1-76.

Taylor, A. Nonverbal communications systems in native North America. *Semiotica,* 1975, *13,* 329-374.

Teodorrson, S. T. Autonomy and linguistic status of non-speech language forms. *Journal of Psycholinguistic Research,* 1980, *9,* 121-145.

Umiker-Sebeok, D. J., and Sebeok, T. A. *Aboriginal sign languages of the Americas and Australia* (Vol. 2). New York: Plenum Press, 1978.

Varney, N. R. Linguistic correlates of pantomime recognition in aphasic patients. *Journal of Neurology, Neurosurgery and Psychiatry,* 1978, *41,* 546-568.

Walker, M., and Nazmi, M. K. Communicating shapes by words and gestures. *Australian Journal of Psychology,* 1979, *31,* 137-147.

Washabaugh, W., Woodward, J., and DeSantis, S. Providence Island sign language: A context dependent language. *Anthropological Linguistics,* 1978, *20,* 95-109.

West, L. *The sign language.* Unpublished doctoral dissertation, Indiana University, 1960.

Wiener, M., Devoe, S., Rubinow, S., and Geller, J. Nonverbal behavior and nonverbal communication. *Psychological Review,* 1972, *79,* 185-214.

Wilkinson, L. C., and Rembold, K. L. The form and function of children's gestures accompanying verbal directives. In P. S. Dale and D. Ingram (Eds.), *Child language: An international perspective.* Baltimore: University Park Press, 1981.

Wundt, W. *The language of gestures.* The Hague: Mouton, 1973. (Translation of *Volkerpsychologie: Eine Untersuchung der Entricklungsgesetze von Sprache, Mythus und Sitte,* Vol. 1, 4th ed., Part 1, Ch. 2. Stuttgart: Alfred Kroner Verlag, 1921.)

Chapter 2

TOUCH
A Bonding Gesture

Richard Heslin and Tari Alper

ONE OF THE MOST interesting aspects of touching as an area of study is that it is susceptible to multiple interpretations. For example, a letter to a well-known columnist exemplifies the change in meaning that can occur between the hand and the shoulder.

> Dear Ann Landers: I have rheumatoid arthritis and must use a walker. Very often when I pass people on the street they pat me on the shoulder as I go by.
>
> In the first place, I feel it is very rude to touch a stranger. It irritates me no end. I resent this demonstration of pity and wish I had the nerve to tell them so—but I haven't. So—will you please tell them for me? Thank you so much, Miss Landers.
>
> —Leave Me Be
>
> Dear L.M.B.: Your letter is an excellent example of what can happen when people don't understand one another.
>
> What you interpret as "pity" is actually compassion. These strangers are trying to tell you they are sorry you are handicapped. The pat is a gesture of caring. I hope in the future you will be able to see it that way [Landers, 1976].

Touching implies interpersonal involvement, but the meaning of that involvement can range from affirmation to "put down," as we see in the preceding interchange. It is complicated by social norms regarding who has permission to touch whom and what is considered to be an appropriate context for such behavior.

In this chapter we will present seven aspects of touch that, for one reason or another, are especially important: (1) cultural differences, (2) the meanings of touch, (3) its relationship to liking, (4) touch as a reflection of an existing social relationship, (5) its role in influencing other people, (6) norms concerning access to people, and (7) measuring a person's attitude toward touch.

Because touching is a behavior—a phenomenon, not a theory—writing about it involves looking at it from a variety of different, disparate, and somewhat unrelated perspectives. The one thing they share is that each of the seven aspects gives a bit more clarity to our concept of what touch means, and what it does, to people.

A CULTURAL FRAMEWORK

In different countries people greet each other differently, look at each other's face for different lengths of time, speak in different tones of voice, and display affection differently (see Williams, 1966). For example, in the midwestern United States one seldom sees either the bear hug or *abrazo* greeting, which is common among Spanish-speaking males, or the carefully graded series of bows used by the Japanese when greeting. Even within a cultural grouping which appears homogeneous from the outside, there may be substantial variability. For example, although Americans tend to contrast the nonverbal style of the Hispanic with that of the "Anglo," Shuter (1976) has found variations within Hispanic cultures as well: Costa Ricans are significantly more likely to touch and hold than Panamanians, who, in turn, are more touch-oriented than Colombians.

Key (1975) cites cultural differences in the interpretation and manifestation of almost every conceivable sound and movement. She describes an eyewitness report collected by Sir James Frazer (1919/1927: 84) of the occurrence of weeping when the Maoris of New Zealand greet or leave friends:

> A great display of outward feeling is made: it commences with a kind of ogling glance, then a whimper, and an affectionate exclamation; then a tear begins to glisten in the eye; a wry face is drawn; then they will shuffle nearer to the individual, and at length cling around his neck. They then begin to cry outright . . . and, at last, to roar outrageously, and almost smother with kisses, tears, and blood.

This description is almost as informative about the British observer as it is about the Maoris, and Frazer's terms ("great display," "outrageously") reflect his own culture's norms concerning proper behavior in greeting and departure.

Another example of the role in touching is given by Hall and Whyte (1960: 7):

An American at a cocktail party in Java tripped over the invisible cultural ropes which mark the boundaries of acceptable behavior. He was seeking to develop a business relationship with a prominent Javanese and seemed to be doing very well. Yet, when the cocktail party ended, so apparently did a promising beginning. For the North American spent nearly six months trying to arrange a second meeting. He finally learned, through pitying intermediaries, that at the cocktail party he had momentarily placed his arm on the shoulder of the Javanese—and in the presence of other people. Humiliating! Almost unpardonable in traditional Javanese etiquette.

In this particular case, the unwitting breach was mended by a graceful apology. It is worth noting, however, that a truly cordial business relationship never did develop.

Although most information about cultural differences in nonverbal behaviors is anecdotal, there are some empirical studies addressing this topic.

For example, in a study of patterns of interaction comparing Arab and American male students, the Arabs were observed to sit closer to one another, maintain a more direct body orientation, engage in greater eye contact, and converse in louder voices than did their American counterparts (Watson and Graves, 1966). Furthermore, members of the Arab pairs occasionally touched one another, whereas touching never occurred between the American conversationalists.

One conclusion we can draw from these reports is that underlying the cultural differences in nonverbal behavior are differences in the meaning given to the behavior by the different cultures. If touching a friend is normative for a culture, then doing it is not an invasion of privacy. But if it is not normative, then it may be a gesture of greater bonding or familiarity than the recipient desires.

Before we get into some recent models and research on the meanings of touch, we want to indicate three early works that are good sources of background material about touching. The early writing on touching ranged widely in search of insights. For example, Montagu's (1971) discussion includes the effects of contact even on the fetus in the womb. He considers the physical and psychological benefits that result from such things as breast feeding, parental and peer touching while the child is growing, and tactile pleasure from bathing. But he also gets into such fascinating peripheral issues as the symbolic role of clothing, sunbathing, and nudity.

Another early view of touching was presented by Frank (1957). He draws together evidence from disparate sources on the impact of touching, and his work serves as a source of hypotheses for more systematic work in this area. Finally, a more anthropological emphasis is given by Kaufman (1971). He applies the kind of structural analysis to touching ("tacemes," "tacemorphs," and "tacemorphic constructions") that has been used with language and has been applied by Birdwhistell (1970) to body movements.

THE MEANINGS OF TOUCH:
A TAXONOMY AND SEX DIFFERENCES

As we said earlier, the nonverbal behaviors that display affect or have norms associated with their manifestations, such as gaze, touch, interpersonal distance, body lean, and body orientation, are open to multiple interpretations. For example, the meaning of a touch is affected by (1) what part of the body touched the other person, (2) what part of the body is touched, (3) how long the touch lasts, (4) how much pressure is used, (5) whether there is movement after contact has been made, (6) whether anyone else is present, (7) if others are present, who they are, (8) the situation in which it occurs (such as a funeral or athletic contest) and the mood created by that situation, and (9) the relationship between the persons involved.

Touching can convey liking, power, and sexuality. All three of these aspects of relating to another person can be somewhat frightening and disturbing. One is in a more predictable and safer world when one keeps one's distance from others. In order to reduce the uncertainty about who can touch whom and what it means, situations and relationships are used as cues to regulate the kind of touch that is to be expected. These situations/relationships can be ordered in intensity.

Heslin (1974) has specified five kinds of situations/relations involving touching. Ranging from the most distant to the most intimate, they are:

(1) Functional/Professional
(2) Social/Polite
(3) Friendship/Warmth
(4) Love/Intimacy
(5) Sexual Arousal

This taxonomy does not deal with the negative touches (such as pinches and punches) which are relatively rare. It emphasizes the effect of (1) the degree of familiarity between the two people, and (2) role expectations. One of the major points of the taxonomy is that the situation/relation breakdown affects what is to be the appropriate interpretation of a touch.

In the *Functional/Professional* relationship, the person is touched in order for the toucher to do something to the receiver. Examples of this kind of relationship are physician-patient, physical therapist-patient, golf professional-student, and beautician-customer. The relationship involved is primarily manipulator-to-object. Although there is a tendency to decry the "cold" manner in which professionals relate to their clients, such a manner is required if it is to be clear that the touching is Functional/Professional rather than conveying a more intense relationship. A particular problem with Functional/Professional touching is that the actual touches used can be fairly intimate and would be quite inappropriate for the degree of acquaintance of the persons involved if the relationship were not Functional/Professional. It is possible in this context to touch intimate areas of a person with whom one is not even acquainted.

There are touching events that can best be categorized under the heading *Social/Polite*. This touching is culturally constrained by norms that prescribe how, when, and whom one should touch. The most usual Social/Polite touch is the handshake (or, in other times and other places, the kiss on the hand), and one of its functions is to acknowledge the humanity of both parties.

Because Social/Polite touching (especially shaking hands) is an act that neutralizes status, it is used to signal that the persons involved are starting off on status levels that manifest each other's personhood. Because it is a recognition of the humanity of the other person, it signals that they will start off as something less extreme than bitter enemies—quite a bit to accomplish with one handshake. (Our proposal that the handshake and other Social/Polite variants of it are status-neutralizing does not contradict Henley's [1973] proposal that touching someone reflects superior status. She is referring to touching that is not reciprocated.)

The *Friendship/Warmth* category occupies a special place in the taxonomy. In a sense, it is the touch relationship around which there is the most uneasiness. It is less formalized than the Social/Polite touch; consequently, a Friendship/Warmth touch may be misinterpreted as indicating love and/or sexual attraction. This is especially threatening in the case of same-sex touching.

We hypothesized that Friendship/Warmth touching will occur less often when friends are alone. This is because with privacy, the likelihood increases that Friendship/Warmth touching will be misinterpreted as love or sexual touching. *We also hypothesized that it is in the areas of Friendship/Warmth that the greatest cross-cultural variability occurs.* The differences in managing Friendship/Warmth touching from culture to culture reflect the differences among cultures in dealing with the potential of illicit or unsanctioned sexuality. For some cultures the fear of such sexuality (homosexuality, heterosexuality that is not sanctioned) is so great that people are willing to forego the warmth and support of touch for the safety of privacy.

The touches that convey *Love/Intimacy* require that the relationship be appropriate for that message if the touch is not to create a disturbance. Laying your hand on the cheek of another person or taking his hand will be interpreted as a loving gesture by most people in the U.S. culture (Nguyen et al., 1975). Figure 2.1 illustrates the expected discomfort that a person will feel when touched by another person. If the relationship between the two persons is very close, as in the case of lovers, then intimate touch will cause no discomfort. In fact, the most discomfort from touch for a person at that level of intimacy would be in receiving a touch that is inappropriately distant for the relationship, such as a handshake. With nonintimate relationships, on the other hand, more intimate touches are expected to be reacted to with more discomfort, especially when the people involved are strangers.

To the extent that a person does not want to make a commitment to the responsibilities of a Love/Intimacy relationship, he or she will be made uncomfortable by touch that assumes that type of bond. Furthermore, males will feel conflict between the behavioral style defined by "masculinity" and the gentler, tender, sensitive behavior expected in a Love/ Intimacy relationship.

The last level of intensity is *Sexual Arousal.* It is the kind of touching that is pleasant because of the sexual meaning and stimulation it conveys. But it can be frightening and arouse anxiety as well. An aspect of the sexual relationship is the physical attraction toward another.

It may be difficult to classify touches that may have components of both Love/Intimacy and Sexual Arousal. The fact that categories overlap for a given person can be demonstrated. For some people touch that means sexual arousal also conveys love. For others, the two concepts are quite distinct. For still others, the more a touch conveys sexual desire, the less it conveys Love/Warmth (Nguyen et al., 1975).

It seems to us that these five levels of intensity of relationship can relate to personalizing and humanizing the other in two possible ways. One model says that *as one moves from Functional/Professional to Sexual Arousal, there is a corresponding increase in the extent to which one individualizes and humanizes the other person.*

An alternative model posits that *the most appreciation of the other as an individual occurs in the Friendship/Warmth relationship.* It is in friendship relationships that people can be themselves; the other levels are less tolerant of idiosyncracies. Freedom to be self-expressive is greater with a

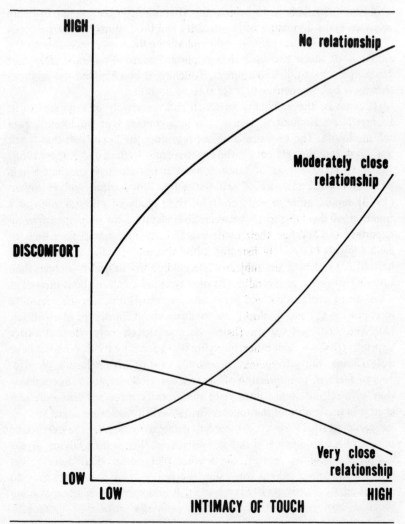

FIGURE 2.1   Affective Response to Touch as a Function of the Intimacy of the
Relationship Between the Toucher and the Recipient, and the Intimacy of the Touch

friend than with a lover, partly because of the high personal involvement a
person has in the success of a love relationship and partly because of the
person's need to restructure the other person to meet his or her own needs
in a love relationship. Even though there are love relationships that
support the individuality of the partners, the second model says that these
relationships are the exception and not the rule. It is our guess that we

could use the extent to which the first model exists in an intimate relationship as a measure of its maturity and the maturity of the partners.

We hope that this typology, by emphasizing the importance of both the function of touch and how the people are relating, makes it clear that touch must be studied in context. Touching is bonding and the relationship must be congruent with it for it to be positive.

Because of the ambiguity of touch and the variety of responses to it, therapists are hesitant to touch even in a context that would encourage self-disclosure. The evidence is mixed regarding the hypothesis that touch and disclosure are related. On the negative side, Jourard and Rubin (1968) found that the extent of body contact is not strongly correlated to a paper-and-pencil measure of self-disclosure. But Jourard and Friedman (1970) report more mixed results in their study of self-disclosure as a function of the "distance" between confederates and participants in an experiment. They had their confederates behave in one of four ways to each subject: (1) merely listening while the subject talks about him- or herself, (2) touching the subject while guiding the subject to a chair, then listening while he or she talks, (3) disclosing information about himself in a variety of professional and personal areas, or (4) touching the subject as in condition (2) and disclosing information about himself as in condition (3). The first two groups (listen only or touch only) do not differ significantly from each other, implying that touch, by itself, does not have a significant ability to increase a person's level of self-disclosure, positiveness of feelings, or impression of the toucher. However, touch in combination with self-disclosure does yield significantly more self-disclosure and change in impression of the toucher than does self-disclosure alone.

Aguilera (1967) reports evidence that seems to support the hypothesis of touching encouraging, if not self-disclosure, then at least talking. Working with psychiatric nurses, she reports that nurses elicit more verbal interaction from a patient when they touch him or her than when they do not. Similarly, Pattison (1973) reports that undergraduate women who are touched during an initial counseling interview engage in more self-exploration than those who are not touched. The findings that touching facilitates talking support the notion that tactile closeness may facilitate psychological, interpersonal closeness. However, as we shall see later, there is a good possibility that some other behavior, such as being friendly and interested, may have helped the relationship.

An effective use of touch, whether in an interpersonal social setting or for therapeutic purposes, seems to require that one first know the *meaning* of touch. People have complained to us, "You know, I'm a toucher. But I often hold back from touching somebody because I'm not sure how that person is going to react to me touching her." Touch can be misinterpreted.

Before we can understand the meaning of touch, we must ask what kind of touch it is that we are considering. Decoding the meaning of a tactile message depends not only on how it is transmitted (mode of touch) but also on where it is applied (area touched). Tactile communication could be misunderstood if a touch (for example, brushing a hand against the outside of someone's thigh) is given different interpretations by the interactors. A touch intended by a woman to convey love might be construed by her male friend as merely an expression of playfulness because of where it is applied.

There have been findings that indicate sex differences in reactions to touch. Women respond positively to having their hand brushed when a library clerk returns their identification card; men do not (Fisher et al., 1976). Women respond positively to a touch on the hand and arm by a nurse during a preoperative instruction session. Men respond negatively (Whitcher and Fisher, 1979).

Thus we find some evidence that women respond more positively than men to being touched. However, when it comes to initiating touch, men are viewed by other persons more positively the more touch they use in greeting, especially with women, whereas for women the results are less straightforward (Silverthorne et al., 1976).

A series of studies has investigated meanings the two sexes give to touch. In the first study (Nguyen et al., 1975), we find that, as expected, men and women agree on what kinds of touch signify sexual desire ($\bar{r}$ = .94). However, men and women differ in their *reactions* to these touches. For men, touches that indicate sexual desire also convey pleasantness, warmth/love, and playfulness ($\bar{r}$ = .59); for women, the more a touch conveys sexual desire, the *less* it is pleasant, warm/loving, playful, or friendly ($\bar{r}$ = -.80; mean correlation calculated using r to z transformation).

It is not clear from that study whether these sex differences in the meaning of touch are due to a general difference between the sexes or to a difference specific to this sample of subjects—college freshmen and sophomores. A follow-up study (Nguyen et al., 1976) on married couples gives us some comparison responses. The average correlations between ratings of "sexual desire" and pleasantness, warmth/love, and playfulness are not as strong for married men ($\bar{r}$ = .22) as they are for unmarried men, an interesting side commentary on men and marriage. But the most striking finding is with women. In contrast to the negative association between sexual desire and pleasant or positive states in the minds of unmarried women, married women have a substantially positive association ($\bar{r}$ = .64) with sexual touching. The aphorism, "familiarity breeds contempt" (or at least, reduces enthusiasm), may be more of a male than a female response to touches from the opposite sex.

One problem with these two studies is that they deal only with touch between intimates of the opposite sex. A third study (Heslin et al., 1982) extends their scope to include touch from strangers and same-sex persons—encounters that are fraught with the potential for miscommunication.

We expect that touch from either a stranger or a same-sex other person will be viewed as unpleasant. Physical intimacy with a person of one's own sex increases the probability of homosexual involvement, while an intimate gesture from a stranger may constitute an unbearable invasion of privacy. On the other hand, the stranger could represent adventure, excitement, and new experiences, and a same-sex other could represent the security and familiarity of one who shares common perspectives and interests. It thus remains to be determined empirically what situations create discomfort.

To understand the meaning of touch, one must consider many factors, not the least of which is whether there is some congruence between the intimacy of the relationship and the intimacy of the nonverbal behavior. This question is raised indirectly by Argyle and Dean's (1965) concept of an equilibrium level of nonverbal intimacy with other persons (see Heslin and Patterson, 1982, for discussion of this concept). Although Argyle and Dean focus on the compensatory mechanisms activated when a component of the equilibrium, such as distance, is varied, the whole notion of equilibrium implies that people try to keep some congruence between how close they feel toward someone and how intimately they behave toward that person.

According to the congruence hypothesis, intimate tactile behavior should be rated negatively when the interpersonal relationship does not warrant it. The kind of touch that should be most sensitive to relational congruence is the stroke, since previous research (Nguyen et al., 1975) has shown it to be the most intimate form.

Intimacy with a member of the opposite sex who is not a close friend raises a set of special concerns. Rytting's (1975) study shows that women do not think in terms of intimate involvement with a man who is not yet a close friend, but men tend to anticipate or consider romantic involvement with women even when they first meet them. Since the present study involves having both men and women react to being touched by strangers as well as close friends, we are able to pursue Rytting's findings and ask, "How *will* men and women rate friendly and intimate touching from an opposite-sex stranger?"

We have ratings by 208 male and female undergraduate students based on the drawing of the body as shown in Figure 2.2—a modification of the figure used by Jourard (1966). The participants were asked to keep in mind the question, "What does it mean to me when a close person

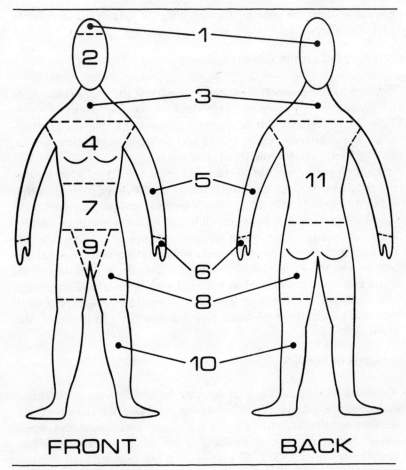

FIGURE 2.2   Figure presented to the Respondents to Identify the Areas of the Body Being Rated

(stranger) of the opposite sex (same sex) touches the indicated area of my body in a certain manner?" Parents, siblings, and relatives were excluded from the category of "close person." This question was answered in terms of (1) each of the eleven body areas depicted in Figure 2.2, (2) four modes of touch (squeeze, stroke, brush—possibly by accident—and pat), and (3) six meaning categories (invasion of privacy, pleasantness, playfulness, warmth/love, friendship/fellowship, and sexual desire)—a total of 264 ratings per person. For example, a respondent indicates (on a seven-point scale) the extent to which he or she agrees or disagrees that when a same-sex stranger pats his or her area 1 (head/forehead), this represents an invasion of his or her privacy. Each person rates the touch from only one kind of person, such as a stranger of the opposite sex.

INTERCORRELATIONS AMONG MEANINGS

Correlations are reported on the respondents' six ratings (invasion of privacy and so on) across the 11 body areas and four modes of touch. Table 2.1 presents the average degree of relationship among the six ratings across the eight conditions generated by combining male or female rater, male or female toucher, and friend or stranger.

Looking at the "range of correlations" column in Table 2.1, we see that the association between any two meanings that might be given to touches received is strongly affected by who is touching and who is receiving the touches. For example, the largest difference between the most negative and most positive correlations is in the ratings of sexual desire and playfulness (from $-.21$ to $.83$). When a woman rates touches from another women who is a friend (FSC), a touch that she rates as indicating sexual desire is definitely not rated by her as playful. When a male rates touch from a woman who is a close friend (MOC), on the other hand, if a touch is seen as indicating sexual desire, then it is very likely to be seen as also playful.

INVASION OF PRIVACY

Jourard (1966) reports that intimate bodily contacts occur almost exclusively with the best friend of the opposite sex. In this study, results are obtained that support Jourard's finding—touches from a close, opposite-sex person are rated as significantly less invasive of personal privacy than touches from a close, same-sex person and from strangers of either the same or the opposite sex.

The stroke, which has connotations of love and sex (Nguyen et al., 1975), is viewed as significantly less invasive of privacy when coming from a close opposite-sex person than when coming from a stranger. This finding is consistent with our hypothesis that psychological comfort/ discomfort is dependent upon the congruence between tactile intimacy and interpersonal intimacy.

As one might expect, a stroke from a close, opposite-sex person is also rated as significantly less invasive of privacy than stroke from a close, same-sex person. This finding supports the notion that situations that may be construed as reflective of homosexual involvement are uncomfortable to most people in this culture.

TABLE 2.1 Touch as a Function of Sex of Recipient/Respondent, Sex of Toucher, and Acquaintanceship

Ratings of Meanings of Touch	Median Correlation Between the Two Meanings	Range of Correlations		Settings for Extreme Correlations		Differences Between High and Low Using r to z Transformation
		Most Negative	Most Positive	Most Negative r	Most Positive r	
Privacy invasion & loving	−.40	−.56	.09	MSS	MOC	.72
Privacy invasion & pleasant	−.37	−.71	.08	FOS	MOC	.97
Privacy invasion & friendship	−.36	−.70	.13	FOS	MOC	1.00
Privacy invasion & playful	.28	−.55	.21	MSS	MOC	.83
Sexual desire & friendship	.21	−.18	.73	FOS & FSC	MOC	1.11
Sexual desire & pleasant	.24	−.21	.79	FOS	MOC	1.28
Sexual Desire & privacy invasion	.29	−.03	.39	FOS	MSC & FSC	.44
Sexual desire & playfulness	.33	−.21	.83	FSC	MOC	1.40
Sexual desire & loving	.36	−.11	.83	FOS & FSC	MOC	1.30
Playful & pleasant	.71	.64	.80	MSS	MOC	.34
Playful & loving	.81	.56	.88	MSS	MOC	.75
Friendship & pleasant	.82	.73	.89	MSS	MOS	.49
Friendship & playful	.82	.76	.90	MOS	FSS	.47
Loving & friendship	.84	.61	.94	MSS	FSC	.76
Loving & pleasant	.85	.70	.93	MSS	MOC	.79

M = male recipient/respondent; F = female recipient/respondent; S = same sex touches; O = opposite sex touches; C = toucher is close friend; S (as third letter only) = toucher is stranger.

NOTE: Correlations are for less intimate areas of the body. Correlations based on ratings involving intimate areas did not differ significantly.

A key question raised in this study is, "What is the effect of familiarity or sex of the other person on perception of touch?" In other words, is fear of a stranger's touch greater than fear of homosexual involvement? Figure 2.3 shows that men and women differ in the importance they give to those two characteristics. In judging the privacy invasion of a touch, men pay more attention to the sex of the toucher than do women. On the other hand, women pay more attention to degree of acquaintanceship than do men.

PLEASANTNESS RATINGS

Looking at the total body, we find that the least pleasant touches are those that come from a same-sex stranger for both sexes, while the most pleasant touches are those that come from opposite-sex friends (Figure 2.4). These discrepancies are particularly evident when touches are applied to sexual areas. Thus, the congruence between a relationship, the situation, and the nonverbal behavior between two people affects psychological anxiety/comfort.

There is, however, one major exception. Men and women differ in their reactions to touches from opposite-sex strangers. As hypothesized, women find significantly less pleasantness in a touch from a male stranger than from a male friend. Men, however, are as comfortable with touch from a woman stranger as from a woman friend. These differences are particularly striking when one considers reactions to touches to the genital areas (Figure 2.4). Such touches are highly pleasant to men regardless of their acquaintanceship with the woman, but they are only pleasant for women when the toucher is a close male friend. Both men and women give the highest mean pleasantness ratings to a stroke of their sexual areas by a close opposite-sex person. However, women give the next highest pleasure ratings to a stroke of their nonsexual areas by a close male friend, while men give the next highest pleasure ratings to a woman *stranger* stroking their *sexual* areas. (Somehow this finding seems relevant to the absence of massage parlors that cater to women.) These differences between the sexes regarding touches from opposite-sex strangers may be caused by the way men view women. As we noted earlier, Rytting (1975) found that men tend not to think in terms of a platonic relationship with a woman. Rather, they consider romantic and physical involvement with a woman much more readily than do women with a man. For men, in this sense, at least, there may not be such a category as a woman "stranger."

The findings of the Heslin et al. (1982) study can be seen to have three major implications. First, touch from a person of one's own sex is generally viewed with uneasiness and anxiety in middle-class American

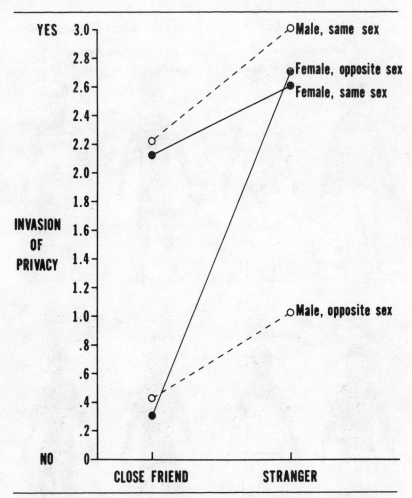

FIGURE 2.3   Rated Extent to Which Men and Women See Touch as an Invasion of Privacy, as a Function of Familiarity or Sex of Toucher

culture. This is particularly true when the other person is a stranger and the touch, because of its modality or the body area touched, has intimate connotations.

Second, congruence between tactile and social intimacy is a significant factor in the psychological receptivity to touch. This is demonstrated in the finding that the same kind of touch (stroke) can be the most and the least invasive of privacy, depending on its congruence with the social relationship.

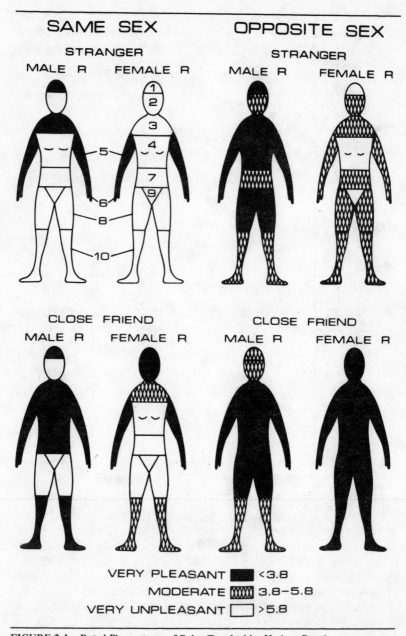

FIGURE 2.4   Rated Pleasantness of Being Touched by Various People

Third, there are important differences between men and women in spite of substantial overlaps in their responses to touch. One significant differ ence relates to the relative importance each sex gives to the degree of familiarity with the toucher and to the sex of the toucher. Men tend to pay greater attention than women to the sex of the other person, whereas women show most concern about the degree of acquaintanceship and less concern about the sex of the toucher.

Women show a marked lack of enthusiasm for touches from a strange man. This finding, taken together with women's greater concern about their bodies when touched (Nguyen et al., 1975), seems to indicate that women view their bodies as more vulnerable than do men. The greater number of violent crimes committed against women by men than vice versa (U.S. National Commission on the Causes and Prevention of Vio- lence, 1969) may be one reason for female caution and sense of physical vulnerability. A second factor may be the cultural norm that a woman's life—body and mind—should be devoted to the care and welfare of her husband and children. Such devotion rules out the possibility of romantic involvement with men who are strangers. As William James has been reported to have expounded in a light moment:

> Higamous, hogamous, women are monogamous
> Hogamous, higamous, men are polygamous.

TOUCHING AND LIKING

Those associated with the "human potential movement" (encounter groups and the like) have long maintained that touching leads to liking. Boderman et al. (1972) tested this belief in a setting divested of the encounter group atmosphere—an "ESP experiment." When a female subject explores the face of a female confederate and has her face explored by the confederate (supposedly to facilitate the extrasensory perception), the subject has a generally more positive attitude toward the confederate than does a subject in a no-touch control condition (Boderman et al., 1972). Thus, it appears we have evidence that touching does, indeed, cause liking.

However, in an attempt to replicate and extend Boderman et al.'s study, Breed and Ricci (1973) proposed that the touch effect may be due to the confederate exuding greater warmth when she touches and is touched by the subjects. When warm or cold demeanor on the part of the confederate is manipulated independently of touching, subjects respond to the warmth and cold variations but not to the touch variations. Breed and

Ricci conclude that there is a good possibility that the Boderman et al. effect is due to the confederate in the touch condition being warmer and more pleasant than in the no-touch condition. Consequently, touch per se may have little or no effect on people. While such an interpretation is certainly consistent with the Breed and Ricci (1973) results, it may still be the case that touching and communication of warmth and caring are inextricably interwined. If that is so, then a separation of them would be an artificiality and does not represent natural situations.

The problem with the above two "ESP experiments" is that they are, to say the least, atypical experiences for the people participating in them and susceptible to attempts by the subjects to act in a way that they consider (1) is expected of them as experimental subjects, and (2) will make them look healthy, bright, and well adjusted. A study by Fisher et al. (1975) is free of these contaminants. They found that when men and women clerks in a university library touch the hand of a patron as they return his or her identification card, this less than half-second touch causes the women patrons not only to like the clerk, but also to feel better and to like the library better than those who are not touched. This finding is a demonstration that even very casual touch by a stranger is noticed, can be more positive than negative, and has the power to increase a person's (1) general sense of well-being and (2) evaluation of the external world. The last effect happens when a person rests his or her hand on a person's shoulder while adjusting a slide projector (Silverthorne et al., 1972). The person likes the slides that are on the screen more while being touched.

It seems then, that touching can lead to liking, but that the relationship between these two sets of variables is complex and susceptible to other influences, such as warmth of the touch and the meaning assigned to it by the recipient.

Are people more likely to touch someone they like? Evidence to support the notion that liking leads to touch is sparse, mostly correlational, and comes from scattered sources. For example, Jourard (1966) found that college students touch and are touched on far more areas of their body by their best friends of the opposite-sex than by their parents or best friends of the same sex. This tendency appears to have gotten even stronger in more recent years (Rosenfeld et al., 1976). This would seem to indicate that these students touch and are touched by those with whom they have the strongest liking relationship. However, our interpretation of Jourard's (1966) findings must be moderated by our awareness that one does not touch even well-liked same-sex others or parents in more than a friendly way because of concern about incest and homosexuality.

SOCIAL REGULATION

The research by Jourard (1966) on reported incidence of touching examines how it is affected by the relationships between the people involved. Research by Heslin and Boss (1980) pursues this question of the importance of the social relationship. Our study is designed to examine nonverbal intimacy as it occurs spontaneously in a natural setting. An airport was the setting and we looked at the greeting and departure rituals there.

In the airport, travelers and persons chosen from among the people who came to meet them or send them off were observed and queried about their relationships. From the types of touch observed, a scale of six levels of intimacy was developed based on the combination of touches seen in the encounter.

0   no touch
I   (a) handshake, or (b) touch on head, arm, or back
II (a) light hug, (b) arm around waist or back, (c) holding hands, (d) kiss on cheek, or (e) two from I
III (a) solid hug, (b) kiss on mouth, or (c) three from I and/or II
IV (a) extended embrace, (b) both kiss on mouth and solid hug, or (c) either kiss on mouth or solid hug and two from I and II
V   (a) extended kiss, (b) extended embrace plus kiss on mouth, (c) extended embrace plus solid hug plus any other, or (d) four or more of any category above II

Levels of intimacy expressed in actual encounters occur with the following frequencies: 0 = 16%, I = 12%, II = 16%, III = 28%, IV = 11%, and V = 18%. Categories 0 and I would have had higher frequencies if there had been strangers in the sample, but as it is, the six levels accounted for good discrimination of the behavior observed, yielding almost a rectangular distribution.

At the most primitive level of closeness is the question of the mere presence when a traveler leaves or returns. Indeed, the intimacy of the relationship between the traveler and a randomly chosen person in his or her greeting or send-off group (for example, mother and daughter) is positively related to the number of times we saw that relationship in our sample. The closeness of the relationship between the two persons also shows a solid correlation with intimacy of the behavior they expressed during their encounter.

There is a nonsignificant tendency for males to initiate touching more than females in cross-sex pairs, and significantly more older people than younger people initiate touch in cross-sex encounters but not in same-sex encounters. These results lend weak support to Goffman's (1967) proposal that persons of higher status have greater freedom to initiate touch with lower-status persons than vice versa. It is consonant with results obtained by Watson (1975; however, his findings are attenuated by methodological difficulties). Watson observed the amount of touching that occurs in a nursing home and reported that high-status persons (nurses) initiated touch with residents more than did lower-status persons (nurses' aides). In this study, nurses were women and nurses aides tended to be men. In contrast, Heslin and Boss's (1980) findings give some (albeit weak) support to Henley's (1973) proposal that males have greater freedom to initiate touch with females than vice versa.

It is also possible that our data are due to avoidance on the part of the females and younger people rather than the power of the male and older people. The fact that in same-sex pairs, older people do not initiate touch more than younger people weakens the status interpretation and supports the proposal that younger people may be manifesting lower attraction toward the initiator than vice versa in a situation in which attraction is a consideration—in cross-sex interactions. Furthermore, the strength or very existence of the hypothesized greater freedom of males to initiate touch has come into question because Smith et al. (1980), Daniel (1978), and Dean et al., (1978) did not find it.

We also found that pairs of women give and receive more solid hugs, score higher on the touch intimacy scale, engage in more frequent contact, and touch each other on the hand, arm, or back more than do pairs of men. Pairs of men shake hands more than pairs of women.

In general, it looks as if there is a slight tendency for higher-status people to initiate touch with lower-status people than vice versa, a slight tendency for older people to initiate touch with younger people than vice versa, and more touching between women than between men. It appears that there is no very strong tendency for men to initiate touch more with women than vice versa.

We found that touching per se is moderately high, in this study, with 60% of all dyads touching in at least some way. When this is compared with Jourard's (1966) and Henley's (1973) American norm of two touches per hour, it is clear that arrival and departure rituals are favorable settings for the study of naturally occurring touch. Another study of airport greeting behavior (Greenbaum and Rosenfeld, 1980) supports such a view: An even higher percentage (83%) of dyads engage in some kind of contact.

However, as can be seen in Table 2.2, there is a general tendency in our study for the more intimate kinds of touch to be relatively infrequent. The

TABLE 2.2   Tactile Involvement Between Traveler and Other

No touch	41	Kiss on cheek	30
Handshake	10	Solid hug	19
Touch on head, arm, back	38	Kiss on mouth	41
Light hug	23	Extended embrace	10
Arm around waist or back	15	Extended kiss	3
Holding hands	12		

*Contact categories in order of increasing intimacy.

NOTE: Numbers refer to the number of dyads (from a total of 103) that engaged in that behavior. The total number of touches is greater than 103 because many dyads engaged in more than one kind of touch.

most severe departures from a monotonic relationship seem to be the handshake, which occurs less often, and a kiss on the mouth, which occurs more often than a linear relationship might predict. We may nevertheless ask if the relationship between the people affects the intimacy of their touching.

We found that, indeed, the intimacy of a relationship and the intimacy of the touch used are positively related. However, Jourard (1966) found that parents do not touch their children much. Jourard's finding is puzzling, since our judges related the parent-child relationship as quite intimate. One possible explanation of this discrepancy between Jourard and our finding is that Jourard's dependent variable, the number of different areas of the body touched, influences his finding of low level of touch between parents and children. The Jourard study ranges from relationships that are close (such as parent-child) to very intimate (best friend of the opposite sex). Our study covers a much wider range of relationships (aunt-nephew to lovers). The most important difference between the two studies is that Jourard examines touch that ranges from moderately intimate to highly intimate (shoulder versus genital area), whereas we study a much narrower range and less intimate touching (handshake versus extended kiss). The kind of touch Jourard is studying (whether some intimate area of the body is touched) would heighten the differences between parent touch and touch with best friend of the opposite sex. The more public touch that we are studying would minimize the differences between parent touch and touch with best friend of the opposite sex.

The research by Jourard (1966) on reported incidence of touch and by us (Heslin and Boss, 1980) on the nature of touching at an airport focuses on how a relationship affects touching. A different way to consider the same question is to see what observers infer about a relationship from seeing interactions involving touch. In one such study, Kleinke et al. (1974) found that "engaged" couples who touch one another are rated more favorably (as more loving and so on) than those who do not touch. The touch implies a bond between the couple that is well understood by observers.

TOUCH AND INFLUENCE

The belief that touch is a medium of influence has a long and ancient history in religion and medicine. It is beyond the focus of this chapter to go into the rich lore surrounding the "laying on of hands" as a healing technique. But this form of nonverbal influence has been practiced by medico-religious persons for many centuries and in diverse cultures.

In recent years there have been attempts to test the efficacy of touch in healing with positive results (Grad et al., 1961; Krieger, 1975), but it will take many studies with supportive findings before such a belief gains wide acceptance. Healing by touch shares with extrasensory perception both an air of mystery and low regard by the scientific community. However, one can more easily find psychological and physiological explanations of healing by touch than similar explanations for some of the extrasensory perception phenomena.

Touch has been found to have three general kinds of influence on people. First, in the right kind of setting touch can make people feel more positive about both external stimuli (Fisher et al., 1976; Silverthorne et al., 1972) and the toucher (Fisher et al., 1976). Second, in the therapeutic setting, touching can help recipients talk to other people especially about themselves (Aguilera, 1967; Pattison, 1973). Finally, touching facilitates influence: People comply with requests more frequently, perform favors more readily (for example, return money found in a phone booth; Kleinke, 1977, 1980), and are more likely to sign a petition and fill out a rating scale (Willis and Hamm, 1980) when they are touched by the requester than when they are not touched.

Why should touching facilitate influence on another person? First, it can imply genuine need, since touching may violate a norm. Research by Baron and Bell (1976) on the distance a requester stands from a potential volunteer supports the implication that the recipient will tend to assume that the toucher is in genuine need. Second, it implies that the requester likes and trusts the person being solicited. The perception of either a great need or a positive attitude would tend to increase compliance.

ACCESS

We can see the regulation of access in whether a person has given permission to another to begin a conversation. A person begins a request of a stranger with an "Excuse me," indicating his awareness that he has violated the privacy buffer of the other person. Similarly, touching another person, if done without invitation or explanation, results in negative reactions, especially from men (Sussman and Rosenfeld, 1978). Because there may be norms about who should touch whom, it is in our interest to explore the touching situation to find out whether such norms do, in fact, exist and what they are. One way of expressing normative expectations is to show people some examples of touching and ask them how they feel about them.

In order to study some of the norms surrounding touching, Major and Heslin (1982) had 66 undergraduates rate eight slides showing silhouettes of people facing each other. In the touch slides one person touches the other on the shoulder.

As can be seen in Table 2.3, touching raises, and being a recipient lowers, the status of a person in the eyes of an observer. It is interesting that there are significant differences in attitude toward both toucher and recipient compared to the more moderate attitudes toward the non-touchers (see also Summerhayes and Suchner, 1978).

How does the theory that touching is a bonding act relate to these findings of favorable attitudes toward touchers and unfavorable attributions to recipients? They are quite compatible if we assume that there are constraints on the initiation of bonding by a lower-status person. There is a bit of indirect confirmation of that notion. Alber (1974) found that people touch more when they are playing a dominant role in a role-playing scene than those who are playing a more submissive role (when the actors are free to use whatever nonverbal behavior fits the scene). A person who initiates touch, then, would be seen as having (1) the status that gives permission to touch, (2) the courage and initiative to exercise that status, and (3) the kind of warm personality that would motivate him or her to express a bonding feeling.

The recipient being rated lower on status, warmth, and assertiveness than people in the no-touch control group is the other side of the coin. It

TABLE 2.3   Ratings of Touchers, Recipients, and Members of Nontouching Control Condition Pairs

	Touch Interaction		No-Touch Control Interaction	
Dimension	Toucher	Recipient	Left Actor	Right Actor
Status/dominance	9.36_a	7.61_b	8.73_c	8.44_c
Warmth/expressiveness	10.01_a	8.25_b	8.99_c	8.87_c
Instrumentality/ assertiveness	10.34_a	7.20_b	8.90_c	8.63_c

NOTE: Within a row, means with different subscripts differ from one another at the .05 level of significance.

is not a statistical artifact or foregone conclusion. Recipients could be rated the same as the control group on these three characteristics. The fact that the recipient is not reciprocating the touch must color our observers' impressions, because they seem to assume that the recipient is (1) at most, of peer status and very likely of lower status in relation to the toucher, (2) passive, and (3) less warm and accepting than not only the toucher but also a person who is simply standing and talking with someone else. In the study of touching by the staff of a nursing home, Watson (1975) points out that touching is used often in the context of criticism of the person being touched, perhaps to reduce the potential for hurt feelings. Once again, we see a dominant and a bonding component of touching. A person who does not reciprocate touch would be low on either relative status or desire to bond with the toucher, or both.

ATTITUDE TOWARD TOUCH

People are concerned about the response of others to their touch and are aware that some of their acquaintances do not touch them. It is clear that attitude toward touch is a characteristic expressive of individual differences (see Anderson and Leibowitz, 1978, for a measure of touch avoidance).

One of us (Heslin, 1982) has sought to develop an instrument that measures attitude toward touch in a differentiated combination of scales. This instrument is composed of three major scales. The first scale, *Tactile Involvement with Nonintimates,* contains 32 items segmented into the following subscales: (1) touching strangers and new acquaintances, (2) touching friends and relatives, (3) being touched by strangers or new acquaintances, (4) being touched by friends or relatives, and all five combinations of these four subscales (1 and 2, 3 and 4, 1 and 3, 2 and 4, and all four together). "Relatives" does not include spouse, and "non-intimates" refers to people other than spouse or lover or most intimate friend.

The second scale is *Nonsexual Touching with Spouse, Lover, or Most Intimate Friend.* It contains 40 items. The subscales include (1) hugging, (2) being hugged, (3) touching his/her hand, (4) having him/her take my hand, (3) putting my arm around his/her shoulder, (5) having him/her put his/her arm around my shoulder, (6) touching his/her face, (7) having him/her touch my face, (8) touching his/her arm, (9) having him/her touch my arm, and eight combinations of the ten subscales.

The third scale measures attitudes toward *Sexual Touching with Spouse, Lover, or Most Intimate Friend.* It has 26 items and these subscales: (1) touch, (2) being touched, and the sum of the two subscales.

It is necessary to break down attitudes toward touch because different processes might be involved in scores on the separate scales and subscales. For instance, a person might be very comfortable touching relatives because that is family practice, but the same person may be uncomfortable with touching a best friend of the opposite sex because of the intimacy involved. Similarly, sex-differences are expected in terms of women feeling more positively toward nonsexual touching with their boyfriends than men would feel with their girlfriends. Yet, we hypothesize that men feel more positively than women toward sexual touching.

Hibbard (1974) investigated the effects of level of romantic love in dating couples on attitudes toward sexual and nonsexual touch using these scales. Those classified as High Love couples on Rubin's (1970) love scale have a more positive attitude toward nonsexual touching than do Low Love couples. High Love couples show a trend toward liking sexual touching more than Low Love couples. There is clearly a significantly more positive attitude toward sexual touching by couples who have engaged in sexual intercourse as compared to those who have not.

CONCLUSIONS

We have looked at touch from a number of perspectives that include how people react to it and the norms surrounding it. There are two points about it that seem clear. First, touch implies a bond between the toucher and recipient. Much of the fascination surrounding touch is over the variety of responses to such a gesture, especially in its relation to the norms connected with it. In many cases, what we are looking at is the variety of responses to a bonding gesture—a gesture that may be appropriate or highly inappropriate, depending on a variety of the characteristics of the situation. The second point follows from the first: The major variance in responses to touching is due to the degree to which the touching is congruent with the intimacy of the relationship betweeen the two people.

An area for future research that seems particularly fruitful concerns the variety of ways of resolving the privacy-intimacy dilemma. Under the assumption that people cannot tolerate excessively high amounts of either intimacy or isolation, research is needed to discover how to measure the need for privacy and the need for intimacy, to examine the relationship between these needs to respond to touching with strangers and intimates, and to examine the notion of multiple modes of satisfying those needs. There are many ways of resolving the intimacy-privacy dilemma, and finding out what kinds of people and what kinds of settings bring about a particular resolution tells us not only something about touching but something about people also. To the extent that a person feels able to control interpersonal situations, he or she will be made less anxious by an unexpected bonding gesture such as touch.

Sex differences in reaction to touch may reflect such important differences in life situations. It is proposed that women approach intimacy with a stranger of the opposite sex with greater caution than do men and that women initially want to slow the process of increasing intimacy until they get to know the man better. In contrast, the fact that a woman may be a stranger may actually add some novelty value in the eyes of a man. How these differing orientations change over the development of a heterosexual relationship should be examined in the future, but it appears at this time that women want more flexibility and freedom in the early stages of a relationship than men and than they themselves want later on. Men, on the other hand, want more freedom at later stages.

REFERENCES

Aguilera, D. C. Relationship between physical contact and verbal interaction between nurses and patients. *Journal of Psychiatric Nursing and Mental Health Services,* 1967, *5,* 5-21.

Alber, J. L. *Tactile communication within dyads.* Unpublished manuscript, Purdue University, 1974.

Andersen, P. A., and Leibowitz, K. The development and nature of the construct touch avoidance. *Environmental Psychology and Nonverbal Behavior,* 1978, *3,* 89-106.

Argyle, M., and Dean, J. Eye contact, distance, and affiliation. *Sociometry,* 1965, *28,* 289-304.

Baron, R. A., and Bell, P. A. Physical distance and helping: Some unexpected benefits of crowding in on others. *Journal of Applied Social Psychology,* 1976, *6,* 95-104.

Birdwhistell, R. L. *Kinesics and context: Essays on body-motion communication.* New York: Ballantine, 1970.

Boderman, A., Freed, D. W., and Kinnucan, M. T. Touch me, like me: Testing an encounter group assumption. *Journal of Applied Behavioral Science,* 1972, *8,* 527-533.

Breed, G., and Ricci, J. S. "Touch me, like me": Artifact? *Proceedings of the 81st Annual Convention of the American Psychological Association,* 1973, *8,* 153-154.

Daniel, S. *An observational study of tactile communication in midwestern America.* Unpublished master's thesis, University of Missouri, Kansas City, 1978.

Dean, L. M., Willis, F. N., and Rinck, C. M. *Patterns of interpersonal touch in the elderly.* Paper presented at the convention of the Western Psychological Association, San Francisco, 1978.

Fisher, J. D., Rytting, M., and Heslin, R. Hands touching hands: Affective and evaluative effects of interpersonal touch. *Sociometry,* 1975, *39,* 416-421.

Frank, L. K. Tactile communication. *Genetic Psychology Monographs,* 1957, *56,* 209-235.

Frazer, J. G. Weeping as a salutation. In *Folk-lore in the Old Testament: Studies in comparative religion, legend and law* (Vol. 2). London: Macmillan, 1919.

Goffman, E. *Interaction ritual.* Garden City, NY: Anchor, 1967.

Grad, B., Cadoret, R. J., and Paul, G. I. The influence of an unorthodox method of treatment on wound healing in mice. *International Journal of Parapsychology,* 1961, *2,* 5-24.

Greenbaum, P. F., and Rosenfeld, H. M. Varieties of touching in greetings: Sequential structure and sex-related differences. *Journal of Nonverbal Behavior,* 1980, *5,* 13-25.

Hall, E. T., and Whyte, W. F. Intercultural communications: A guide to men of action. *Human Organization,* 1960, *19,* 5-12.

Henley, N. M. Status and sex: Some touching observations. *Bulletin of the Psychonomic Society,* 1973, *2,* 91-93.

Heslin, R. *Steps toward a taxonomy of touching.* Paper presented at the convention of the Midwestern Psychological Association, Chicago, May 1974.

Heslin, R. *An instrument to measure attitudes toward touching.* Unpublished manuscript, Purdue University, 1982.

Heslin, R., and Boss, D. Nonverbal intimacy in airport arrival and departure. *Personality and Social Psychology Bulletin,* 1980, *6,* 248-252.

Heslin, R., Nguyen, T. D., and Nguyen, M. L. *The meaning of touch: The case of the stranger and the same sex other person.* Unpublished manuscript, Purdue University, 1982.

Heslin, R., and Patterson, M. L. *Nonverbal behavior and social psychology.* New York: Plenum Press, 1982.

Hibbard, J. A. *Attitudes toward sexual and non-sexual touch in dating couples as a function of level of romantic love.* Unpublished master's thesis, Purdue University, 1974.

Jourard, S. M. An exploratory study of body-accessibility. *British Journal of Social and Clinical Psychology,* 1966, *5,* 221-231.

Jourard, S. M., and Friedman, R. Experimenter-subject "distance" and self-disclosure. *Journal of Personality and Social Psychology,* 1970, *5,* 278-282.

Jourard, S. M., and Rubin, J. E. Self-disclosure and touching: A study of two modes of interpersonal encounter and their inter-relation. *Journal of Humanistic Psychology,* 1968, *8,* 39-48.

Kaufman, L. E. Tacesics, the study of touch: A model for proxemic analysis. *Semiotica,* 1971, *4,* 149-161.

Key, M. R. *Paralanguage and kinesics (nonverbal communication).* Metuchen, NJ: Scarecrow Press, 1975.

Kleinke, C. L. Compliance to requests made by gazing and touching experimenters in field settings. *Journal of Experimental Social Psychology,* 1977, *13,* 218-223.

Kleinke, C. L. Interaction between gaze and legitimacy of request on compliance in a field setting. *Journal of Nonverbal Behavior,* 1980, *5,* 3-12.

Kleinke, C. L., Meeker, F. B., and LaFong, C. L. Effects of gaze, touch, and use of name on evaluation of "engaged" couples. *Journal of Research in Personality,* 1974, *7,* 368-373.

Krieger, D. Therapeutic touch: The imprimatur of nursing. *American Journal of Nursing,* 1975, *75,* 784-787.

Landers, A. *Journal and Courier* (Lafayette, Indiana), November 13, 1976.

Major, B., and Heslin, R. Perceptions of same-sex and cross-sex touching: It's better to give than to receive. *Journal of Nonverbal Behavior,* 1982, *6,* 148-162.

Montagu, A. *Touching: The human significance of skin.* New York: Columbia University Press, 1971.

Nguyen, M. L., Heslin, R., and Nguyen, T. The meaning of touch: Sex and marital status differences. *Representative Research in Social Psychology,* 1976, *7,* 13-18.

Nguyen, T., Heslin, R., and Nguyen, M. L. The meanings of touch: Sex differences. *Journal of Communication,* 1975, *25,* 92-103.

Pattison, J. E. Effects of touch on self-exploration and the therapeutic relationship. *Journal of Consulting and Clinical Psychology,* 1973, *40,* 170-175.

Rosenfeld, L. B., Kartus, S., and Ray, C. Body accessibility revisited. *Journal of Communication,* 1976, *26,* 27-30.

Rubin, A. Measurement of romantic love. *Journal of Personality and Social Psychology,* 1970, *16,* 265-273.

Rytting, M. B. *Self-disclosure in the development of a heterosexual relationship.* Unpublished doctoral dissertation, Purdue University, 1975.

Shuter, R. Proxemics and tactility in Latin America. *Journal of Communication,* 1976, *26,* 46-52.

Silverthorne, C., Micklewright, J., O'Donnell, M., and Gibson, R. Attribution of personal characteristics as a function of the degree of touch on initial contact and sex. *Sex Roles,* 1976, *2,* 185-193.

Silverthorne, C., Noreen, C., Hunt, T., and Rota, L. The effects of tactile stimulation on visual experience. *Journal of Social Psychology,* 1972, *88,* 153-154.

Smith, D. E., Willis, F. N., and Gier, J. A. Success and interpersonal touch in a competitive setting. *Journal of Nonverbal Behavior,* 1980, *5,* 26-34.

Summerhayes, D., and Suchner, R. Power implications of touch in male-female relationships. *Sex Roles,* 1978, *4,* 103-110.

Sussman, N. M., and Rosenfeld, H. M. Touch, justification, and sex: Influences on the aversiveness of spatial violations. *Journal of Social Psychology,* 1978, *106,* 215-225.

U.S. National Commission on the Causes and Prevention of Violence. *Violent crime.* New York: George Braziller, 1969.

Watson, O. M., and Graves, T. D. Quantitative research in proxemic behavior. *American Anthropologist,* 1966, *68,* 971-985.

Watson, W. H. The meaning of touch: Geriatric nursing. *Journal of Communication,* 1975, *25,* 104-112.

Whitcher, D., and Fisher, J. Multidimensional reaction to therapeutic touch in a hospital setting. *Journal of Personality and Social Psychology,* 1979, *37,* 87-91.

Williams, T. R. Cultural structuring of tactile experience in a Borneo society. *American Anthropologist,* 1966, *68,* 27-39.

Willis, F. N., Jr., and Hamm, H. K. The use of interpersonal touch in securing compliance. *Journal of Nonverbal Behavior,* 1980, *5,* 49-55.

Chapter 3

NONVERBAL VIOLATIONS OF EXPECTATIONS

Judee K. Burgoon

CONVENTIONAL WISDOM suggests that the key to success in communication is to obey the rules. Those who follow society's norms and strictures will be better received—or so the argument goes. Goffman (1959), for instance, contends that successful self-presentations depend on adhering to decorum requirements, following the rules of conduct associated with a particular performance. Thibaut and Kelley (1959), applying a rewards and cost analysis, likewise argue that norm violations increase costs in social encounters by reducing the predictability and regularity of interaction. Indeed, much popular literature on how to achieve success is grounded in the notion of scrupulously heeding social norms.

However, conformity is not necessarily always the best strategy. Small groups research, for example, reveals circumstances in which one may achieve better results in interpersonal exchanges by deviating from, rather than conforming to, expected behavior. For example, individuals in leadership roles not only have the freedom to deviate (colorfully labeled "idiosyncracy credits"), but also are expected to do so (see Blau, 1960; Hollander, 1958, 1960; Homans, 1950). Kiesler (1973) confirmed this in two experiments showing that high-status individuals are expected to behave independently (that is, not to follow the group's consensus) and achieve greater attraction when they do so. Meanwhile, low-status individuals are expected to conform to the group's norms and are seen as more attractive when they eschew deviation. Moreover, under circumstances in which unpredictability might be preferred (as when it connotes creativity), members net greater esteem through violations, regardless of status. In short, for some people and some situations, engaging in a violation can be more advantageous. The same conclusion was reached in a small groups study by Bradley (1980), which showed that interaction behaviors that violate initial expectations in a positive way (in this case, by demonstrating competence counter to one's perceived status) lead to greater influence and acceptance.

A second line of research, on language intensity, also attests to the possible beneficial effects of violations. Studies show that positive violations, often in the form of unexpectedly temperate (nonintense) messages, foster greater attitude change and more favorable evaluations of the communicator, while negative violations have a boomerang effect (see Brooks, 1970; Burgoon, 1975; Burgoon and Chase, 1973; Burgoon and Stewart, 1975). Burgoon and Miller (1982) find these patterns to be sufficiently consistent to warrant developing an expectancy interpretation of language and persuasion.

These examples from communication literature demonstrate that the counterintuitive recommendation of engaging in a violation may sometimes actually be the best policy for maximizing one's effectiveness in interpersonal encounters. The same thesis formed the basis of the theoretical model and associated program of research to be reported here on the communicative effects of proxemic violations of expectations. The model was formulated out of the belief that nonverbal communication phenomena are sorely in need of theoretical perspectives to explain them and that an expectancy approach could provide one such organizing framework. This chapter reviews the original model and its revisions, the nine experiments my associates and I have conducted so far to test the model, and several experiments conducted by others that can be reinterpreted to fit the model. It concludes with a discussion of the model's extension to other nonverbal behaviors and the basic principles that should be applicable.

THE THEORETICAL MODEL

Factors such as (1) the participant's sex, age, race, status, and degree of acquaintance, (2) the situation's degree of formality, topics, and task requirements, and (3) environmental constraints all play a role in defining what is the normative distance for a given conversation. Not only do people recognize these norms and attempt to comply with them; violations by others prompt marked changes in behavior and evaluations (see Dietch and House, 1975; Efran and Cheyne, 1974; Evans and Howard, 1973; Heston, 1974; Patterson et al., 1971). However, the nature of these reactions ranges from highly positive to highly negative, offering conflicting evidence as to whether violations have favorable or unfavorable communication consequences.

The apparent regularities in the *use* of space and the contradictory results on the *effects* of such use prompted the development of a theoretical model to explain the role of proxemics in interpersonal communication (Burgoon, 1978; Burgoon and Jones, 1976). The pivotal propositions in the early formulations were:

(1) Expected distancing in a given context is a function of (a) the social norms and (b) the known idiosyncratic spacing patterns of the interactants.
(2) The effects of violations of expectations are a function of (a) the reward-punishment value of the initiator of a violation, (b) the direction of deviation, and (c) the amount of deviation.

As explained in those formulations, expectations are assumed to be the result of a person's experience with normative behaviors in society and any knowledge of the unique proxemic patterns of those with whom he or she interacts. (This means that with strangers, the norms alone serve as a guide; with increasing familiarity comes greater recognition of individual differences.) Expectations reflect our predictions about how others will behave; they serve as an adaptation level or comparison level for a given context. So long as the expectations are realized, awareness of proxemic behavior is presumed to be relatively subconscious. Once they are violated, though, the model predicts that the person will become aroused physiologically and psychologically and attempt to restore homeostasis or balance.

The manner in which one reacts to violations is posited to depend on the characteristics of the perpetrator of the violation, whether the violation is closer or farther than expected, and its extremity. In the early formulations, we proposed that an individual who is well regarded, of higher status, more attractive, and so forth (that is, more rewarding to interact with) can better afford to engage in a violation than an individual who provides punishment or no rewards, and that such an individual may actually improve communication outcomes (such as attraction, credibility, comprehension, and persuasion) through a moderate, close violation. The model predicted that extreme close violations and far violations have deleterious effects. For individuals with low reward value, we hypothesized that the most favorable outcomes are achieved by conforming to expectations or adopting a distance slightly farther than the expected.

The rationale underlying these predictions invoked three considerations: (1) the process of arousal labeling, (2) the message value of proxemic shifts, and (3) competing privacy and affiliation needs. We proposed that the arousal created by a violation of expectations is ambiguous in nature and that whether the victim of a violation responds negatively or positively depends on cues in the environment that are used to interpret and label the arousal. If, in an activated state, the victim is in the presence of a rewarding individual or is receiving positively valued messages, he or she should attach positive connotations to the arousal and respond in a favorable way. Conversely, if the activation occurs in the presence of a nonrewarding interactant or is accompanied by the receipt of negatively valued messages, the activation should take on negative affect and be responded to in a negative fashion. The possible messages associated with proxemic changes therefore become relevant. We contended that a movement closer by a highly regarded individual carries affiliative and acceptance meanings, giving it a positive value. The same movement by a negatively regarded individual may be somewhat threatening, connote intrusion on one's privacy, or even suggest a deviant or socially unskilled personality, all of which contribute to such a move being assigned negative value. Because individuals are assumed to have competing affiliative and privacy needs that must be kept in proper balance, the model argued that an extremely close distance adopted by a highly regarded individual also ultimately takes on privacy invasion and threat connotations, resulting in such an extreme violation turning into a negative message. As for far deviations, we suggested that they carry meanings of disinterest and rejection and therefore become increasingly negative in meaning as they become more extreme, regardless of who commits them.

This, then, was the original model and the thinking underlying it. The model has since undergone revisions in both the hypothesized relationships between distance and communication outcomes and the underlying explanations of the relationships. Those changes will unfold as they developed in the nine experiments that have directly tested the model to date.

EXPERIMENTAL TESTS OF THE MODEL

THE FIRST TEST

Because expectations based on norms are such a key element of the distancing model, its first test began with an attempt to identify norms (Burgoon, 1978). Forty subjects, interacting with confederate interviewers, established normative and "threat" distances for male-male, male-female, and female-female interactions. These distances, along with "close" (six inches nearer than the norm) and "far" (six feet) conditions, formed the four distance conditions for the subsequent experiment. In the experiment itself, 70 subjects, who were seated at one of the preset distances from a male or female confederate, received positive or negative kinesic and vocal feedback while creating sentences from 20 adjectives. The two feedback conditions served as the reward manipulation. Afterward, subjects attempted to recall as many of the 20 adjectives as possible within one minute and rated the confederate on attraction and credibility.

Five hypotheses were tested. The first, that reward produces more positive outcomes than nonreward, was strongly supported. When the confederates gave positive feedback, they were seen as more physically, socially, and task attractive, more competent, more sociable, more composed, more extroverted, and of higher character than when they gave negative feedback. Only recall was unaffected. The second hypothesis, that the effects of distance and reward are interactive rather than additive, and the third hypothesis, that a threatening distance consistently produces more negative consequences than a normative distance, were not supported. The final two hypotheses, which tested the separate nonlinear distance predictions for the reward and nonreward conditions, did receive some support. When confederates were rewarding, three outcomes showed a nonlinear relationship with distance. For the character dimension of credibility, ratings were higher at the close and far distances. For physical attraction, they were higher at the close and norm distances. For social attraction, they were highest at the threat distance. Thus, deviations generally improved perceptions of the violator, regardless of their extremity. The means for nonsignificant effects showed similar patterns. Conversely, when confederates were nonrewarding, an inverted-U pattern frequently emerged. Composure was highest at the norm distance, character was rated higher at the norm and far distances, and physical attraction was highest at the close distance. All other credibility and attraction ratings peaked at the norm distance (although the results were statistically nonsignificant).

This pilot effort brought three issues to the fore. One was that a far violation may be beneficial rather than injurious when committed by a rewarding individual. There were enough favorable ratings at the far distance (in addition to higher recall scores) to raise questions about the original prediction that distal violations by a rewarding individual carry negative connotations. Second, the results similarly raised questions about the predicted negative consequences at an extremely close distance under reward conditions. It was possible either that a truly threatening distance was not achieved in this experiment or that the extremity of a deviation is less salient than the fact that one has occurred. These two alternatives needed to be probed in the next experiment. Third, the lack of significance for many effects, while partly due to low statistical power, led to a reevaluation of using preset normative distances. The literature on norms suggests that they are highly complex and that for any two interactants, a host of factors need to be taken into consideration. The use, then, of an averaged distance for all male-male dyads, for instance, fails to take account of all the other factors that would typically dictate the expected conversational distance for each pair. The net result of this approach was to increase error variance. I concluded that future experiments must allow the normative distance to be defined by the actual participants themselves rather than by a separate sample of subjects.

REVISING AND RESTRICTING THE MODEL

The First Experiment. The next two experiments to test the model were similar in many ways to the pilot test (Burgoon et al., 1979). The first used the same task and dependent measures. This time, however, 100 subjects sat along a benchlike series of chairs that permitted them to select any distance they wished from the confederate. We assumed that whatever distance they adopted would be the perceived norm and a distance at which they felt comfortable. Once seated, the confederate stood to give the subject an information sheet, covertly recorded where the subject was sitting, and returned to one of four distances. In the norm condition, the confederate returned to his or her original spot. In the close and far conditions, the confederate moved eighteen inches closer or farther than the norm. In the threat condition, the confederate moved to within six inches of the subject. We hoped that such extremity, combined with a change to side-by-side seating in this experiment, would provide a more definitive test of a highly invasive violation. The confederate's move to a new distance was also designed to appear as an intentional act on the part of the confederate, making the manipulation more congruent with our view of distance alterations as potential communicative acts.

We tested four operationalizations of reward: physical attractiveness, gender composition of the dyad, racial composition of the dyad, and subject's initially chosen distance. Past research (including that on physical attraction and quasi-courtship) led us to predict that physically attractive confederates, opposite-sex dyads, same-race dyads, and closer initially selected distances would be more rewarding. To manipulate the gender and race variables, we used 12 white and black male and female confederates.

The first four hypotheses tested main effects for the different reward operationalizations. Physical attractiveness proved to enhance perceptions of character, sociability, composure, extroversion, social attraction, and physical attraction. Sex composition of the dyad affected recall, cross-sexed dyads exhibiting higher scores. Racial composition of the dyad failed to affect communication outcomes, as did initial distance adopted, indicating that these two considerations by themselves are insufficient to define interaction as more or less rewarding. Instead, there were numerous blocking effects for interviewers in the latter three sets of analyses, revealing that uncontrolled elements of the interviewers' demeanor were accounting for considerable variance and outweighing the proposed demographic factors as influences on communication outcomes.

As for the two hypotheses regarding distance and reward interactions, only in those cases in which different levels of reward materialized could the interrelationships between reward and distance be tested. Among the six credibility and attraction dimensions affected by physical attractiveness, three showed distance by reward interactions. The most attractive interviewers were seen as most sociable at the threat or far distances, most composed at the threat distance, and most physically attractive at the threat, far, or close distances. By contrast, the least attractive interviewer earned the highest sociability, composure, and attraction ratings at intermediate distances. Dyadic gender composition failed to produce a significant interaction for recall.

Although not hypothesized, there were also several main effects for distance. Interviewers were seen as more extroverted when they moved to threat or far distances, more task attractive at the close and far distances, and of higher character at the far distance. Violations thus accrued some beneficial effects apart from the reward level.

We drew five conclusions from this experiment. First, such demographic characteristics as race and sex by themselves do not constitute reward. Neither does voluntarily selected distance correspond to anticipated rewards or level of personal regard for another. More likely, a number of other factors—such as personal needs, assumptions about appropriate distancing, and other interpersonal characteristics—come into play. These findings, coupled with the significant differences among interviewers, suggested the need for a more narrow definition of reward and for subsequent investigations to explore facets of interviewer demeanor that might define an interaction as rewarding.

Second, the results did confirm the importance of physical appearance as a contributor to reward. Third, also congruent with the model, where reward and distance interactions were testable, the nonrewarding condition consistently showed more positive outcomes at the norm or intermediate distances.

Fourth, contrary to the model's predictions, confederates who offered greater rewards tended to improve their credibility through distance violations, regardless of the direction and extremity of the violations. Combined with the results of the first experiment, these findings led us to rethink the model. It was apparent that far violations were often producing positive rather than negative effects. We surmised that perhaps the far violation communicated greater status, thereby increasing the reward value of the violator and encouraging more favorable outcomes. Similarly, extremely proximal violations were also producing positive results much of the time. It was possible that we had still failed to achieve a truly threatening distance or that one is not achievable in the laboratory without being so contrived and obvious as to be meaningless. Apart from this methodological explanation, though, it occurred to us that once people are engaged in a conversation, they may be more tolerant of an extremely close approach, or the extremity of the deviation may be less significant than the fact of its occurrence (a possibility raised by the first study). We were therefore ready, at this juncture in testing violation effects, to revise the model and simply predict that violations are preferable to norm conformity for initiators who are rewarding.

Finally, the mixed pattern of results across dependent measures suggested a need to probe for the intervening mechanisms that might account for the differences.

The Second Experiment. The next study was designed to examine more closely what cues signal reward and, secondarily, to see if the model applies to observers of interactions as well as to participants. Subjects (N = 148) this time were observers of a live, ostensibly spontaneous interview between two students. In actuality, the interviews were staged by two confederates using the same sentence creation task, but with prearranged replies. Interviews took place at a rectangular table, with the "interviewer," who was to be the focus of attention, facing obliquely toward a one-way observation mirror. Interviewers adopted one of four distances and presented as the reward manipulation either smiles, head nods, smiles and nods, or no facial cues after selected sentences. Subjects completed the same credibility, attraction, and recall measures as used previously.

The data analyses produced significant reward effects for seven dependent variables (with interviewee and interviewer effects covaried from the analyses). Smiles proved to be the most effective reward cue and effectively enhanced perceived sociability, character, extroversion, competence, task attraction, social attraction, and physical attraction, as compared to the absence of positive facial cues. These consistent attraction and credibility effects underscored the importance of nonverbal elements of a person's communication repertoire as contributors to reward value.

Distance violations failed to have any effects on observers. While the analyses of separate reward cues significantly reduced statistical power, offering one explanation for the results, we also considered it possible that distance adjustments have less impact on observers' attributions than on those of participants. In particular, we thought observers might have focused more on cues emanating from the interviewer alone (such as the feedback) and less on actions that could be seen as jointly defined by interviewer and interviewee (as distance might be regarded). Additionally, the absence of any negative reaction on the part of the interviewee might have led observers to disregard the violation. Regardless of the explanation, the results encouraged us to return to participant studies in the future.

EXPLORING THE ROLE OF DISTRACTION

In previous reports, we had mentioned the possibility that distance violations might serve as distraction. The next experiment (Stacks and Burgoon, 1981) pursued this thought. We believed a combination of arousal and distraction might provide a fuller explanation of violation effects. We also expanded the set of communication outcomes of interest to include persuasion. It seemed a logical extension to see if the interpersonal evaluations we had been studying would translate into social influence effects.

It has long been recognized that the mere presence of others alters a person's behavior. Known as social facilitation, the changing of a context from a nonsocial to a social one (through the introduction of a species-mate) can actually either impair or facilitate learning and task performance. Various explanations have been offered for these effects, including an alertness reflex, increased drive or arousal, and increased distraction. (For recent summaries of theoretical perspectives on social facilitation and the role of distraction, see Zajonc, 1980, and Sanders, 1981). In simple terms, the distraction position argues that the presence of others distracts one's attention from the task at hand and toward the source of distraction, while simultaneously heightening drive, due to the competing demands for attention placed on the individual.

The significant implication of this body of research for understanding violation outcomes is that if such social effects occur prior to any interaction taking place, they are bound to carry into the interaction itself, causing even more pronounced mediating effects. Consequently, it is useful to identify any characteristics or actions of individuals, particularly those that are an ever-present and normal part of discourse, that promote arousal and distraction.

Such human sources of distraction have rarely been studied in the persuasion arena. Rather, the types of distractions used have often been environmental in nature (such as flashing lights) or atypical of normal human interaction (such as audiotaped messages or heckling from an audience). Research has shown that such blatant forms of distraction can actually make individuals more susceptible to messages counter to their beliefs, presumably by reducing their ability to dispute the message mentally (see Baron et al., 1973; Breitrose, 1966; Brock, 1967; Festinger and Maccoby, 1964; Osterhouse and Brock, 1970; Weyer, 1974). Distractions have been well documented to increase persuasion so long as they are moderate in degree; extreme distractions show an opposite, inhibitory effect.

Less is known about more subtle, natural forms of distraction that might be akin to social facilitation effects. Where communicator or message factors have been taken into account (see Burgoon et al., 1978; Kiesler and Mathog, 1968; Zimbardo et al., 1970), research has indicated that the communicator's credibility and the focus of attention (whether on the task or the communicator, and on positive or negative characteristics of each) mediate distraction effects.

This body of research led us to reexamine the violations model from a distraction perspective. It was our belief that two key elements of the model—reward and distance deviations—might be natural sources of distraction in interpersonal interactions. We assumed they would act as moderate distractions, having the power to redirect attention away from the verbal message without actually impairing reception of it. We reasoned that changes in expected social behavior or extraordinary personal characteristics (such as being extremely beautiful or ugly) should, by virtue of their unusualness, arrest attention and draw it toward the deviant behavior or characteristic. Hence, a distance violation would be distracting, as would extremes in reward/punishment characteristics.

In the case of distancing violations, we went further. Coupling our belief in the arousing value of distance violations with the distraction research related to focus of attention and communicator credibility, we advanced the following reasoning. A distance violation that is of sufficient magnitude to arouse a person should cause its victim to search the context for explanations, since the behavior's meaning by itself should be somewhat ambiguous. Attention should center on communicator and message characteristics as holding possible clues to the behavior (assuming no environmental attributions can be made). In the case of a rewarding violator, the situation should be infused with favorable interpretations because the arousal is taking place in the presence of a favorably regarded other. Positive meanings may be attributed to the behavior as well (for example, the move may be seen as a relational message of affiliation or power). Compared to a nonviolation situation, the favorable communicator and nonverbal message features should be made more salient through the violation distracting attention away from the topic of discussion and toward the interpersonal characteristics. At the same time, the distraction should inhibit refutation of the persuasive message, the violator's positive credibility preempting source derogation as a form of counterargument. The net result should be more favorable evaluations of, and susceptibility to persuasion by, the violator.

In the case of a nonrewarding violator, the distraction should focus more attention on negative communicator characteristics and lead to unfavorable attributions about the behavior and its source. While the distraction should interfere somewhat with counterarguing the persuasive message, the shift of attention to negative personal characteristics should prompt source derogation as an alternative mechanism for resisting the message. Hence, a violation should reinforce negative evaluations and make the reactant more resistant to persuasion than if the violation were committed by a rewarding individual.

These lines of argument led us to hypothesize two separate curvilinear relationships between distance and communication outcomes: for rewarding initiators, a U curve, and for nonrewarding initiators, an inverted-U curve. We similarly predicted a U curve relationship between distance and distraction, positing distraction to be greater under violation conditions. We continued to hypothesize a main effect for reward on communication outcomes and added a predicted main effect for reward on distraction.

From among 12 volunteers who were rated on physical attraction scales, we chose as confederates the two males and two females whose physical attractiveness, grooming, and clothing produced significantly different levels of physical appeal. This became the reward operationalization, with the same appearances held constant throughout the experiment. Distance was manipulated in the same way as in Burgoon et al. (1979). The 350 subjects reported to an apparent waiting room where a confederate confided that he or she had to give a speech in class shortly and asked if the subject would mind listening to the memorized speech while they waited for the experiment to begin. After the speech, the two were separated and the subject told that reactions to the other participant were required before proceeding to the experiment.

The first two hypotheses tested the critical assumptions of this experiment, that distance deviations and physical appearance are arousing and distracting. A multiple regression analysis of the five-item distraction measure on distance and reward produced significant main effects for both variables. Distraction was greatest at the threat and far distances, as predicted, and for the extremes of attractiveness, the least attractive confederate generating the most distraction and discomfort. Consistent with our belief that such distractions would be moderate in nature, none of the distraction means exceeded the midpoint of the scale.

The third hypothesis of a main effect for reward on credibility, attraction, and message acceptance was likewise supported for seven of the eight credibility and attraction dimensions but not for message acceptance. The mean ratings, however, showed the three most attractive confederates to be very similar, while the fourth consistently received less favorable evaluations. We decided that only the fourth confederate could be regarded as representing nonreward for the distance by reward tests. The proposed U and inverted-U curves were tested separately for each confederate. For the two most attractive confederates, who were considered to represent high reward value, there were a few significant relationships and several trends. The patterns did not all conform to a U, but the best results consistently occurred at the far or threat or both distances. Composure, extroversion, competence, sociability, social attraction, and message acceptance all tended to be higher in the violation conditions. These results offered some support for the concept of violations enhancing interpersonal evaluations and persuasion, but inasmuch as some of the patterns were linear rather than curvilinear, they did not offer resounding support for the U curve prediction. As for the nonrewarding confederate, no significant effects obtained in the analyses.

Again, the necessity of testing distance effects separately for each confederate substantially reduced statistical power and weakened our ability to detect subtle variations across distances. Nevertheless, the results showed distance violations working to alter perceptions and receptivity to the verbal message. Perplexing to us was the finding of distance effects in the high reward condition but not the low reward condition, whereas previously the low reward condition had more consistently shown such effects. That any appeared, combined with the supportive distraction results, encouraged us to persevere. We resolved, however, to work toward inducing greater differences between the high and low levels of reward, as we were convinced this was part of the problem in the low reward condition (in other words, that it may have been statistically but not meaningfully different from the other three). We also resolved to return to having the same people manipulate both levels of reward, since it was possible that uncontrolled aspects of the confederates' vocal and kinesic demeanor mediated the effects of physical attractiveness.

DISTRACTION AND SOCIAL COMPARISONS

The next experiment continued the examination of distraction as an explanatory mechanism and the role of violations in a persuasion context (Burgoon et al., 1981). It also expanded the number of participants to three persons and considered how a violation might be regarded against the comparison level of another group member who did not engage in a violation. The previous studies had all essentially treated a confederate as his or her own control, comparing a given confederate's results from one distance condition to the same confederate's results from another distance condition. We were curious to see if distance violations would have the same effects if we introduced a second confederate who did not deviate. We were especially interested in the *differences* in reactions to the two confederates; that is, we wanted to compare the confederate not only to self across distances, but also to another nondeviating confederate at each distance. We hypothesized that given two rewarding group members (the confederates), the deviating one would achieve greater credibility, attraction, and persuasion through distance violations, relative to the stationary one and relative to the norm condition. Our thinking was that the contrast effect would make the positive features of the violation all the more evident. With two nonrewarding group members, we hypothesized that the deviating one would experience lesser credibility, attraction, and persuasion through violations, relative to the stationary member and to the norm condition. We again hypothesized a main effect for distance on distraction, predicting that a violation would distract attention away from all messages being sent, and a main effect for reward on communication outcomes. We did not predict a distraction effect for reward, since both confederates were to be matched on that variable and we thought that might neutralize its distractive potential.

The study was conducted simultaneously at two locations, half of the 179 subjects coming from the University of South Alabama and half from Michigan State University. In each location there were two male and two female confederates.

The experiment was set up under the guise of studying jury decisions with groups of different sizes. Subjects were told that they would be participating in a three-person group, that the other two members had already arrived and had been assigned responsibilities for arguing the prosecution's or defense's position on a murder trial, and that they were to enter the group as undecided members. They were given a synopsis of the case, which was based on an actual trial. Transcripts from the trial were used to construct the arguments that were memorized and presented by the two confederates. The arguments were carefully counterbalanced and pretested to ensure relative equality.

When subjects entered the experimental room, they were ushered to a chair with limited mobility (so that they could not adjust to any subsequent violations) and were joined by the two confederates, who had been working in opposite corners in the back of the room. The confederates initially took positions equidistant from the subject. Once a certain point in the scripted discussion had been reached, the deviating confederate adjusted his or her distance and maintained that distance for the remainder of the interaction. Subjects were encouraged to speak early in the introductory stage of the interaction and were free to interject questions or comments as the discussion proceeded, but otherwise the discussion was prearranged and constant across conditions. Following the discussion, the subject completed the attraction, credibility, persuasion, and distraction measures while the confederates were told to work on preparing the opposite position for a second discussion. In reality, each confederate presented only one side of the case throughout the experiment.

Reward level was manipulated in several ways. In the high reward condition, the two same-sex confederates who were paired wore "dressy" clothes and were well-groomed, the females wearing makeup. In the low reward condition, they wore dirty jeans and T-shirts and were poorly groomed, females wearing no makeup and males going unshaven. Rewarding confederates introduced themselves as seniors with a prestigious major who had come from an upper-division communication course and who had prior jury experience. Nonrewarding confederates introduced themselves as freshmen with an undecided major (but likely to go into a less prestigious field) who had come from an introductory communication course and had no previous jury experience. Rewarding confederates also expressed enthusiasm for the task and expressed interest nonverbally through forward body lean, while nonrewarding confederates said they expected the task to be dull and communicated disinterest through more rigid, erect postures. Because none of the earlier experiments had found the "threat" distance actually to be treatening, we reduced the distance conditions to three: far, norm, and close. Deviations were 18 inches closer or further than the normative distance. Confederates alternated between deviating and remaining stationary.

Results showed significant differences among confederates on physical attraction, social attraction, sociability, and extroversion. Confederate effects also repeatedly interacted with reward and distance, confounding the tests of the hypothesized relationships. The hypothesized main effect for reward materialized only for physical attraction (which at least attested to the effectiveness of the attractiveness manipulation). Instead, there were reward by confederates interactions for most measures. Consistently, the midwestern confederates achieved better results in the high reward condition as predicted. They were rated more persuasive, composed, trustworthy, sociable, socially attractive, and task attractive in the high reward condition and achieved more concurrence with their side of the case. The southern confederates, however, tended to achieve better results in the low reward condition (this reversal often being confined to the two females). We concluded that the hypothesis was supported in the midwestern replication but not the southern.

Because these confounded reward findings jeopardized the distance tests, we inspected the means in the reward versus nonreward conditions to try to make sense of these unusual results. Our inspection revealed the southern confederates to have very high ratings (above the midpoint of the scale) regardless of reward condition. In other words, low reward did not "take" in the southern sample. On a post hoc basis, we surmised that the more casual, "natural" appearance of the confederates in the low reward condition may have been so unusual on the Mobile campus as to have been a kind of positive violation of expectations. Alternatively, it may have fostered a sense of homophily. The confederates' sociable demeanor also apparently leaked into their performance, overriding manipulated disinterest. Because there was no truly low reward condition in the southern group, we could only test the nonreward distance hypothesis among the midwestern sample. We therefore chose to test all distance effects separately in the two samples.

For the persuasion dependent measures, rewarding confederates from both locations improved acceptance of the verdict they advocated through a far violation, and the midwestern confederates also improved message acceptance with a close violation, relative to the norm condition. Moreover, rewarding confederates were seen as more persuasive in the two violation conditions when compared to both the norm and the stationary confederates. For rewarding confederates, then, violations were definitely a better persuasion strategy and even improved their effectiveness relative to another rewarding group member who conformed to the norm. For nonrewarding confederates, distance violations had marginal impact on actual message acceptance, but perceived persuasiveness was lowered by a violation compared to conforming to the norm. The violating confederates were also rated as less persuasive than the nondeviating confederates. Results were therefore consistent with our hypothesis of violations having detrimental effects for nonrewarding group members.

For the credibility and attraction measures, rewarding southern confederates were evaluated as more sociable, extroverted, socially attractive, and task attractive when they engaged in a violation than when they conformed to the norm, a pattern consistent with the U curve hypothesis. Rewarding midwestern confederates instead showed a linear pattern of obtaining the highest ratings in the far condition and the lowest in the close condition on character, sociability, extroversion, composure, social attraction, physical attraction, and task attraction. The rewarding southern confederates were also seen as least composed at the close distance. When the deviating and nondeviating confederates were compared to each other, the one who engaged in a violation earned higher competence, sociability, physical attraction, and task attraction scores than the one who did not, despite the fact that they both offered interpersonal rewards. Thus the results were highly supportive of violations working to improve one's perceived credibility and attraction in an absolute sense and relative to other, equally rewarding individuals, but they were mixed on whether or not the pattern was a U curve. A far violation was more reliable as an effective strategy than was a close violation.

As for nonrewarding confederates, violations had negligible impact in altering the confederate's own credibility and attraction ratings but caused him or her to lose ground relative to the other, nondeviating confederate on competence, sociability, task attraction, and physical attraction. Apparently the comparison to a conforming group member led not so much to more negative evaluations of the deviant as to more positive evaluations of the conformer.

Finally, the test of distance on distraction failed to show any significant differences across conditions, but there was a trend toward greater distraction in the high reward condition, particularly at the far and close distances. There were some other main effects for distance, but they were usually overridden by the distance by reward and distance by confederate interactions.

What conclusions were we able to draw from this investigation? First, while physical attractiveness, status, expertise, and expressed interest generally are more rewarding, any manipulations of reward must take into account such factors as the social milieu, perceived similarity, and positive violations of expectations that can enter into the reward mix. Despite our best efforts to induce low reward in this experiment, the southern confederates were able to counteract totally the manipulations through a friendly manner, a "neater" appearance (they could not bring themselves to be as "grubby" as the midwestern confederates) and possibly an unexpectedly refreshing self-presentation. However, even the unkempt midwestern confederates received more favorable evaluations than we would have liked, which suggests that their communication behaviors may also have inadvertently improved their evaluations. This made us all the more aware of elements of reward emanating from the interaction itself that we either needed to control better or to study directly.

Second, the results strongly demonstrated that for someone who is relatively rewarding to begin with, engaging in a distance violation can be more effective in gaining message acceptance, credibility, and attraction than conforming to the norm and may even advance one's position relative to an equally rewarding but conforming other. This has significant implications for interactions involving three or more people, because it means that the contrast between deviant and nondeviant behavior helps rather than harms the well-regarded individual. Conversely, for someone who is less well regarded to begin with, engaging in a violation is more risky business. In this study, engaging in a violation did not seriously jeopardize the deviant's own attraction and credibility, but it did undermine persuasiveness. Moreover, the main beneficiary of the deviation was the other, conforming group member, who was made to look good by contrast, not an outcome one would wish to bestow on one's adversary.

Third, while these results reaffirmed the differential effects of violations for rewarding versus nonrewarding individuals, they were more equivocal on the shapes of the relationships between distance and communication outcomes. In the high reward condition, there were both U-shaped and linear relationships, the far distance consistently emerging as the most desirable distance—a notable finding in itself, given the original model's prediction that far violations would be detrimental. One explanation for the sometimes linear relationship is that the confederates were less comfortable with the close violation, a conclusion bolstered by the lower scores on composure in this condition across all confederates, and that they therefore gave off cues that undermined their performance in that condition. Another possibility is that in this adversarial context a close violation is seen as somewhat intimidating and aggressive, thus reducing its effectiveness in this particular kind of situation. Whatever the explanation, the mixed patterns reinforce the need to consider more carefully the nature of the communication setting before specifying the pattern of relationship between distance and each communication outcome of interest.

Finally, the results did not replicate the previously found distractive effect of distance violations, but they did unexpectedly concur with the previous finding of elements of reward having some distractive ability. In retrospect, the nature of the task—requiring the subject to listen to two opposing sets of arguments and to arrive at a verdict—may have minimized detectable distance effects, since the distraction measure applied to the entire situation and not to the deviant's message alone. That there was still some elevation of distraction at far and close distances in the high reward condition, where many of the other significant effects were also occurring, at least lent modest encouragement to our continued faith in distraction as a mediating mechanism.

TAKING TO THE FIELD

At the same time that we were conducting the small group jury study, we also undertook three field experiments (Burgoon and Aho, 1982). We felt it important to take the model out of the laboratory, with its possible distorting effects, and test it in more realistic communication settings. We were simultaneously interested in extending the model beyond *outcomes* of communication to actual behaviors exhibited *during* an interaction. Of special interest were those behaviors that might serve as indicants of arousal and distraction.

Each of the three experiments was done as a class project. To allow students some latitude in designing a study that met their interests, we let the first two groups select dependent measures of interest to them from among a list of those we had identified as potentially useful; in the last experiment, we arbitrarily included any behaviors that had not been included in the first two. Thus, for the sake of education, experimental consistency was sacrificed.

The First Experiment. This study looked at the behaviors of 70 television salesclerks when ostensive customers of varying reward levels maintained or violated the normative distance. (We thought it fitting to use salespeople as the objects of our manipulations, since the reverse is usually the case.)

In the high reward condition, the two male and two female confederates introduced themselves as homeowners looking for a high-quality cabinet set, with price no object, and dressed in formal, attractive clothing to underscore their status. In the low reward case, they said they were students looking for an inexpensive portable television to use in their dorm, to be purchased on credit, and they wore casual, nondescript clothing. Three distance conditions were again used to keep the manipulations manageable and realistic. The distance adopted by the salesperson when he or she first approached the confederate constituted the normative distance. This was maintained for the first minute of interaction. A close violation was then instituted by halving the distance between the two parties, while a far violation was created by doubling the initial distance.

During the five minutes or so that confederates allowed the salespeople to show them the merchandise, trained coders posing as casual shoppers surreptitiously recorded the subject's behaviors. All of the following were counted or rated during the one-minute baseline period and after each of the succeeding four minutes: number of distance adjustments made by the salesperson; amount of self-touching, amount of other-touching, amount of eye contact, and amount of smiling, all recorded on a semantic differential scale ranging from constant to none; verbosity (brief/lengthy, short/wordy); interest in the interaction (apathetic/interested, withdrawn/involved); tension (cool/bothered, relaxed/tense); and vocal volume (soft/loud). At the end of five minutes, the confederate asked the salesperson for permission to use the store's phone, and then, regardless of whether permission had been granted, announced that the spouse/roommate would have to see the set and concluded the conversation. Coders recorded the salesperson's compliance with the request (yes or no) and rated apparent willingness to comply (unwilling/willing).

Because an initial analysis revealed no confounding sex or confederate effects prior to the distance manipulation, we used change scores (premanipulation score to averaged postmanipulation score) to analyze all variables with multiple measurements. The behaviors we thought could qualify as positive communication outcomes (that is, would conform to the model's predictions) were compliance, interest, loudness, smiling, eye contact, touching of the confederate, and possibly verbosity. We expected the others to be more an indication of activation and distraction and therefore possibly only to show a main effect for distance. Results tended to support this division.

The reward manipulation effectively altered behavior. When the confederate conveyed greater status, attractiveness, and purchasing power, 88% of the salespeople agreed to the phone request, compared to 58% when the confederate was less rewarding. Salespeople also seemed more willing to comply, showed greater interest in the confederate, were more verbose, adjusted their distance fewer times, and smiled more at the rewarding than the nonrewarding confederates.

Within the high reward condition, interest, loudness, verbosity, and smiling were all affected by distance violations. Interest was most pronounced at the close distance but was much lower at the far distance; loudness increased in both violation conditions, as did talkativeness; smiling was somewhat greater toward female confederates in the violation conditions but not toward males. Within the low reward condition, interest was marginally higher in the norm condition, vocal volume increased in the norm and far conditions, and verbosity decreased as distance increased. Female confederates also received more touch from the salesperson in the two violation conditions and male confederates received the most in the norm condition. Just the reverse occurred with willingness to comply with the request—males got the most cooperation in the two violation conditions, while females received more in the norm condition.

As for measures of arousal and distraction, tension increased as distance increased, but only in the low reward condition. Distance adjustments were more frequent in the two violation conditions and were especially evident in the low reward condition. Self-touching also increased in the two violation conditions, particularly at the far distance.

As a composite, these results offered good evidence of the applicability of the violations model to more natural communication settings. Cues of reward were effective in eliciting more positive responses from people (perhaps because they raised the specter of a tried-and-true incentive—money). Both overt helping behavior (compliance with the request) and nonverbal indicators of liking and interest increased with the presentation of rewards. Distance violations also succeeded in inducing salespeople to show more interest, to talk louder, and to smile more at females when the customer appeared to be a good prospect for a big sale. Conversely, salesclerks showed less interest, touched female customers more, touched male customers less, and increased their helpfulness to the males but reduced it for the females when the deviating customer was not such a good prospect. They also became less talkative, spoke louder, and showed more tension as less rewarding customers moved further away.

These results generally supported the violations model, but they introduced two tempering considerations: gender differences and nonverbal norms for compensation and reciprocity. We had noted sex differences before, but the finding here of different nonverbal reactions to male versus female customers corroborated other research that has found many sex differences in nonverbal communication patterns. It hinted that use of nonverbal behaviors as dependent measures might often be fraught with these confounding differences and that it might be necessary to adjust predictions to take gender norms into account. In the same vein, some of the patterns of results suggested that some nonverbal behaviors were less influenced by our experimental manipulations than by their normal relationship to other nonverbal cues. It is well recognized that many nonverbal cues operate as a unit, some compensating for distance increases—as in the case of eye contact increasing to compensate for increased distance—and others showing reciprocity—as in close distances evoking greater verbal output. These norms would explain the failure to find eye contact effects, as well as the sustained volume at the far distance and greater verbosity at the close distance, regardless of reward level. These norms, too, might therefore have to be taken into account when making predictions about complexes of nonverbal behaviors.

A final contribution of this investigation was the discovery of differential levels of arousal across conditions. Distance violations evinced greater activation and possible discomfort, as revealed through more frequent distance adjustments and self-touching. The increased loudness at a close distance and increased verbosity at a far distance in the high reward condition, as well as the increased tension at a far distance in the low reward condition, could also be taken as signs of violations heightening activation. This pattern affirmed the crucial assumption of the model, namely, that distance violations are arousing. The additional finding of differences in amount and nature of activation across the two reward levels also concurred with the earlier hypothesis of reward elements having the potential to arouse and distract. Thus the focus on interaction behaviors in this experiment proved useful in supporting not only the model's predictions but the underlying explanations for the effects as well.

The Second Experiment. The next experiment similarly employed salespeople as subjects, this time in retail clothing stores. The 49 subjects were approached by a male or female graduate student who either dressed in expensive, formal clothing (indicative of wealth) and sought a cashmere sweater, possibly with a designer label, as a gift for a sibling (high reward condition) or dressed in typical student garb (jeans) and sought an inexpensive, synthetic sweater as the gift (low reward condition). The coders, again posing as casual shoppers, recorded or rated the following behaviors during a one-minute baseline period and again two minutes after the distance manipulation: distance adjustments, smiling, self-touching, evident body tension, random bodily activity, and facing (measured as indirectness of head orientation). At the close of each interaction, they rated verbosity and recorded the length of the interaction and compliance with the confederate's phone request.

Analyses of baseline data showed no differences by experimental condition but did reveal female salespeople initially to engage in more self-touching and all salespeople to average a greater initial distance from the female than from the male confederate (three-inch difference). Except for these two behaviors, change scores became the dependent measures where applicable.

The presentation of reward cues again evoked more favorable responses: Salespeople confronted by the more affluent-appearing confederate agreed more often to the phone request (65 percent, compared to 32 percent in the low reward condition), smiled more, were more talkative, faced the customer more directly, spent more time with him or her, showed less tension and bodily activity, and adjusted the distance fewer times. Greater reward, then, elicited more helping behavior, more nonverbal indications of liking and interest, fewer indications of negative forms of arousal (such as discomfort and anxiety), and some evidence of positive arousal in the form of greater loquaciousness.

Within the high reward condition, the effects of distance on those behaviors that qualified as favorable communication outcomes were all confounded by sex. Clerks became increasingly indirect in their facing as the female customer increased proximity but became increasingly more direct with the male customer in both violation conditions. Clerks were also more verbose with the female at the far distance and more so with the male at the norm distance. And total interactions were actually longer with the male at the norm and far distances, but with the female at the two extreme distances. Within the low reward condition, there was only a linear relationship between facing and distance such that orientation became more indirect as proximity increased, a pattern commonly found in the compensation literature.

Behaviors indicative of arousal likewise showed confounding effects by gender. Distance adjustments were greater in the two violation conditions, but in the high reward condition, the male customer prompted more adjustments at the close distance, while the female prompted more at the far distance (a pattern that might be interpreted to mean that males seem more threatening at a close distance and females seem uncharacteristically nonaffilative at a far distance). Body tension was again primarily evident in the low reward condition, where it was pronounced at the far and especially the close distances, the latter being particularly great with the male customer. Overall amount of random bodily activity was similarly highest at the close distance, but that was largely due to the male customer in the low reward condition; for the female, activity increased with both kinds of violations, regardless of reward level.

The results continued to support the efficacy of reward cues in altering interaction behaviors and helping responses in a realistic communication context and reinforced the arousal function of distance violations. Unfortunately, they also repeated the previous mediating effects of gender and possibly compensation and reciprocity norms, while failing to duplicate the same patterns as the previous experiment. It was becoming increasingly apparent that the interrelationships among the nonverbal behaviors, and the norms governing their presentation, were very complex. We concluded that greater clarity might be achieved by returning to the laboratory, where we could videotape the nonverbal cues and inspect them more closely. Before we decided that, however, the third experiment was already in progress.

The Third Experiment. This last one was the most ambitious of the three and also the least successful. In brief, we interviewed 104 automobile, appliance, furniture, and stereo salespeople about consumers and major purchases. Three male and three female confederates, each joined by two coders to pose as a three-person interview team, manipulated reward through physical and verbal cues of expertise. Coders, under the guise of recording brands and prices, rated verbosity, interest, tension, relevance (irrelevant/relevant, unrelated/related), flexibility (inflexible/flexible, unchangeable/changeable), task orientation (socially oriented/task-oriented, personal/ideational), seven vocalic behaviors, and six kinesic behaviors. Duration of the interaction was also recorded.

Analyses produced significant or near-significant confederate effects that overrode or interacted with reward for every single variable. Close inspection of the means for each confederate uncovered the fact that two males who had been received more favorably during the baseline period were typically obtaining better responses in the low reward than in the high reward condition. This pattern stood as strong testimony to the nullifying impact of individual and sex differences in demeanor on our experimental manipulations. These differences warrant further investigation in the future, but for the time being they nixed our ability to test differential distance curves. We were left looking at main effects for distance.

There were three of consequence. Tension increased, while task orientation and relevance decreased, in the two violation conditions. In other words, the salespeople were more distracted, unsettled, and socially oriented when the confederate moved to the far or close distance. Although the two previous experiments had already confirmed the arousal effect of distance violations, the relevance and task orientation findings were the first to support a distraction effect more directly. This support for both the arousal and distraction components of our rationale made the labor of this experiment more worthwhile. We were ready, however, to return to the greater control of the lab.

CHECKING ASSUMPTIONS

The latest experiment (Burgoon and Hale, 1982) in this research program is, at this writing, still in the preliminary stages of analysis and so will be discussed only briefly. In assessing what we had come to know and what questions were still unanswered at this point, we decided at least three things needed to be incorporated into the next study: (1) exploration of what messages are actually attributed to distance violations, (2) expansion of the violation to include not just proximity but also other nonverbal cues that are typically part of the proximity complex, and (3) determination of whether the model applies to friends as well as strangers. Our interest in the meanings associated with violations stemmed from our invocation of a status explanation for the success of far violations without knowing if, in fact, such attributions were being made, and our recognition that we had never directly tested whether distance violations carry the connotations we have ascribed to them. Our interest in expanding the violation to include additional cues arose from our suspicion that a distance violation by itself might be too subtle to render consistently the communication effects we had predicted, coupled with the realization from the field experiments that the confederates themselves might be inadvertently compensating for the distance violations by adjusting eye contact, body lean, vocal intensity, and so forth. By bringing all such immediacy cues (cues signaling approach and involvement) under control in the experiment, we thought we might achieve a more potent proximity manipulation. Finally, we recognized that one shortcoming of the research program so far had been its exclusive concentration on interactions among strangers. We decided it was time to see if the model was applicable to more familiar relationships.

In capsule version, subjects were pairs of friends who interacted once with each other and once with someone else's friend to yield 99 friend and stranger dyads. In each dyad, we took aside one individual to become a confederate, whom we then trained to engage in a high immediacy violation (consisting of close interpersonal distance, nearly constant eye contact, forward body lean, and vocal and facial cues of interest), a high nonimmediacy violation (consisting of a far interpersonal distance, infrequent eye contact, backward body lean, and vocal and facial cues of disinterest), or no violation (consisting of encouragement to maintain as normal an interaction pattern as possible). Each confederate subject committed only one type of violation across his or her two interactions. Likewise, each naive subject was exposed to only one type of violation across the two interactions. This permitted direct comparison of reactions to a given type of violation when committed by a friend as opposed to a stranger. The friend interactions were assumed to be the high reward condition; the stranger interactions, the low reward condition.

Discussion topics were one of four social-moral problems (for example, a sibling had stolen a piece of jewelry from a friend) about which the pair was to arrive at a consensus recommendation for resolution. During the interactions, confederate and naive subjects were videotaped on a split screen. Following the interactions, all subjects rated their partners on credibility, attraction, and four dimensions of relational messages that tapped the degree of dominance and control, intimacy/attraction/trust, emotionality/arousal/composure, and detachment that were being communicated. The videotapes were subsequently also rated by naive observers on their perceptions of the subjects' credibility, attraction, and relational messages and by trained coders on a host of nonverbal variables.

The preliminary results on the "victim's" own perceptions of the violator are what deserve note at this point because they have significant implications for the violations model. It appears that regardless of whether the violation is committed by a stranger or a friend, it has somewhat more negative consequences than conforming to the norm, especially if it is a nonimmediate (distal) type violation. Moreover, the more a violation is seen as communicating status and dominance, the more negative rather than positive it is regarded. Perceptions of increased status, then, are not a likely explanation of the favorable results occuring at far distances in the previous studies. Rather, it seems more likely that distance violations by themselves are highly ambiguous and require their victims to search the social context for other clues as to their meaning. When reward cues are available, the violation takes on a positive force; when the cues are more negative, the violation produces negative consequences. The present reversal of positive effects in the high reward condition, then, could be explained by the presence of the other immediacy cues making the violation less ambiguous. In the case of the far violation, the presence of other negative messages of disinterest might have led the subject to assign more negative meaning to the situation; in the case of the close violation, the combination of cues might have produced an overload situation, finally achieving a more threatening kind of violation and consequently producing more negative perceptions of the violator.

If these tentative conclusions are borne out in the final analyses, they will make an important contribution to our understanding of the nature of violations, for they suggest that the most successful violation might be one that is so subtle and ambiguous in nature as to not dictate the current definition of the interpersonal relationship itself but to redirect attention to other social cues that *will* define the positiveness or negativity of that relationship. Whether other nonverbal cues could function in the same subtle manner as proxemic shifts would then need to be investigated.

ANCILLARY EMPIRICAL SUPPORT
FOR THE MODEL

Before drawing conclusions about the viability of the conversational distancing model, some other proxemics research that is potentially relevant to the model should be noted.

In their 1976 review, Sundstrom and Altman summarized proxemic research running the gamut from reactions to spatial invasion and effects of invasions on the invader, to norms for comfortable interaction and compensation for violations of distancing norms. Based on their analysis of this literature, along with the relationship of proximity to friendship, attraction, and stress, they proposed a model of the relationship between distance and comfort. Their model specifies three different forms of relationship: one for encounters with strangers not involving interaction, one for interactions with strangers, and one for interactions with friends. Interestingly, the two curvilinear relationships proposed for conversations with strangers and friends are almost identical to that proposed in our initial model for reward and punishment. While the Sundstrom and Altman model is limited only to the dependent variable of comfort and therefore does not speak directly to the communication outcomes that have been of interest in our line of research, their depiction of stranger interactions operating optimally at an intermediate distance and friend interactions operating at a closer distance without experiencing discomfort comports with some of the major tenets of our model. In fact, if it could be shown that far violations among friends simultaneously produce discomfort and positive communication outcomes, then their model would be totally compatible with our revised model.

At about the same time that Sundstrom and Altman were developing their model and Steve Jones and I were working on ours, Konečni et al. (1975) conducted four field experiments that produced results consistent with our predictions in the low reward condition. They tested the effects of violating or not violating the personal space of a pedestrian at a crosswalk. Not only does a violation cause pedestrians to cross the street faster, a finding interpreted as evidence of arousal strengthening the dominant response of crossing the street; it also reduces helping behavior, especially if the violation is of long duration and the "lost" object to be returned is of little value. Greatest helping generally occurs when the confederate adopts an intermediate distance (five feet) from the victim; it is considerably lower at one and two feet and drops off again somewhat at a ten-foot distance, thus producing a curvilinear pattern totally consistent with our low reward condition.

Two subsequent experiments by Smith and Knowles (1979) partially replicated the Konečni et al. procedures and results. Smith and Knowles tested two alternate explanations for the effects of personal space invasions. One category they identify, arousal explanations, considers the stress of discomfort caused by physical closeness to be the primary mediator of reactions to invasions. Included within this category are the two-factor arousal-labeling models (arousal leading to a search for causes and subsequently labeling the arousal based on what cognitive interpretations are made). The second category of explanations gives primacy to cognitive mediators, specifically expectations about distancing that derive from cultural norms. When these expectations are violated, so this line of argument goes, they are interpreted as rude, inappropriate, or threatening and trigger a variety of negative responses, including heightened arousal. (It should be apparent at this point that both of these perspectives are incorporated in our model.) To test these two alternatives, Smith and Knowles modify the pedestrian violation procedure in the following ways.

The distance manipulation is reduced to two levels (four inches or five feet). The characteristics of the violator are manipulated to either provide plausibility for the invasion (by having the invader appear as an artist, carrying an open sketch pad with a partially completed sketch of the scene across the street) or not (in the latter case, having the invader carry the pad closed at the side). A second, noninvading confederate who is to be the target of helping behavior half the time is also added. Either the invading or noninvading confederate drops a pen in the street. In the second experiment, yet a third confederate, posing as in interviewer, obtains questionnaire impressions of the invader from the subject.

If the nonartist condition can be seen as the least rewarding or acceptable of the two types of encounters, then the results correspond nicely with our own. The nonartist who engages in a close violation produces faster escape speeds, is regarded as more inappropriate and receives less help in retrieving the lost pen than either the artist who engages in a close violation or confederates who do not engage in a violation. An invasion also reduces the amount of help given to the noninvading confederate. The authors interpret these findings as substantiation for both arousal and cognitive mediators of reactions of spatial intrusions, the reduced helping of the noninvader serving as evidence of general arousal and the differential effects for the artist versus the nonartist serving as evidence of cognitive recognition of differences in the two situations. Their conclusions reinforce our model, as does their specific pattern of results.

Further support comes from Baron and Bell (1976; Baron, 1978), who find opposite effects on helping behavior in circumstances approximating our high reward condition. Baron and Bell (1976) originally set out to show that violations reduce helping behavior, consistent with the Konečni et al. findings. However, their first experiment found the opposite: Confederates who approach subjects in a cafeteria at a one-and-a-half-foot distance and ask for assistance with a research project actually receive more help than those who approach from a three- to four-foot distance. A follow-up study indicated that the closer distance communicates a greater need for help. Baron (1978) then developed another experiment in which apparent need for help was actually manipulated. When the confederate communicates a legitimate need for assistance, the close distance again elicits more help than the far distance and is accompanied by more positive affective reactions. When the apparent need is low, the trend is for greater voluntarism at the far rather than the close distance. If need for assistance is seen as somewhat analogous to reward and a four-foot distance is equated with the normative distance, then the pattern of results is highly compatible with our predictions of gaining better results through

a violation if one is in a positively regarded circumstance and gaining better results through conformity to the norm if one is in a more negatively regarded circumstance.

Another study that includes a manipulation highly comparable to one of our reward manipulations was conducted by Schiffenbauer and Schiavo (1976). Their independent variables are two levels of distance (two or five feet) and three levels of feedback (positive, neutral, and negative). Subjects, who engage in a problem-solving task with a confederate, show greater liking for the confederate in the positive feedback condition if the confederate takes the close rather than the far distance. They show equal liking at both distances when feedback is neutral and are more favorable toward the confederate at the far than the close distance when the feedback is negative. Storms and Thomas (1977) similarly find through three experiments that a confederate who is "friendly" (based on feedback given) or similar to the subject is better liked at a close (twelve inches) distance than a far (thirty inches) distance, while "unfriendly" or dissimilar confederates are better liked at the far than close distance. The distance identified as far in these two arrangements is within the normative range and therefore makes the results congruent with our model.

One final consonant finding comes from Imada and Hakel (1977), who find that interviewers view as more warm and enthusiastic those interviewees who adopt immediate (close) seating positions than those who adopt more nonimmediate ones. They are also far more likely to recommend the proximal interviewees for a job (80 percent of the time, compared to only 19 percent for the distal ones).

CONCLUSIONS

The initial empirical and theoretical support for the proposed model, the results from the nine tests of it conducted to date, and the auxiliary support from other proxemic studies make is possible to draw a number of conclusions at this point about the model's soundness. These conclusions can be divided into those that endorse elements of the model and those that specify limitations on it. First, the supporting conclusions:

(1) *Those characteristics and behaviors of an initiator that contribute to interpersonal rewards mediate communication processes and outcomes.* Central to the violations model is the proposition that those actions and attributes of an initiator that define the interpersonal encounter as rewarding or nonrewarding determine whether a violation will have positive or negative consequences. Critical to the model's efficacy, then, is evidence that there are such factors that produce differential communication con-

sequences and can be construed as elements of reward. Across the experiments that have been summarized here, the following initiator attributes, all defined on an a priori basis as contributing to the reward value of an interaction, have proven to affect a reactant's communication behaviors and perceptions: (a) *positive and negative feedback* (including verbal and nonverbal acts), which influences the three dimensions of attraction (task, social, physical), liking and five dimensions of credibility (competence, character, sociability, composure, extroversion); (b) *physical attractiveness* (including facial attractiveness, grooming, and attire), which also consistently affects all the attraction and credibility dimensions; (c) *the presence or absence of smiling and head nods,* shown to affect the three dimensions of attraction and all but the composure dimension of credibility; (d) *implied socioeconomic status and purchasing power,* shown to affect helping behavior, nonverbally expressed interest, verbosity, frequency of smiling, directness of facing, duration of the interaction, amount of distance adjustments, amount of apparent tension, and amount of random bodily activity; and (e) *attitudinal similarity,* shown to increase liking. It should be noted that this consistent reward effect, coupled with its mediation of distance effects (outlined next), also supports the Smith and Knowles (1979) thesis of cognitive mediators of distancing effects, if one draws the additional assumption that these reward characteristics are cognitively recognized by reactants.

(2) *Given a rewarding initiator, optimal communication outcomes are achieved by violating the expected distance rather than conforming to it.* Initiators who engage in a distance violation obtain better results, compared to when they conform to the norm, on all of the following dependent measures in one or more of the studies cited: the three dimensions of attraction, the five dimensions of credibility, message acceptance, persuasiveness, liking, helping behavior, endorsements for a job, interest, verbosity, vocal volume, and (for females only) smiling. For those measures used in more than one experiment, there is no consistent pattern of a single distance condition being preferable for a given dependent measure. Rather, every one of the violation conditions emerges at some point as the superior one. Across all these studies, then, the composite picture is of more beneficial consequences accruing to the initiator who moves either further or closer than the normative (expected) distance.

(3) *Given a nonrewarding initiator, optimal communication outcomes are achieved by conforming to the distance norm rather than violating it.* In one or more studies, the norm emerges as the most favorable position for the following dependent variables: physical attraction, character, sociability, composure, persuasiveness, helping behavior, willingness to help, liking, perceived appropriateness of behavior, interest, vocal volume, ver-

bosity, and touch from another. Most often, the pattern that emerges is an inverted U.

(4) *Given two or more members in a group who are of equal reward value, one who is favorably regarded and engages in a violation will gain better results than an equally well-regarded one who conforms to the normative distance; conversely, a poorly regarded violator will obtain worse results than a poorly regarded conformer.* This companion to the previous two conclusions is an important discovery of this program of research. It reveals that the contrast between deviation and nondeviation may actually intensify the effect of the violation. In the case of a rewarding individual, a violation may give him or her an edge over other participants. This finding might begin to explain the cycle whereby deviant members in a group acquire more idiosyncracy credits, enabling them to engage in yet more violations. By contrast, in the case of the nonrewarding member, the violation enhances perceptions of other group members, thereby reducing the violator's relative social influence.

(5) *Distance violations are arousing.* This pivotal assumption of the model is substantiated through reactants' manifestations of greater tension, more self-touching, more frequent distance adjustments, and faster crossing times at traffic intersections when initiators adopt deviant distances. The greater extroversion attributed to distance violators might also be taken as indirect evidence of an arousal effect.

(6) *Distance violations are distracting.* This conclusion is founded on the direct increases in reported distraction when violations occur as well as the observed decreases in the relevance of verbal comments and the shifts from a task orientation to a more personal, social orientation when a violation is experienced.

(7) *Distance violations carry messages.* This is the third critical assumption, along with the arousal and distraction value of violations, in the model's theoretical explanation for the effects of violations. In supporting this third assumption, the relational messages data move us closer toward validation not only of the model's predictive utility but also of its explanatory power.

The next conclusions begin to delimit the model:

(8) *Engaging in interaction may increase an individual's tolerance of an otherwise threatening distance.* The original model posited that a threat threshold exists beyond which intrusions from others produce physical and psychological discomfort. Our failure to find hypothesized negative reactions at such "threat" distances and the frequent discovery of opposite, positive reactions to a rewarding individual who adopts such a distance suggests that, in contrast to personal space invasion studies (which involve no communication between parties), the mere act of making social

contact may redefine the context sufficiently to ameliorate the threat properties of the situation. It may make extreme proximity more acceptable and even desirable. We suspect that a prolonged invasion of personal space will still produce detrimental consequences, but since in normal conversations few people would tolerate such an intrusion without making some adjustment on their own to compensate for it, it seems more reasonable to confine the model's predictive domain to typical communication encounters and to abandon any references to a threat distance.

(9) *The shape of the relationship between distance and communication consequences may differ across consequences.* The original model proposed two separate curvilinear relationships between distance and communication outcomes, one for reward and one for "punishment," both of which showed more negative consequences at extreme distances. When it became apparent after the first few experiments that the data were not fitting the high reward curve, the model was revised to predict more of a U-shaped curve in the high reward condition; the low reward prediction was simplified to an inverted U. Now, after many more experiments, it appears that a U pattern may not be applicable to all communication consequences across all communication contexts. In some instances, a linear pattern obtained; in others, a two-cycle quadratic or other nonmonotonic relationship appeared. Thus, while some form of violation is typically optimal in high reward conditions, violations both closer and farther are not always equally advisable. By the same token, while intermediate distances are typically the most effective in low reward conditions, the norm condition is not exclusively the best position. In retrospect, it was premature to specify the exact shape of the relationships before the model was put to serious empirical test. Not until the model is tested across a greater variety of communication contexts will it be possible to postulate the form of relationship for each communication behavior or outcome of interest. Even if a U curve proves to offer the best overall description of the relationships, it is probable that there will still be differences as to whether a proximal or distal violation is preferable in a high reward condition for a given consequence or situation, as there will still be exceptions to the norm being the preferred position in a low reward situation. There will no doubt also be consequences for which distance violations will have marginal, if any, impact. Fortunately, across the several experiments that have been conducted so far, almost every dependent measure has at some point showed significant effects for distance and/or reward.

(10) *The model's predictions must take into account norms based on gender, compensation effects, and reciprocity effects.* The field experiment results showed nonverbal communication patterns to be influenced

by these considerations, sometimes to the point of negating any impact for distance adjustments. These factors must therefore be recognized in future hypotheses.

(11) *Assessments of reward value must take into account not only initial sources of reward but also those derived through the interaction itself.* The recurrent differential effects across confederates, despite our efforts to maintain a high degree of control, indicate that individual differences in demeanor and communication style can be potent sources of reward. These need to be studied more fully and factored into the determination of net reward value of an initiator.

The final conclusion suggests the relevance of the violations model to other kinds of violations:

(12) *Violations appear to be an effective strategy so long as they are accompanied or followed by other positively valued actions that can compensate for any negative connotations they carry.* The reversal of the high reward pattern in the experiment involving manipulation of multiple immediacy cues suggests that a far violation, when accompanied by other negatively valued messages, may no longer be acceptable. The success of such violations in previous studies may have depended on the ambiguity of the message. When presented in the midst of other reward cues, the violation may take on more positive connotations or override the other positive cues in the environment to which it calls attention. This principle of violations being effective only when other compensatory cues are available may also explain some of the research findings on the effects of deviant dress. Some studies show that unconventional attire yields *less* helping behavior and compliance—for example, individuals dressed in "hippie" or radical attire receive fewer rides when hitchhiking, get fewer signatures on petitions, are able to distribute fewer campaign leaflets, and have more difficulty obtaining change for a dime than those dressed formally or conventionally (Crassweller et al., 1972; Darley and Cooper, 1972; Keasy and Tomlinson-Keasy, 1973; Raymond and Unger, 1972). Others find deviant dress to produce *more* attitude change (Cooper et al., 1974; McPeek and Edwards, 1975). The key seems to be that in the latter cases, the unconventional appearance sets up negative expectations that are then violated in a positive way when the individual presents a coherent message or unexpected point of view, whereas in the former cases, no countervailing positive cues are present. The continued affirmation of this principle in future studies would argue for limiting violations to one mode at a time and accompanying them with offsetting sources of reward.

In sum, the research to date demonstrates that there are circumstances in which violations of expectations may indeed be preferable to conforming to the norm. Moreover, the research findings are consonant with the underlying explanations for their efficacy that are advanced in the proxemic violations model. It remains to be seen whether the model's principles will find generalizability to other kinds of communication violations as well. The conclusions drawn to date hold the promise of having wider applicability than to proxemic behavior alone.

REFERENCES

Baron, R. A. Invasions of personal space and helping: Mediating effects of invader's apparent need. *Journal of Experimental Social Psychology*, 1978, *14*, 304-312.

Baron, R. A., Baron, D. H., and Miller, N. The relation between distraction and persuasion. *Psychological Bulletin*, 1973, *80*, 310-323.

Baron, R. A., and Bell, P. A. Physical distance and helping: Some unexpected benefits of "crowding in" on others. *Journal of Applied Social Psychology*, 1976, *6*, 95-104.

Blau, P. M. Patterns of deviation in work groups. *Sociometry*, 1960, *23*, 245-261.

Bradley, P. H. Sex, competence and opinion deviation: An expectation states approach. *Communication Monographs*, 1980, *47*, 101-110.

Breitrose, H. S. *The effect of distraction in attenuating counter arguments.* Unpublished doctoral dissertation, Stanford University, 1966.

Brock, T. C. Communication discrepancy and intent to persuade as determinants of counterargument production. *Journal of Experimental Psychology*, 1967, *3*, 269-309.

Brooks, R. D. The generalizability of early reversals of attitudes toward communication sources. *Speech Monographs*, 1970, *37*, 152-155.

Burgoon, J. K. A communication model of personal space violations: Explication and an initial test. *Human Communication Research*, 1978, *4*, 129-142.

Burgoon, J. K., and Aho, L. Three field experiments on the effects of violations of conversation distance. *Communication Monographs*, 1982, *49*, 71-88.

Burgoon, J. K., and Hale, J. A. *Effects of immediacy violations on credibility, attraction and relational messages.* Unpublished manuscript, Michigan State University, 1982.

Burgoon, J. K., and Jones, S. B. Toward a theory of personal space expectations and their violations. *Human Communication Research*, 1976, *2*, 131-146.

Burgoon, J. K., Stacks, D. W., and Burch, S. A. The role of interpersonal rewards and violations of distancing expectations in achieving influence in small groups. *Communication, Journal of the Communication Association of the Pacific*, 1982, *11*, 114-128.

Burgoon, J. K., Stacks, D. W., and Woodall, W. G. A communicative model of violations of distancing expectations. *Western Journal of Speech Communication*, 1979, *43*, 153-167.

Burgoon, M. Empirical studies of language intensity: III. The effects of source credibility and language intensity on attitude change and person perception. *Human Communication Research*, 1975, *1*, 251-256.

Burgoon, M., and Chase, L. J. The effects of differential linguistic patterns in messages attempting to induce resistance to persuasion. *Speech Monographs*, 1973, *40*, 1-7.

Burgoon, M., Cohen, M., Miller, M. D., and Montgomery, C. L. An empirical test of a model of resistance to persuasion. *Human Communication Research*, 1978, *5*, 27-39.

Burgoon, M., and Miller, G. R. An expectancy interpretation of language and persuasion. In H. Giles and N. St. Clair (Eds.), *The social and psychological contexts of language*. Hillsdale, NJ: Lawrence Erlbaum, 1982.

Burgoon, M., and Stewart, D. Empirical investigations of language intensity: I. The effects of sex of source, receiver, and language intensity on attitude change. *Human Communication Research*, 1975, *1*, 244-248.

Cooper, J., Darley, J. M., and Henderson, J. E. On the effectiveness of deviant- and conventional-appearing communicators. *Journal of Personality and Social Psychology*, 1974, *29*, 752-757.

Crassweller, P., Gordon, M. A., and Tedford, W. H. Jr. An experimental investigation of hitchhiking. *Journal of Psychology*, 1972, *82*, 43-47.

Darley, J. M., and Cooper, J. The "Clean for Gene" phenomenon: The effects of students' appearance on political campaigning. *Journal of Applied Social Psychology*, 1972, *2*, 24-33.

Dietch, J., and House, J. Affiliative conflict and individual differences in self-disclosure. *Representative Research in Social Psychology*, 1975, *6*, 69-75.

Efran, M. G., and Cheyne, J. A. Affective concomitants of the invasion of shared space: Behavioral, physiological and verbal indicators. *Journal of Personality and Social Psychology*, 1974, *29*, 219-226.

Evans, G. W., and Howard, R. B. Personal space. *Psychological Bulletin*, 1973, *80*, 334-344.

Festinger, L., and Maccoby, N. On resistance of persuasive communications. *Journal of Abnormal and Social Psychology*, 1964, *68*, 359-366.

Goffman, E. *Presentation of self in everyday life*. Garden City NY: Doubleday, 1959.

Heston, J. K. Effects of anomia and personal space invasion on nonpersonal orientation, anxiety and source credibility. *Central States Speech Journal*, 1974, *25*, 19-27.

Hollander, E. P. Conformity, status, and idiosyncracy credit. *Psychological Review*, 1958, *65*, 117-127.

Hollander, E. P. Competence and conformity in the acceptance of influence. *Journal of Abnormal and Social Psychology*, 1960, *61*, 365-369.

Homans, G. C. *The human group*. New York: Harcourt Brace, 1950.

Imada, A. S., and Hakel, M. D. Influence of nonverbal communication and rater proximity on impressions and decisions in simulated employment interviews. *Journal of Applied Psychology*, 1977, *62*, 295-300.

Keasy, C. B., and Tomlinson-Keasy, C. Petition signing in a naturalistic setting. *Journal of Social Psychology*, 1973, *89*, 313-314.

Kiesler, S. B. Preference for predictability or unpredictability as a mediator of reactions to norm violations. *Journal of Personality and Social Psychology*, 1973, *27*, 354-359.

Kiesler, S. B., and Mathog, R. B. Distraction hypothesis in attitude change: Effects of distractiveness. *Psychological Reports*, 1968, *23*, 1123-1133.

Konečni, V. J., Libuser, L., Morton, H., and Ebbesen, E. B. Effects of a violation of personal space on escape and helping responses. *Journal of Experimental Social Psychology*, 1973, *11*, 288-229.

McPeck, R. W., and Edwards, J. D. Expectancy disconfirmation and attitude change. *Journal of Social Psychology*, 1975, *96*, 193-208.

Osterhouse, R. A., and Brock, T. C. Distraction increases yielding to propaganda by inhibiting counterarguing. *Journal of Personality and Social Psychology,* 1970, *15,* 344-358.

Patterson, M. L., Mullens, S., and Romano, J. Compensatory reactions to spatial intrusion. *Sociometry,* 1971, *34,* 11-121.

Raymond, B. J., and Unger, R. K. The apparel oft proclaims the man: Cooperation with deviant and conventional youths. *Journal of Social Psychology,* 1972, *87,* 75-82.

Sanders, G. S. Driven by distraction: An integrative review of social facilitation theory and research. *Journal of Experimental Social Psychology,* 1981, *17,* 227-251.

Schiffenbauer, A., and Schiavo, R. S. Physical distance and attraction: An intensification effect. *Journal of Experimental Social Psychology,* 1976, *12,* 274-282.

Smith, R. J., and Knowles, E. S. Affective and cognitive mediators of reactions to spatial invasions. *Journal of Experimental Social Psychology,* 1979, *15,* 437-452.

Stacks, D. W., and Burgoon, J. K. The role of nonverbal behaviors as distractors in resistance to persuasion in interpersonal contexts. *Central States Speech Journal,* 1981, *32,* 61-73.

Storms, M. D., and Thomas, G. C. Reactions to physical closeness. *Journal of Personality and Social Psychology,* 1977, *35,* 412-418.

Sundstrom, E., and Altman, I. Interpersonal relationships and personal space: Research review and theoretical model. *Human Ecology,* 1976, *4,* 47-67.

Thibaut, J. W., and Kelley, H. H. *The social psychology of groups.* New York: John Wiley, 1959.

Weyer, R. A. *Cognitive organization and change: An information processing approach.* Hillsdale, NJ: Lawrence Erlbaum, 1974.

Zajonc, R. B. Compresence. In P. B. Paulus (Ed.), *Psychology of group influence.* Hillsdale, NJ: Lawrence Erlbaum, 1980.

Zimbardo, P., Snyder, M., Thomas, A., Gold, A., and Gurwitz, S. Modifying the impact of persuasive communication with external distraction. *Journal of Personality and Social Psychology,* 1970, *16,* 669-680.

Chapter 4

CONVERSATIONAL INVOLVEMENT
Approaching and Avoiding Others

Joseph N. Cappella

SOME CONVERSATIONS seem to be very stimulating, involving their participants in mind as well as body and voice. Other conversations are plodding, dull, and lifeless, involving the participants only in the superficial routines and rituals necessary to manage the back-and-forth flow of information. In the former case, the partners might describe themselves and one another as animated, aroused, and involved, while in the latter case distant, separated, and uninvolved are more appropriate descriptors. The reasons for involving conversations might include interest in or even passion over the topic, excitement over the presence and interest of the partner, or the intellectual high of mutual discovery. However, the involvement may not be so positive; threats, strong disagreements, confrontations, and passionate conflicts are as involving in mind, body, and voice as are mutual discovery and explorations, shared excitement, or mutual intimacy. They are simply not as pleasant.

This chapter is about involvement in conversations. How do people show their involvement in their words, bodies, and voices? Can partners move one another either toward greater involvement in the conversation or toward greater distance and inactivity? The answers to these two questions lead to a third question: Why does involvement develop mutually in some circumstances, unilaterally in others, and sometimes not at all? These questions are the topics of the three sections of this chapter.

AUTHOR'S NOTE: I would like to thank John O. Greene for his help with literature reviewing, from which parts of this chapter have profited.

DEFINING INVOLVEMENT IN
HUMAN INTERACTIONS

In order to give involvement an intelligent and reasoned hearing, we must be precise in describing it. The first concern must be with the verbal and nonverbal signs of involvement. Second, we must define what it means for involvement to spread from one person to another; this infectiousness will be termed "mutual influence."

THE SIGNS OF INVOLVEMENT

The research on judgments that people make about relationships is quite extensive. It indicates that at least one of the judgments concerns affiliation or liking for the other person, and one concerns activity, intensity, or their more static versions, potency and status (Bales, 1970; Bochner et al., 1977; Carson, 1969; Triandis, 1977; Wish et al., 1976; Wish and Kaplan, 1977). Thus, people seem to categorize others in relationships as liked, potent, and possibly active or intense.

Unfortunately, much less information exists about how people judge the character of the interactions that they observe or in which they participate. Mehrabian (1972) identified the three most important dimensions of verbal and nonverbal behavior to be affiliation, responsiveness, and relaxation. Norton's (1978) self-report measure of communicators' interaction styles found behavior groupings that were labeled dramatic and animated, attentive and friendly, and relaxed. Wish et al. (1980) had people judge the interactors in twenty one- to two-minute interactions (most of which were taken from the documentary "American Family"). They concluded that the judgments included a power category, labeled ascendancy, an evaluative factor concerned with friendliness and hostility, and an arousal factor concerned with the intensity of each person's behavior. Despite the different labels and different procedures used by various researchers, there is some consensus about how people judge human interaction. They judge interactions as more or less affiliative, more or less active or animated, and more or less relaxed.

These studies indicate the different types of categories that people might use to classify interactions. They do not indicate on which behaviors judges focus to make these classifications. Not only do we want to know that certain judgments are reached; we also want to know what the behavioral basis of the judgment is. What behaviors are interactants manifesting that lead to judgments about how affiliative, animated, or relaxed they are?

Mehrabian (1972) has given systematic attention to this question. Affiliation is primarily cued by touching, close interpersonal proximity, forward lean of the body, eye contact, and orientation of the body toward the other interactant. Activity or animation is primarily cued by vocal activity, speech rate, and speech volume. Relaxation is cued by asymmetry of arm and leg positions, sideways lean, backward recline of the body and relaxed hand and neck positions. Much subsequent research has upheld these claims (Harper et al., 1978), although most studies have considered how people judge only one of the cues in a specific situation and for restricted ranges of the behavior.

My discussion of judgments thus far could produce two erroneous implications. The first is that affiliation and activity-animation are independent, separate judgments about interaction because they seem to be based on different behaviors. The second is that being perceived as affiliative and friendly in interaction depends on exhibiting all the above affiliation signs frequently and intensely. Both implications are incorrect and even a bit foolish.

The second implication seems logical enough. If people watching an interaction make judgments of how affiliative and active-animated the participant is on the basis of certain behaviors, why shouldn't the participants in an interaction arrive at the same conclusions? What I wish to argue is that the usual nonverbal and vocal cues of affiliation do not signal positive or negative interpersonal attitudes in and of themselves; rather, they are signals of involvement with the other person and with the situation. The quality of the involvement, whether positively or negatively toned, will depend on the situation, the expectations of the participants, and the intensity of the behavior itself.

Both the anecdotal and scientific evidence for such a claim is strong. Imagine two impassioned lovers greeting one another in public after a long separation. They are likely to touch, to spend time in physical proximity, to gaze at one another, to orient their bodies toward one another, to have a great deal to say, and to be animated in saying it. Now imagine a divorcing husband and wife engaged in an impassioned custody battle over children, home, and resources. They too will touch, gaze, be near physically, be oriented toward one another, and be vocally animated. They will, of course, be more likely to gaze with sneers rather than smiles and to touch with malice rather than nurturance. Clearly, the behaviors commonly identified with affiliative and friendly interactions are equivocal. Without other information they cannot be reliably interpreted as signs of positive attitude toward the other person.

The research literature supports these anecdotes. Gaze has been the most thoroughly researched. Ellsworth (1975) maintains that gaze alone is a sign of neither positive attitude nor threat but rather of involvement with the other person. She bases this claim on her research on gaze under various positive and negative conditions. An already unpleasant interaction will lead to more negative evaluations when gaze is present than when it is reduced (Ellsworth and Carlsmith, 1968). On the positive side, a stare from a person clearly in need of specific assistance leads to more helping than either no staring or staring when the required assistance is unclear (Ellsworth and Langer, 1976). Gaze involves and arouses the other person but does not produce greater approach or avoidance of its own accord.

A similar type of result has been obtained with touching behavior in a nurse-patient interaction (Whitcher and Fisher, 1979; see also Heslin and Alper's chapter in this volume). Male and female patients awaiting surgery were either touched or not by a female nurse during the preoperative instruction period. Reports of anxiety over the surgery were greater for the touched males as opposed to the touched females and greater for the untouched females as opposed to the untouched males. More remarkably, the touched males showed greater increases in blood pressure than did the untouched males, while the reverse held for the females. In general, touch per se had neither positive nor negative effects. The type of effect depended on its interpretation in the circumstances.

My point is that the usual signs of affiliation do not carry such information in themselves but rather are indices of involvement with the other and involvement in the situation. The quality of the involvement will depend on factors such as situational cues, the relationship between the interactants, and individual preferences. Despite these suggestions, the evidence remains that in neutral social situations observers judge the interactants to have a more positive attitude toward each other when the behavioral cues of involvement are present. How can we account for these findings?

An account can be offered when we consider the second unwarranted implication from the earlier discussion of affiliation and activity-animation: that the two dimensions of judgment are independent of one another. In a recent series of studies on words used to describe moods, feelings, and temporary states, Russell (1980) found that two major dimensions of judgment were used: pleasure-displeasure and degree of arousal. More important, his results warn us that these judgments are not completely separate, falling in a circular array around the pleasure-displeasure and degree-of-arousal axes. Near neighbors of the terms "aroused" and "excited" are, to one side, "happy" and "delighted" and, to the other side, "afraid" and "alarmed." Near neighbors of the terms "bored," "tired," and "sleepy" are the terms "calm" and "serene" and, to the other side, "depressed," "gloomy," and "sad." This consistent arraying of judgmental terms implies that perceptions of high involvement accompany perceptions of intensely positive and intensely negative emotions and that perceptions of noninvolvement accompany the more inactive emotional states, both positive and negative. In other words, involvement and intensity of subjectively felt emotions go hand in hand.

The study by Russell was concerned only with descriptive categories, not with actual behaviors. Shrout and Fiske (1981) asked about the relationship between eight families of nonverbal behaviors exhibited by persons in a dyadic interaction and judges' ratings of these persons on "social evaluation" adjectives from the Adjective Check List (Gough and Heilbrun, 1965). Five nonverbal variables (smile number, filled pause rate, nod rate, gaze number, and short vocal back-channel rate) accounted for much of the variation in the evaluation judges made of both male and female targets. Of special interest is the finding that all the significant predictors of social evaluation are activity variables (that is, rates and frequencies rather than average or total durations). The authors believe, and I concur, that nonverbal activity produces positive social evaluation because attention is drawn to the more active persons making positive attitudes more positive. Persons emitting social behaviors frequently or rapidly may also be viewed as more responsive to their partners and more attractive as a result (Davis and Perkowitz, 1979). The implication of this study is *not* that any nonverbal activity in any amount will be evaluated positively but that other-directed behaviors (such as smiling and gazing) exhibited in moderation will.

I hope that my claims about nonverbal behavior and involvement are now clear. Identifying kinesic (proximity, lean, orientation, gestural activity, smiling, gazing, laughing, and touch) and paralinguistic (speech rate, speech latency, loudness, and speech duration) signs with various interpersonal attitudes is not useful and is even misleading. Rather, they signal a degree of involvement in the situation and involvement with the other person whose emotional tone depends on situational factors, relationship stage, and individual differences. Involvement, arousal, and behavioral excitation are associated with both positive and negative emotions and attitudes. The simplistic notion that a more positive attitude is cued by more touching or more gaze must be purged from our thinking about nonverbal behavior. It is not that these behaviors are irrelevant as cues of attitude and emotion but that they have a more complex relationship to the quality of the emotional response than some writers have led us to think. I propose, modestly, that they be labeled more neutrally as signs of involvement rather than signs of affiliation. Verbal intimacy (either as self-disclosure or intimate questions) should also be included with nonverbal signs of involvement. Intimate topics can occur as easily in intensely positive or intensely negative situations. In either case, an intimate discussion topic is highly involving.

TRANSMITTING INVOLVEMENT

In some conversations, like some relationships, the partners seem to be ideally suited to one another, although the precise behavioral basis for this fit is usually obscure to both participants and observers. Phrases such as "being in touch" and "operating on the same wavelength" are common descriptors. With some pairs, the melding and blending of interactional style develops over time; with other pairs, it never develops.

What about the blending and melding of verbal and nonverbal involvement? Do people adjust their levels of behavioral involvement in response to the involvement expressed by the other person? If they do, what are these adjustments like? To answer these questions, some definition and terminology is necessary.

If a person adjusts his or her involvement in response to changes in the other person's involvement, then the two are *influencing* one another's involvement level. Six cases of influence are possible and are summarized in Table 4.1. If person A increases the level of expressed involvement, then B can respond by increasing, decreasing, or not changing the level of involvement. In the first case, B is matching (or reciprocating) A's change; in the second case, B is compensating for A's change; in the third case, B is uninfluenced by A. Whenever one of the persons increases his or her level of involvement, that person is said to be *approaching*, regardless of what the other person is doing; whenever involvement decreases, the person is *avoiding.* Notice that the definitions of compensation and reciprocation depend on how B responds to A's change, whereas the definitions of approach and avoidance depend only on the change in one's own behavior.

The bottom half of Table 4.1 describes the other three cases of influence in response to a decrease in A's expressed involvement. Notice that matching results either when increases in involvement are followed by increases or when decreases are followed by decreases; the same is true for compensation.

Reviews of matching and compensation in involvement (Cappella, 1981; Patterson, 1973, 1976) have found that the overwhelming majority of studies have investigated responses to increases in involvement. Our knowledge about responses to decreases in involvement is scant. Notice also that whether B is approaching or avoiding A does not determine the type of influence A has on B. Rather, it is the combination of A's and B's changes that defines the type of influence.

TABLE 4.1   Types of Influence and Response in Dyadic Adjustments of Involvement Level

A's Involvement	B's Response	Type of Influence	Type of Response
Increase	Increase	Matching (Reciprocity)	Approach
	Decrease	Compensation	Avoid
	Remain Same	None	Neither
Decrease	Increase	Compensation	Approach
	Decrease	Matching (Reciprocity)	Avoid
	Remain Same	None	Neither

The definitions in Table 4.1 are sufficient for the purposes of this discussion. The researcher should be warned that definitions of matching and compensation in terms of act sequences are quickly becoming obsolete in the face of advancing methodology for studying behavior patterns (Cappella, 1980; Gottman, 1979, 1981).

RESEARCH ON MUTUAL INFLUENCE IN VERBAL AND NONVERBAL INVOLVEMENT

Several reviews, written in the last ten years, have summarized what is known about people's responses to the levels of involvement exhibited by their partners (Cappella, 1981; Patterson, 1973, 1976). I will summarize those reviews, updating them with studies not considered in the reviews themselves. Only studies that focus on behavioral responses to levels of involvement are included.

OBJECTIVE SPEECH

Objective speech refers to features of the spoken word that can be measured with little inference, including speech rate, loudness, duration of vocalization, speech latency (duration of pauses between speaker switches), and pauses (apart from latency). In the thirty or so studies reviewed by Cappella (1981), strong evidence for matching on speech rate, latency, pausing, and loudness was found. The experimental work of Matarazzo and his colleagues (Matarazzo and Weins, 1972) supports the finding that increases as well as decreases in speech latency are matched. Speech duration does not show as clear a pattern. Several studies have found positive but insignificant matching on the duration of vocalization[1] (Welkowitz and Feldstein, 1969). When analyzing the behavior of individual pairs of dyads, some investigators have found certain pairs compensating in utterance and vocalization duration (Cappella and Planalp, 1981; Matarazzo et al., 1968). It may be that dyads tend to match utterance duration in general but that particular pairs may fall into compensatory patterns that remain hidden in the typical group-level analyses.

Some recent additional evidence continues to support these conclusions. Putman and Street (forthcoming) asked subjects to play the role of an interviewee who was trying to create an impression (competent/ incompetent, liked/disliked). In creating a likable-competent impression, interviewees and interviewers converged speech rates ($r = .66$), showing nonsignificant tendencies to converge in the likable condition ($r = .38$). In a second study (Putman and Street, forthcoming), interviewers and interviewees showed a positive correlation on speech rate and turn duration and a positive, but nonsignificant, correlation on response latency.

Street et al. (1981) studied intensively four 3½-year-old children in conversation with six or eight different adults. All four children showed matching in average speech latency to the adult interlocuter across conversations, and the three most talkative showed strong matching in average speech rate across conversations. The least talkative child actually compensated in speech rate. Matching on speech rate and response latency within interactions was strong for three of the children and positive but nonsignificant for the fourth.

Warner et al. (1979), employing a powerful but demanding design, had eight people interact with one another in all possible pairs on three different occasions. The percentage of time each pair spent talking was coded. Warner et al. found that speakers adjusted their percentage of talk to their partners in a compensatory fashion that was not reproduced from conversation to conversation with the same pair. When one person held the floor more in conversation 1, the other person held it less than normal for that person; the pattern might be reversed but remain compensatory in other conversations. These results are in agreement with the findings of Cappella and Planalp (1981) and Matarazzo et al. (1968).

GAZE

The earlier review of responses to gaze uncovered only nine studies that manipulated level of gaze (Cappella, 1981). The general pattern of findings, although weak, was that increases in gaze tend to produce reciprocal responses: more gaze and longer durations of speech were returned. The situations producing these findings were uniformly positive or at least neutral in tone. Gaze is not always reciprocated, however. Greenbaum and Rosenfeld (1978) found that female drivers who were stared at by a male confederate at an intersection compensated in response to that gaze by leaving the intersection quickly, breaking away from the confederate's gaze before departing. Thus, in neutral or positive social encounters, gaze is reciprocated, while threatening or anxiety-producing settings evoke compensatory responses to gaze increases.

Studies not reported in my earlier review offer further support of the matching response to gaze in neutral and positive social situations. Sodikoff et al. (1974) found that subjects interacting with an interviewer who did not look at them gazed less, employed a less direct body orientation, and leaned away more than subjects who interacted with an interviewer who did gaze at them. Schneider and Hansvick (1977) had people give a five-minute monologue about themselves to a confederate who either increased or decreased gaze from the first to the second half of the monologue. The confederate's gaze tended to elicit more gaze from the subjects than the confederate's gaze aversion. The decrease of the subject's returned gaze was strongest when the confederate decreased gaze rather than increased it. No effects from the confederate's gaze on the standing distance of the subjects were found.

Noller (1980) studied the gaze patterns of high-, medium-, and low-adjusted couples during discussions of their marriages. Correlations between the average duration of husband's gaze while speaking and wife's gaze while listening (as well as for the husband listening and wife speaking) were positive for all groups, indicating matching. The correlations for the well-adjusted couples were substantial; those for the poorly adjusted couples were positive but nonsignificant.

Coutts et al. (1980) instructed their confederate either to increase gaze toward the subject or let it remain natural in each of two conditions: agreement and disagreement. The increase in gaze led to more returned gaze and more smiling from the subjects than when there was no change. This reciprocity effect occurred in both the agree and disagree conditions—in fact, more strongly in the disagree condition.

These four studies underscore the conclusions about responses to gaze. In neutral and positive social interactions, gaze begets gaze, as well as other involvement responses. However, gaze is not an unequivocal signal for approach. Like Ellsworth et al. (1972), Elman et al. (1977) found that a lengthy stare directed at a stranger on an elevator will increase walking speeds away from the elevator as opposed to the no-stare condition. Interestingly, when the confederate also wears a smile, walking speeds also increase over control but are intermediate between the control and stare-plus-no-smile group.

PROXIMITY

Responses to increases in proximity have been researched extensively. In thirty-six studies that manipulated proximity, the consistent general finding is that compensation results from increased proximity (Cappella, 1981). As proximity increases, people increase their distance, leave the area more quickly, gaze less, orient their bodies more indirectly, and decrease their durations of speaking. However, increased distance is not a universal sign of avoidance. Greenbaum and Rosenfeld (1978) found that a subgroup of their subjects actually gazed more when the confederate was at a close as opposed to far distance. This small subgroup was probably more affiliative because they verbalized to the staring confederate at the traffic intersection. In interactive situations, Aiello (1972), Skotko and Langmeyer (1977), and Stone and Morden (1976) found female subgroups showing signs of matching.

Other studies, not reviewed in Cappella (1981), provide added support for the above claims. Coutts and Ledden (1977) had a female interviewer increase, decrease, or not alter her distance from her female interviewees during a discussion. When distance was decreased, subjects gazed and smiled less than when distance was unaltered. When distance was increased, they gazed and smiled more while showing more direct body orientation and more forward lean than when the distance remained the same. This study is unique in that compensatory responses were observed for increases as well as decreases of interpersonal distance.

Aiello (1977) replicated his earlier findings on gaze responses to distance. As distance increased from 2.5 to 6.5 to 10.5 feet, the males compensated by increasing their gaze; the females increased gaze from 2.5 to 6.5 feet and then decreased gaze from 6.5 to 10.5 feet. Sundstrom and Sundstrom (1977) found similar sex differences in degree of compensation to strangers. But the females compensated more when the stranger did *not* ask permission to be seated than when they were asked, while the males showed greater compensation when they *were* asked permission. The females may have found close approach less invasive when the stranger established personal contact by asking permission, while the males may have found the stranger's contact in the permission condition more invasive precisely because a relationship was established. Sex differences in reactions to close and far approach indicate the importance of individual differences in the effects of the distance signal.

The only evidence contrary to the trend toward compensatory reactions to excessively far and close distances comes from Chapman's (1975) study of children listening to humorous audiotapes. He found that children gazed at one another and laughed more when they sat near rather than far from their partners. I do not find this evidence directly contra-dictory. The children wore headphones and were not interacting; Chap-man's results are related to audience contagion more than to social interaction.

OTHER INVOLVEMENT BEHAVIORS

Other signs of involvement might also exhibit patterns of mutual influence. For example, Condon and Ogston (1966, 1967) have speculated that changes in the movement of body parts are synchronized between interactants. McDowall's (1978) data, however, suggest that motion synchrony does not occur beyond chance.[2] The simpler hypothesis that rates of object- and body-focused gestures are matched in interaction has never been tested, even though there exists good reason for such specula-tion (Cappella, 1981). Reciprocal touching may develop in some condi-tions, as Whitcher and Fisher (1979) observed for hospital encounters of female nurses and female patients. Male patients tended not to reciprocate the nurses' simple touches. Little direct or indirect research has been addressed to these relatively peripheral signs of involvement.

SUMMARY

The overview presented in this section permits some general and impor-tant conclusions about mutual influence and involvement. First, mutual influence exists across a variety of signs and involvement, from the automatic, such as speech latency, to the deliberate, such as other-directed gaze. Second, mutual influence is both reciprocal and compensatory. Certain changes in involvement, such as gaze, tend to produce reciprocal responses, while others, such as proximity, tend to produce compensatory responses. Third, the response produced by each verbal and nonverbal sign of involvement depends on the situational, individual, and relational con-text in which the sign is emitted. By this statement I do not mean to imply that the effect is indeterminate. Rather, the intensity and even the quality of the response depends on the behavior relative to the situational, individual, and relational expectations. For example, males almost always compensate to changes in distance, while females may show signs of matching. Threatening social situations (strangers at an intersection) will not produce reciprocal responses to intense gaze, but neutral and positive social interactions do.

Fourth, changes in certain signs of involvement tend to be reciprocated (objective speech and gaze), while others tend to elicit compensatory responses (proximity).

Together, these conclusions set the demands for an explanation of how mutual influence occurs. Any explanation failing to account for one or more of the above conclusions must be rejected as inadequate.

EXPLAINING MUTUAL INFLUENCE PROCESSES

Every attempt to explain why mutual influence occurs in verbal, nonverbal, and vocal behaviors has found it necessary to enter the psyches of the influencing and influenced organisms to posit various mediating processes (Cappella and Greene, forthcoming; Patterson, 1976 and forthcoming; Street and Giles, 1982). The task I undertake in this section is not to set forward the correct explanation but to describe the possible processes mediating person B's response to a change in A's involvement. I believe that an accurate explanation of mutual influence will be forged from these mediating processes in the future.

Precisely what about mutual influence in involvement needs explanation? The task is *not* to explain how situational, relational, and individual differences produce differences in a person's expressed level of involvement. These factors do exert such an influence, but that influence occurs apart from or in addition to the influence of the partner's change in involvement. Rather, the task is to explain how a partner's expressed level of involvement, embedded, as it is, within the situational, relational, and individual context, acts on the person to produce a response leading to greater approach or avoidance. Thus, any explanation must be concerned with (1) the effect of A's involvement change on B and (2) how the changes in B's internal state are translated into a response of greater approach or greater avoidance. There will be much more to say about the former than the latter.

THE EFFECTS OF A's CHANGE IN INVOLVEMENT

Three types of effects are likely from a change in expressed involvement: physiological, affective, and attributional. The first refers to changes in arousal level as indexed by heart rate (HR), blood pressure (BP), electroencephalogram (EEG), electrocardiogram (EKG), galvanic skin response (GSR), electromyograph (EMG), and other signs of heightened activity. The second refers to positive and negative sentiments, preference, and attraction to the partner. The third refers to the inferences and categorization that the observer (person B) makes about A over and above general likability. For example, trait inferences (say, that those who interrupt are egocentric) have implications for positive and negative evaluations of the source as well as inferences about the source's motives. Let us take up each of these classes of effects in turn, remembering that it is not A's behavior per se that produces these effects but A's behavior relative to the situational, relational, and individual difference context.

INVOLVEMENT CHANGE AND AROUSAL

Speech and Arousal. No direct, unconfounded evidence exists to support the claim that speech activity affects the arousal of listeners. The kind of evidence needed would show that various levels of speech rate, loudness, and the like, unconfounded by content, are monotonically related to arousal states.

All other evidence is indirect. A recent study by Goldband (1981) found that subjects' GSRs to unusually long latencies by interviewers were greater than GSRs to normal latencies. Zimny and Weidenfeller (1963) found that musical pieces presumed to differ in their degrees of activity or tempo produced positive increments in GSR as tempo increased but had no effect on heart rate. This result agrees with earlier work (Ellis and Brighouse, 1952; Henkin, 1957). The effects of verbal content on various measures of arousal have been demonstrated by Smith et al. (1954), Wallerstein (1954), and Gaviria (1967).

The scant evidence shows monotonically increasing arousal effects for stimuli differing in tempo and differences in arousal between spoken verbal material and its absence. Although suggestive, these data cannot be said to make a strong case for the arousing affects of speech activity. Arousal and activation are presumed to occur whenever the organism mobilizes for performing a task. Thus, arousal increments in listening states can be attributed to attention and comprehension efforts (Kahneman, 1973) just as easily. Studies that equalize task demands across conditions but manipulate speech activity variables could unconfound the arousal-inducing effects of speech from other cognitive efforts. The tempo studies come close to doing so but manipulate musical rather than speech tempos.

Proximity and Arousal. Patterson's (1976) review of effects of proximity on arousal concludes that variations in proximity can produce arousal changes. However, only McBride et al. (1965) provide substantiating direct evidence, while Dabbs (1971) finds no effect on palmar sweating and Efran and Cheyne (1974) find none on heart rate. These negative results are mitigated, Patterson notes, by significant increases in subjects' arousal as they anticipate interaction and by observed differences in indirect, behavioral indicators of arousal in the close versus the far condition.

Since Patterson's review, several other direct sets of evidence have solidified the case for the arousing effects of close interpersonal distance.

In a series of convincing studies, Aiello and his colleagues (Aiello et al., 1975, 1977, 1979) have shown that when individuals are placed in group settings, their skin conductance levels are higher in small than in large rooms, are higher in groups than when alone, are highest for those with preferences for large interpersonal distances in crowded conditions, and are higher for most male and female fourth-, eighth-, and eleventh-graders in crowded conditions.

Using EEG measures of arousal, Gale et al. (1975) found that arousal increases as proximity increases from 2 through 32 feet in five steps. D'Atri (1975) studied three prison institutions that differed in housing methods between dormitory (close) and cell (far) settings. The blood pressure of prisoners was higher in the dormitory conditions than in cell conditions, while pulse was significantly higher in only one of two possible comparisons (the other was in the same direction).

The effects of situational factors on arousal can also be demonstrated. Walden and Forsyth (1981) found higher blood pressure in close than in far distance group settings when the group had been administered a placebic drug and told that it had no side effects. However, when a comparable group was told that the drug did have side effects, the blood pressure was higher in the far than in the near condition. The latter group may have felt that the close condition provided greater opportunity to monitor the effects of the drug on the other people, reducing anxiety about the drug's effects and thereby decreasing the BP level for this group over the elevated BP of the distant group.

Gaze and Arousal. Four studies provide direct evidence on the gaze-arousal relationship. Nichols and Champness (1971) found that the number and amplitude of GSR responses was greater when subjects gazed into one another's eyes than when they averted gaze. Similar results on averted versus constant gaze have been reported with measures of EEG (for which decreases are indicative of greater arousal; Gale et al., 1972, 1975) and of HR (Kleinke and Pohlen, 1971). Coutts et al. (1980) found that HR was greater when the confederate increased gaze than when gaze remained the same. Indirect evidence indicates that excessive gaze can decrease the latency of subjects' flight from the arousing starer (Ellsworth et al., 1972) and can result in stronger feelings of tension and anxiety (Schaeffer and Patterson, 1980). Patterson (1976) reports on several other sources of supporting, but indirect, evidence.

Other Expressive Behaviors and Arousal. Few of the other expressive behaviors (body movement, orientation and lean, smiling, touch) have been studied to determine their impact on physiological arousal. Gale et al.

(1972) report that the experimenter's smile reduced subjects' EEGs in comparison to their resting EEG levels. Increased touch by female nurses of patients before surgery showed that males' later blood pressure was elevated, while that of females was depressed compared to the male and female no-touch groups respectively (Whitcher and Fisher, 1979). Patterson et al. (1981) found that increases in intimacy by a confederate, due either to gaze or to a combined lean, touch, and increased gaze, resulted in greater skin conductance response and skin conductance level over baseline, especially in the early sections of the interaction. That further research on this topic is necessary on pragmatic grounds alone is demonstrated by Lynch et al.'s (1977) research on arhythmic heart rates of heart patients in response to the mere presence of medical personnel.

Arousal-Arousal Covariation. If changes in involvement tend to produce arousal increments and if involvement changes are either matched or compensated, then interactors should exhibit positive correlations in their arousal levels during interaction. DiMascio et al. (1955) report a positive correlation between patient and therapist pulse rates during periods of concordance and a negative correlation during periods of discord. Coleman et al. (1956) found similar average heart rates for patient and therapist during moments judged to be emotional ones. Chin EMG levels were found to be similar for both the recipient and the giver of praise and criticism (Malmo et al., 1957).

Nowlin et al. (1968) measured free fatty acid levels and heart rate of both the passive (questioning) and active (answering) members of a controlled conversation. Both measures exhibited parallel changes for each person over the test intervals. The most impressive research on this question is that of Kaplan et al. (1963, 1964). In the first study, groups of four persons were assembled on the basis of a priori liking and disliking. The group with members who disliked one another exhibited a greater number of pairs with positive versus nonsignificant correlations on GSR than the groups with neutral or positive liking. These findings were replicated in a dyadic setting by Kaplan et al. (1964: 108), leading them to conclude that physiological covariation may be "an index of consensual affective investment in the study of social interaction." Given the criticisms of Lacey (1959), more well-designed experiments are necessary before such a claim can be trusted. Nonetheless, the covariation of physiological activity during interaction is necessary evidence for any arousal-mediated explanation.

Taken as a whole, the evidence for involvement change producing arousal in interaction is strong. Any explanation of mutual influence across the various involvement behaviors must give a role to arousal. Most do (Cappella and Greene, forthcoming; Patterson, 1976 and forthcoming).

INVOLVEMENT CHANGE AND AFFECT

The most obvious principle relating involvement levels to affective responses is that both excessively high and excessively low levels of involvement are less preferred than intermediate levels. What determines the boundaries of excess include situational norms, relationship stage, and individual differences. What is too close in an elevator with one's colleagues may not be close enough in private with one's spouse. This relationship between involvement level relative to a normative standard and affective response is the classic inverted-U relationship between arousal potential and preference (Berlyne, 1967) or stimulus intensity and hedonic tone (Eysenck, 1973; see also Burgoon in this volume). It agrees with our intuitions that unusual, nonnormative, and, indeed, deviant behaviors are less preferred and their perpetrators less attractive to us. Does the scientific evidence support these intuitions?

Few studies have manipulated enough levels of expressed involvement (there must be at least three) to provide relevant information on the inverted-U curve to affective response. Smith et al. (1975) found a curvilinear relationship between speech rate and an evaluative factor that they labeled benevolence. As the rate increased from below-normal to normal speech rates, ratings increased but decreased as rates increased beyond the normal range (see also Brown, 1980). Hayes and Meltzer (1978) have speculated that the relationship between participation in discussion and evaluation of the participant is curvilinear. No direct data support this claim, but adjective studies of interpersonal judgment do (Hayes and Sievers, 1972). Although gaze may lead to greater or lesser attraction to the gazer as a function of other cues (Ellsworth and Langer, 1976), these findings of positive association and negative association typically involve only two levels of gaze. Assessment of curvilinearity is therefore impossible. However, both Cook and Smith (1975) and Argyle et al. (1974) found that increasing gaze from another beyond "normal" and "spontaneous" limits respectively revealed decrements in liking for the excessive gazer after initial increases.

Research on person's affective reactions to interpersonal proximity are similar to the results on gaze. When persons are asked to evaluate social settings (as observers) in which distance between interactants is a prominent cue, they tend to label close distances as a sign of greater attraction than far distances (Mehrabian, 1968a; Kelly, 1972). When they experience close interpersonal distances negatively (as crowded or as interfering with their goals), then attraction and liking toward the other are inversely related to proximity (Griffith and Veitch, 1971; Worchel and Teddlie, 1976) and expectations about the interaction can significantly alter affective reactions (Schiffenbauer and Schiavo, 1976).

The vast majority of studies manipulate only two levels of distance.[3] Patterson and Sechrest (1970), however, found that ratings of friendliness increased as distance decreased from eight to four feet, but decreased from four to two feet. These data suggest that while persons identify proximity as a sign of affect, actual intrusions are experienced positively or negatively as a function of expectations, with the possibility that intermediate distances are most positive in general. Thompson et al. (1979) obtained almost identical results on preference for distance in two- and four-person groups.

Results for other expressive behaviors and the affective reactions they induce are not available at sufficient levels to conclude anything about curvilinearity. In infant-adult interaction, studies by Fogel (1977), Stern et al. (1977), and DeBoer and Boxes (1979) suggest that infants' signs of positive expression (smiling, visual attention, vocalization, and body motions) are stimulated by the mother's facial, visual, and vocal activity. But when that stimulation becomes excessively repetitious, nonresponsive (Brazelton et al., 1975) or too exaggerated, the infant reduces signs of positive affective involvement (Stern, 1974).

It is important to recognize that I am *not* claiming that certain absolute levels of involvement are preferred or excessive. Rather, what makes a distance too close or a gaze too intense is the behavior relative to what is expected on the basis of situational norms, relationship between the interactors, and individual preferences. Without this concept of involvement relative to expectation, we are forced into the untenable position that a given level of involvement has a specified effect independent of its circumstances. As claimed at the outset of this chapter, such a position is absurd.

INVOLVEMENT AND ATTRIBUTION

People not only have preferences for certain involvement levels and are differentially attracted to the excessively involved actor, but also make inferences about actors' traits, motivations, and qualities on the basis of limited observation of their behavior. Although a long history of research links various involvement behaviors to immediate qualities of the actor (for example, voice and personality), studies of more indirect inferences have only recently been undertaken under the title of implicit personality research (Ebbesen and Allen, 1979; Hastie and Carlston, 1980). This research will become useful for understanding the processes of mutual influence as evidence linking trait attributions to specific behaviors (Pavitt and Haight, 1982) and as the structure and organization of implicit theories about personality accumulates.

We know that people develop expectations about others on the basis of their actions and act in accord with those expectations (Kelley, 1950). What we do not know is how these expectations filter through the network of implicit assumptions about human behavior producing expectations that, correctly or incorrectly, move far beyond the observational base for such expectations. As Patterson (forthcoming) points out, these expectations can be self-confirming with the perceiver treating the partner in a way that elicits behavior confirming the initial expectation (Snyder et al., 1977).

B's RESPONSES TO AFFECTIVE, PHYSIOLOGICAL, AND COGNITIVE CHANGES

The research evidence discussed above indicates that a change in A's level of expressed involvement can produce affective, physiological, and cognitive-attributional changes in B. But what would lead B to respond to these internal changes with greater behavioral approach toward or avoidance of A?

The answers that have been given to this question about the production of involvement responses have been embarrassingly simple or so general as to defy empirical testing. Let us consider each answer in turn.

EQUILIBRIUM THEORY

In 1965, Argyle and Dean (1965) proposed a theory that had profound impact on empirical research on compensation: Equilibirum Theory. The theory has been amended by Argyle and Cook (1976) and by Firestone (1977) but basically remains the same. The domain of the theory is the set of affiliative behaviors: gaze, distance, touch, lean, verbal disclosure, and so on. Its claims are simple. Once an equilibrium level of desired affiliation is established in a dyad, excessive levels of affiliative behavior by one partner lead the other partner to compensate in order to maintain the equilibrium level of intimacy. The reason for the compensatory response is that the perpetual balancing act between internal forces toward approach and avoidance has swung in the direction of avoidance for the moment. But the theory gives no flesh to the bones of approach and avoidance forces. We do not know what psychological mechanisms are referred to, nor do we know how to measure the degree of these forces. As a consequence, this theory explains by appealing to processes that, in themselves, can offer no greater understanding of why compensatory (or reciprocal, in the later versions) processes occur.

AROUSAL LABELING

Patterson (1976) proposed an important amendation of Equilibrium Theory with his Arousal Labeling (AL) model of reciprocity and compensation. The domain of this theory is also the affiliative behaviors. AL takes into account the findings that a change in a person's level of involvement can produce physiological arousal in the partner. Whether this arousal leads to approach or avoidance depends on how the arousal is labeled by the experiencer. If the arousal is labeled positively, then reciprocal responses should occur; if the arousal is labeled negatively, then compensatory responses should occur. The label attached to the arousal is presumably found in the search of the environment. Excessive intimacy in a situation that is labeled as friendly and even loving should produce reciprocal responses. In a threatening situation, the same intimacy and its associated arousal would be labeled negatively and avoided.

In this way, AL theory is a significant advance over Equilibrium Theory. The approach and avoidance forces are replaced by physiological responses that receive a cognitive label. The hypotheses are clear, and the intervening mechanisms are all directly measurable. The simple assumption that positive affect leads to reciprocity and that negative affect leads to compensation is never critically evaluated. The behavioral response is assumed to follow the affective response.[4]

SPEECH ACCOMMODATION THEORY

Giles has engaged in a lengthy program of research on the processes of accommodation and adaption in speech (Giles and Powesland, 1975; Giles and Smith, 1979). Street and Giles (1982) have provided a recent update of this theory, whose domain is the objective speech variables plus dialect and pronunciation. They maintain that people will converge

> towards the speech patterns believed to be characteristic of their recipients when they (a) desire their social approval and the perceived costs of so acting are proportionally lower than the rewards anticipated; and/or (b) desire a high level of communicational efficiency, and (c) social norms are not perceived to dictate alternative speech strategies. (p. 29)

People diverge

> from those believed characteristics of their recipients when they (a) define the encounter in intergroup terms and desire a positive ingroup identity or (b) wish to bring another's speech behaviors to a personally acceptable level. (p. 30)

Although the domain of the theory is limited, the production mechanisms might apply to other involvement behaviors as well. The mechanism of Speech Accommodation Theory (SAT) seems to be a conscious willing of divergence or convergence rather than a more automatic response to the situation.

Street and Giles (1982) claim that, despite the language of SAT, these processes are quite automatic, called into play from the procedural storehouse of memory with the proper cue. Their account may or may not be valid, but it certainly will be very difficult to evaluate empirically. I have no doubt that with effort and practice people can force themselves to reciprocate or compensate to another's behavior. In the absence of such deliberate action, the invocation of automatic procedures stored in memory does not explain how the automatic procedures got into memory, why they have one procedural content (for example, reciprocating for efficiency) rather than another, or how procedural knowledge translates into procedural action.

DISCREPANCY-AROUSAL THEORY

Simple observation suggests that people adjust their levels of involvement to one another rather rapidly during conversation. These quick adjustments might be called moment-to-moment influence (Cappella, 1980; Cappella and Planalp, 1981). Such rapid action sequences leave no room for the slow cognitive judgments of certain explanations (Giles and Powesland, 1975; Giles and Smith, 1979; Patterson, 1976). Quicker, less cognitively ponderous reactions must be build into the explanations. Discrepancy-arousal (DA) theory (Cappella and Greene, forthcoming) is designed with this purpose in mind. The domain of the theory is all involvement behaviors. DA holds that involvement behaviors by A that deviate from an expected level (set by situational, relational, and individual factors) give rise to a change in arousal level. If the change in arousal over baseline is small to moderate, it is experienced as affectively positive and reciprocated; if the change in arousal is extreme, it is experienced as affectively negative and compensated (Berlyne, 1967; Stern, 1974).

DA is a modification of AL in which quicker responses are expected because the "decision" to reciprocate or compensate is a direct result of change in arousal mediated by affective reaction and not the result of a cognitive search after arousal has occurred. Three types of evidence can be marshaled to support the tenets of DA: the arousal-affect relationship, the affect-involvement relationship, and the arousal-involvement relationship.

Arousal-Affect. The arousal-affect linkage follows directly the one proposed by Berlyne (1967), which he based on the work of Wundt (1874), McClelland et al. (1953), and Haber (1958); it is similar to the proposal of Fiske and Maddi (1961). Berlyne is primarily concerned with arousal changes as reinforcers, which, he notes, are related to learning, to the experience of pleasantness and preference, to the evocation of positive and negative approach and avoidance behaviors, and to response energizing and discrimination. He conceptualizes arousal as a nonspecific energizing drive; since most reinforcers have been identified by their ability to reduce or increase various drives, changes in arousal become prime candidates for reinforcing agents.

In supporting his case, Berlyne first notes that there is considerable evidence that decreases in arousal are rewarding. On the other hand, some less conclusive evidence suggests that arousal increases will also have reward value. One reason for this could be that the increased arousal that accompanies stimulus change is quickly followed by arousal reduction, and it is this reduction that is rewarding. Berlyn supports the arousal increase-reward relationship by citing numerous studies that build a convincing, if circumstantial, case. That the amount of arousal change is crucial for determining the rewarding or aversive character of the arousal change follows from animal research (for example, Schneirla, 1959, 1965), from research by Sokolov (1964) on the orienting and defensive responses, from research on pleasantness ratings of stimulus sequences and other collative variables (such as that of Maddi, 1961), from research on the intensity of brain stimulation, and from studies of verbal learning.

In addition to these studies on adults, research on infants provides evidence on the arousal-affect linkage. The positiveness of the infant's behavioral response seems to parallel conditions of moderate arousal as opposed to low or high arousal. Hopkins et al. (1976) found that papier-mâché figures moderately discrepant with a familiar standard exhibited the greatest positive vocalization and least fretting from infants. These stimuli were also most highly attended. McCall and Kennedy (1980) rated the quality of infant's affect (on the basis of smiles, vocalizations, and movements) in response to male faces differing in typicality. Behavioral affect followed visual attention, with most positive affect displays associated with conditions of greatest attentional involvement.

These remarkable social responses to what are essentially cognitive problems for the infant (that is, assimilating new information) have been explained by Zelazo (1972) and McCall (1977) in similar ways. Both suggest that the infant's attempt to match a new stimulus to an existent schema requires cognitive effort that, when successful, results in smiling and possibly vocal bursts. This is not to say that smiling, vocalization, and other infant actions occur only in response to successful assimilation of new information but rather that this mechanism ties learning, cognitive exploration, social behavior, and mother-infant attachment together.

The link to arousal is made by Sroufe and Waters (1976). They build a convincing argument that at least one infant behavior, smiling, comes as a result of the release of tension built up in the process of assimilating new stimuli. Thus, this affective response is possibly a direct response to arousal decrease and may not only control the infant's arousal but also make possible exploration of the environment and secure attachment to the primary caretaker (Stechler and Carpenter, 1967). If this explanation is correct, then the expressive responses to stimulation that are labeled as social signs of affect by adults may be serving the infant's cognitive functions in reaction to arousal changes.

The evidence for the arousal-affect relationship, while circumstantial for the most part, is encouraging. At a minimum, we are probably safe in claiming that large changes in arousal over baseline expectations are probably experienced as aversive, while moderate changes attract interest and curiosity.

Affect-Involvement. Perhaps the least controversial element of the DA model is the hypothesis that experienced affect toward another and the intensity or duration of various expressive behaviors directed toward that other covary positively. The research is voluminous but will be summarized briefly here. Attraction to an interviewer tends to produce shorter pauses, shorter response latencies, and greater speech rates (Siegman 1978: 218-220; 1979). More attractive discussion partners elicit greater gaze than less attractive ones (Exline and Winters, 1965), and those strongly in love engage in more mutual gaze than those less strongly in love (Rubin, 1970).

Physical proximity is one of the most well-established signs of positive affect. High school students who like one another interact at closer distances than those who do not (Aiello and Cooper, 1972). Mehrabian's (1968a, 1968b; Mehrabian and Friar, 1969) subjects took up positions closer to hypothetical others who were imagined as more positive than to those imagined to be more negative. In situations with mixed-sex couples, standing distance was less for dating couples who were affectively more positive than those affectively negative (Byrne et al., 1970). Couples who are more intimate with one another sit closer (Cook, 1970) and stand nearer when interacting (Heska and Nelson, 1972; Willis, 1966). Other expressive behaviors are less well researched, although touch (Whitcher and Fisher, 1979), direct postural orientation (Clore, cited in Patterson, 1978), and smiling (Argyle, 1975) are associated with positive affect toward an interactant.

Arousal-Involvement. The discrepancy-arousal model predicts that the intensity and duration of various expressive behaviors should be predictable from arousal changes. The relationship between these two (which is mediated by affective reaction) should be an inverted U function. Such a function is reminiscent of the arousal-performance curves described in the activation literature (Berlyne, 1960; Fiske and Maddi, 1961; Duffy, 1962; Kahneman, 1973) but in this case are presumed to be mediated by affective reactions rather than attentional mechanisms (Easterbrook, 1959). Ideally, evidence for covariation between arousal change and expressive response would have manipulated at least three levels of arousal and preferably four. Unfortunately, most studies manipulate only two levels of arousal which can give information only on the rising or falling edge of the deduced inverted-U curve.

Objective aspects of speech have been widely studied in response to manipulations of arousal and anxiety. Siegman (1978) has offered a comprehensive and intelligent review of this research. He concludes that the most parsimonious explanation of the relationship between anxiety arousal and rate, latency, speech disturbances, and pauses is an inverted-U function.

The most suggestive evidence for a curvilinear relationship derives from studies by Fenz and Epstein (1962) on latency to response and by Cook (1969) on speech rate. In the Fenz and Epstein study, parachutists were asked to respond to stimulus cards that increased in anxiety provocation for parachutists from neutral to moderate and then to very high. Latencies decreased and then increased as the U-shaped response curves should for the parachutists but showed opposite tendencies for a control group of nonparachutists.

Cook sampled subjects high and low on trait anxiety and manipulated state anxiety by introducing intimate interview topics in the second period of a three-period interview. Those low in trait anxiety increased their speech rates during the arousing middle section of the interview, while those high in state anxiety decreased their rates in the middle section. Those high in trait anxiety are presumed to be overly aroused by the anxiety-provoking questions, which have a debilitating effect on their speech rates. Those low on trait anxiety are presumably activated by the anxiety of the intimate questions.

Studies on the covariation of arousal and other expressive behaviors are sparse. Brady and Walker (1978) manipulated subjects' felt anxiety by inducing them to focus on their own performance while being observed. Subjects in the high anxiety condition stood further apart than those in the low anxiety condition. Subjects in the high anxiety condition exhibited a greater speech disturbance ratio as well. Nesbitt and Steven (1974) reasoned that the intensity of stimulation would increase distance between persons waiting in a line. They found, not surprisingly, that loud clothes and heavy scents prompted bystanders to maintain greater distances than did conservative dress and normal scents.

Arousal, particularly that associated with anxiety, seems to be negatively related to gaze. Jurich and Jurich (1974) reported a very high positive correlation between gaze aversion and sweat print under conditions of variable anxiety provocation. Daly (1978) found that more socially anxious subjects looked less while talking during an interview than did less socially anxious subjects. Hutt and Ounstedt (1966) observed that autistic children spent less time studying face drawings in a playroom than did normal children. They interpret this result as an attempt by the autistic children to regulate their arousal, since it is presumed that they are typically in a "state of high physiological and behavioral arousal" (p. 355). While these studies on gaze and distance show primarily a negative relationship to arousal, it is easy to conceive of (and a delight to partake in) social encounters in which positively experienced arousal prompts greater gaze and closer proximity.

Only a few other expressive behaviors have been related to the arousal state. Jurich and Jurich's (1974) correlational study obtained positive correlations between sweat print and posture shifting and sweat print and hand motions toward the head. Sainsbury (1955) separated psychiatric interviews for 16 patients into stressful and nonstressful periods and recorded heart rate and gestural activity in all periods. Stressful periods exhibited greater gestural activity than nonstressful periods in all 16 interviews, with 14 significant. Heart rate was also greater in stressful periods in 13 of 16 interviews, with 9 significant; 3 interviews showed no differences in heart rate between stress and nonstress segments. Increases in stress also seem to increase the fundamental frequency of voice (Scherer, 1977), and tension release may account for smiling in newborn and older infants (Sroufe and Waters, 1976).

Studies of the arousal-expressive response relationship suffer from manipulating too few levels of arousal to conclude anything about the proposed curvilinearity. With only two levels of arousal or anxiety, one can only guess about what edge of an inverted U is being tested. On the positive side, covariation between arousal and expressive response has been observed in speech variables, gaze, distance, verbal disclosure, and body movements. Speech rate and response latencies are best understood as having an inverted-U relationship to arousal; gaze, proximity, and verbal disclosure decrease as anxiety moves from low to high; bodily activity increases from nonstressful to stressful times.

SUMMARY

In order to explain mutual influence in conversation, any account must be concerned with the effects of A's involvement behavior on B and with the translation of B's reaction into behavioral approach or avoidance. Equilibrium Theory appeals to the relative balance of approach and avoidance forces in explaining responses; SA Theory appeals to perceptions, goals, and social norms as cues to automatic procedures held in memory; AL suggests that the label applied to one's arousal from a cognitive search of the environment and memory for cues produces reciprocal or compensatory responses; DA maintains that the degree of arousal change determines the quality of experienced affect which, in turn, determines the quality of response, reciprocal or compensatory. Which theory will ultimately be most successful in accounting for mutual influence in involvement depends on contrastive empirical tests. Such a test between AL and DA is currently being carried out in our laboratory. Regardless of the results of that test, any future explanation of mutual adjustment of involvement must rely on and account for affective, physiological, and attributional changes produced by the other's involvement and how those changes result in behavioral response.

PRAGMATICS OF MUTUAL INFLUENCE

A great deal of evidence on the existence and pervasiveness of mutual influence processes and their explanations has been reviewed in this chapter. It is fair to ask whether the presence or absence of reciprocal or compensatory involvement matters in the pragmatic concerns of conversational and relational partners.

RESULTS OF MUTUAL INFLUENCE

The presence of reciprocal patterns of involvement may have implications for the development of attraction and positive attachment generally in adult dyads. Noller (1980) studied married couples who were classified as high, moderate, and low adjusted, recording gaze patterns during discussion. She found high positive correlations between males' gaze while speaking and females' gaze while listening (as well as the reverse categories) for the highly and moderately adjusted couples but insignificant correlations between male and female gaze for the low adjusted couples.

In a more controlled environment, Street (1982) had judges listen to tape-recorded interviews in which the interviewer and interviewee converged, partially converged, maintained, or diverged their speech rates, latencies, and durations. The judges evaluated the interviewee most negatively when there was divergence on rate, latency, and utterance duration. More generally, Warner (1979) has speculated that individuals have a baseline tempo for activity that must be adjusted in interactions with others in order for there to be a smooth, flowing interaction (Chapple, 1970). Warner suggests noncomplementary tempos may make interactions awkward and stressful, thereby filtering out certain pairs as unattractive to one another. I believe that Warner's speculations may be meritorious, but I argue that symmetrical rather than complementary tempos are necessary over the duration of the lengthy conversations that lay the foundation for relationships. Complementary periods of activity should occur with turn-taking, but, over several turns, one partner cannot be passive and leaden while the other is animated and vibrant without some negative perceptions arising.

This work suggests that positive orientations arise as partners are "in sync" with one another in terms of overt expression of involvement. It might be that positive and negative reactions would arise in helping relationships (doctor-patient, counselor-advisee, teacher-student) when the members of the pair exhibit reciprocal and compensatory patterns of involvement, respectively. Perceptions of empathy and identification in these contexts could result from the observation that the other's behavior or the other's reaction to the situation is similar to one's own. Speculating further, it would be fruitful to explore the patterns of involvement reciprocity and involvement compensation not only as the basis of initial attraction between persons, but also as a source of satisfaction and dissatisfaction with the other as a long-term partner.

On the other hand, compensatory reactions may be necessary to control the overly intrusive or overly stimulating actions of another. They are the necessary behavioral means of regulating excessive interaction and contact and of preserving autonomy.

Research by Davis (Davis and Martin, 1978; Davis and Perkowitz, 1979) suggests that the reason for the more positive outcomes from matched rather than compensatory levels of involvement may be the perception of responsiveness—more specifically, appropriate responsiveness. Davis and Perkowitz (1979) had confederates respond to either 33% or 66% of the subject's questions, finding that attraction was highest to the more responsive confederates regardless of the frequency of response (4 or 8). This finding was replicated with 80%-20% response rates in a second study. Davis and Martin (1978) had dating or stranger pairs give pleasurable shocks to their partners under conditions in which the partner was verbally responsive or not as the pleasant shock was being administered. They found that for dating pairs, both males and females gave more pleasurable shocks to responsive than to unresponsive partners. But for the stranger pairs, the females actually gave fewer pleasurable shocks to the responsive rather than the unresponsive partner (the males did not exhibit any difference in administering pleasure to the responsive and unresponsive partners). Responsiveness seems to be important in determining attraction and in giving positive reward. However, sheer responsiveness, when inappropriate, may actually have a detrimental effect on positive reactions.

Davis's work is very suggestive for the role of reciprocal and compensatory involvement in the assessment of communicative competence. However competent communicators behave, they certainly do not exhibit a lack of responsiveness to the other. The person who consistently neither responds in kind nor withdraws from the demonstrated involvement of another person is surely incompetent by this pattern of unresponsiveness. Specifically, we would expect that demonstrations of involvement, when within the bounds of appropriateness, would be reciprocated. Involvement and interest should beget involvement and interest. When involvement levels are deficient or excessive, outside the bounds of appropriateness, then perhaps the actions of the competent actor are to reintroduce normative levels of involvement by approaching or avoiding. At a minimum, however, the close ties between involvement and responsiveness make the lack of reciprocal or compensatory adjustments in involvement a certain sign of communicative incompetence.

CONCLUSION

A relatively straightforward question has guided the content of this essay: Do people catch one another's involvement when they interact? The answers that have been provided range across large bodies of research literature. The reason for such breadth of coverage results from two words in our guiding question: *involvement* and *interaction.* The first describes a function that a variety of verbal, nonverbal, and vocal behaviors can serve. Consequently, the range of behaviors that must be treated is broad. This approach contrasts sharply with the study of individual behaviors that are known to serve numerous functions.

The second word, *interaction,* forces us to consider if, when, and how involvement changes by one are associated with involvement changes by the other. In taking up such considerations, we have had to pry into individuals and ask about the affective, cognitive, and physiological changes that a change in another's involvement brings about; further, how do those internal changes result in a behavioral response to greater, lesser, or no change in level of approach? In short, by addressing the functions that behaviors serve and how they are sequenced, the Pandora's box of social interaction has been opened. I hope that future rummaging in the box will uncover treatments of other functions (control, regulation, task orientation) in the context of interaction.

NOTES

1. An important difference exists between vocalization duration and utterance duration as they are usually measured. Utterance duration includes all pauses while speaking, except the latency between speaker switches. Vocalization duration excludes pauses altogether and is the time spent in vocalization while holding the floor.

2. Gatewood and Rosenwein (1981) have criticized McDowall's work as irrelevant to the fundamental hypotheses and basic methods and definitions employed by Condon.

3. Burgoon (this volume) argues that the inverted-U relationship holds primarily for nonrewarding persons, while a U-shaped relationship between deviations and outcomes best describes the data for rewarding sources.

4. In Patterson's (forthcoming) most recent theory, the production component does not receive any treatment at all. Rather, instabilities in the interaction due to mismatched goals, functions, or levels of involvement intensity lead to compensatory adjustments that will presumably lead to stable and synchronous interactions.

REFERENCES

Aiello, J. R. A test of equilibrium theory: Visual interaction in relation to orientation, distance, and sex of the interactants. *Psychonomic Science,* 1972, *27,* 335-336.

Aiello, J. R. A further look at equilibrium theory: Visual interaction as a function of interpersonal distance. *Environmental Psychology and Nonverbal Behavior,* 1977, *1,* 122-139.

Aiello, J. R., and Cooper, R. E. Use of personal space as a function of social affect. *Proceedings of the 80th Annual Convention of the American Psychological Association,* 1972, *7,* 207-208.

Aiello, J. R., Derisi, D. T., Epstein, Y. M., and Karlin, R. A. Crowding and the role of interpersonal distance preference. *Sociometry,* 1977, *40,* 271-282.

Aiello, J. R., Epstein, Y. M., and Karlin, R. A. Effects of crowding on electrodermal activity. *Sociological Symposium,* 1975, *14,* 43-57.

Aiello, J. R., Nicosia, G., and Thompson, D. E. Physiological, social, and behavioral consequences of crowding on children and adolescents. *Child Development,* 1979, *50,* 195-202.

Argyle, M. *Bodily communication.* New York: International Universities Press, 1975.

Argyle, M., and Cook, M. *Gaze and mutual gaze.* Cambridge: Cambridge University Press, 1976.

Argyle, M., and Dean, J. Eye contact, distance, and affiliation. *Sociometry,* 1965, *28,* 289-304.

Argyle, M., Lefebvre, L., and Cook, M. The meaning of five patterns of gaze. *European Journal of Social Psychology,* 1974, *4,* 125-136.

Bales, R. F. *Personality and interpersonal behavior.* New York: Holt, Rinehart & Winston, 1970.

Berlyne, D. E. *Conflict, arousal, and curiosity.* New York: McGraw-Hill, 1960.

Berlyne, D. E. Arousal and reinforcement. In D. Levine (Ed.), *Nebraska Symposium on Motivation.* (Vol. 15). Lincoln: University of Nebraska Press, 1967.

Bochner, A. P., Kaminski, E. P., and Fitzpatrick, M. A. The conceptual domain of interpersonal communication behaviors. *Human Communication Research,* 1977, *3,* 291-302.

Bowlby, J. *Attachment and loss* (Vol. 1). New York: Basic Books, 1969.

Brady, A. T., and Walker, M. B. Interpersonal distance as a function of situationally induced anxiety. *British Journal of Social and Clinical Psychology,* 1978, *17,* 127-133.

Brazelton, T. B., Tronick, E., Adamson, L., Als, H., and Wise, S. *Early mother-infant reciprocity. Parent-Infant Interaction.* Ciba Foundation Symposium 33. Amsterdam: Elsevier, 1975.

Brown, B. L. Effects of speech rate on personality attribution and competency evaluations. In H. Giles (Ed.), *Language: Social psychological perspectives.* London: Pergamon Press, 1980.

Byrne, D. C., Ervin, R., and Lamberth, J. Continuity between the experimental study of attraction and real-life computer dating. *Journal of Personality and Social Psychology,* 1970, *16,* 157-165.

Cappella, J. N. Structural equation modeling: An introduction. In P. R. Monge and J. N. Cappella (Eds.), *Multivariate techniques in human communication research.* New York: Academic Press, 1980.

Cappella, J. N. Mutual influence in expressive behavior: Adult and infant-adult dyadic interaction. *Psychological Bulletin,* 1981, *89,* 101-132.

Cappella, J. N., and Greene, J. O. A discrepancy-arousal explanation of mutual influence in expressive behavior for adult-adult and infant-adult interaction. *Communication Monographs,* forthcoming.

Cappella, J. N., and Planalp, S. Talk and silence sequences in informal conversations: III. Interspeaker influence. *Human Communication Research,* 1981, *7,* 117-132.

Carson, R. C. *Interaction concepts of personality.* Chicago: Aldine, 1969.

Chapman, A. J. Eye contact, physical proximity, and laughter: A reexamination of the equilibrium model of social intimacy. *Social Behavior and Personality,* 1975, *3,* 143-155.

Chapple, E. D. *Culture and biological man: Explorations in behavioral anthropology.* New York: Holt, Rinehart & Winston, 1970.

Coleman, R., Greenblatt, M., and Solomon, H. C. Physiological evidence of rapport during psychotherapeutic interviews. *Diseases of the Nervous System,* 1956, *17,* 71-77.

Condon, W. S. An analysis of behavior organization. *Sign Language Studies,* 1976, *13,* 285-318.

Condon, W. S., and Ogston, W. D. Sound film analysis of normal and pathological behavior patterns. *Journal of Nervous and Mental Disease,* 1966, *143,* 338-347.

Condon, W. S., and Ogston, W. D. A segmentation of behavior. *Journal of Psychiatric Research*, 1967, *5*, 221-235.

Cook, M. Anxiety, speech disturbances and speech rate. *British Journal of Social and Clinical Psychology*, 1969, *8*, 13-21.

Cook, M. Experiments on orientation and proxemics. *Human Relations*, 1970, *23*, 61-76.

Cook, M., and Smith, J.M.C. The role of gaze in impression formation. *British Journal of Social and Clinical Psychology*, 1975, *14*, 19-25.

Coutts, L. M., and Ledden, M. Nonverbal compensatory reactions to changes in interpersonal proximity. *Journal of Social Psychology*, 1977, *102*, 283-290.

Coutts, L. M., Schneider, F. W., and Montgomery, S. An investigation of the arousal model of interpersonal intimacy. *Journal of Experimental Social Psychology*, 1980, *16*, 545-561.

Dabbs, J. M. Physical closeness and negative feelings. *Psychonomic Science*, 1971, *23*, 141-143.

Daly, S. Behavioral correlates of social anxiety. *British Journal of Social and Clinical Psychology*, 1978, *17*, 117-120.

D'Atri, D. A. Psychophysiological responses to crowding. *Environment and Behavior*, 1975, *7*, 237-252.

Davis, D., and Martin, H. J. When pleasure begets pleasure: Recipient responsiveness as a determinant of physical pleasuring between heterosexual dating couples and strangers. *Journal of Personality and Social Psychology*, 1978, *36*, 767-777.

Davis, D., and Perkowitz, W. T. Consequences of responsiveness in dyadic interaction: Effects of probability of response and proportion of content-related responses on interpersonal attraction. *Journal of Personality and Social Psychology*, 1979, *37*, 534-550.

Deboer, M. M., and Boxes, A. M. Signal functions of infant facial expression and gaze direction during mother-infant face-to-face play. *Child Development*, 1979, *50*, 1215-1218.

Dimascio, A., Boyd, R. W., Greenblatt, M., and Solomon, H. C. The psychiatric interview: A sociophysiologic study. *Diseases of the Nervous System*, 1955, *16*, 2-7.

Duffy, E. *Activation and behavior.* New York: John Wiley, 1962.

Easterbrook, J. A. The effect of emotion on cue utilization and the organization of behavior. *Psychological Review*, 1959, *66*, 183-201.

Ebbesen, E., and Allen, R. B. Cognitive processes in implicit personality trait inferences. *Journal of Personality and Social Psychology*, 1979, *37*, 471-488.

Efran, M. G., and Cheyne, J. A. Affective concomitants of the invasion of shared space: Behavioral, physiological, and verbal indications. *Journal of Personality and Social Psychology*, 1974, *29*, 219-226.

Ellis, E. S., and Brighouse, G. The effects of music on respiration and heart rate. *American Journal of Psychology*, 1952, *65*, 39-47.

Ellsworth, P. C. Direct gaze as a social stimulus: The example of aggression. In L. Kramer, T. Alloway, and P. Pliner (Eds.), *Nonverbal communication of aggression.* New York: Plenum, 1975.

Ellsworth, P. C., and Carlsmith, J. M. The effects of eye contact and verbal content on affective response to a dyadic interaction. *Journal of Personality and Social Psychology*, 1968, *10*, 15-20.

Ellsworth, P. P., Carlsmith, J. M., and Henson, A. The stare as a stimulus to flight in human subjects. *Journal of Personality and Social Psychology*, 1972, *21*, 302-311.

Ellsworth, P. C., and Langer, E. J. Staring and approach: An interpretation of the stare as a nonspecific activator. *Journal of Personality and Social Psychology,* 1976, *33,* 117-122.

Elman, D., Schulte, D. C., and Bukoff, A. Effects of facial expression and stare duration on walking speed: Two field experiments. *Environmental Psychology and Nonverbal Behavior,* 1977, *2,* 91-99.

Exline, R. V., and Winters, L. C. Affective relations and mutual glances in dyads. In S. Tomkins and C. Izard (Eds.), *Affect, cognition, and personality.* New York: Springer, 1965.

Eysenck, H. J. Personality and the law of effect. In D. E. Berlyne and K. B. Madsen (Eds.), *Pleasure, reward, and preference.* New York: Academic Press, 1973.

Fenz, W.D.J., and Epstein, S. Measurement of approach-avoidance conflict along a stimulus dimension by a thematic apperception test. *Journal of Personality,* 1962, *30,* 613-632.

Firestone, I. J. Reconciling verbal and nonverbal models of dyadic communication. *Environmental Psychology and Nonverbal Behavior,* 1977, *2,* 30-44.

Fiske, D. W., and Maddi, S. R. A conceptual framework. In D. W. Fiske and S. R. Maddi (Eds.), *Functions of varied experience.* Homewood, IL: Dorsey Press, 1961.

Fogel, A. Temporal organization in mother-infant face-to-face interaction. In H. R. Schaffer (Ed.), *Studies in mother-infant interaction.* New York: Academic Press, 1977.

Gale, A., Lucas, B., Nissim, R., and Harpham, B. Some EEG correlates of face-to-face contact. *British Journal of Social and Clinical Psychology,* 1972, *11,* 326-332.

Gale, A., Spratt, G., Chapman, A. J., and Smallbone, A. EEG correlates of eye contact and interpersonal distance. *Biological Psychology,* 1975, *3,* 1237-1245.

Gatewood, J. B., and Rosenwein, R. Interactional synchrony: Genuine or spurious? A critique of recent research. *Journal of Nonverbal Behavior,* 1981, *6,* 12-29.

Gaviria, B. Autonomic reaction magnitude and habituation to different voices. *Psychosomatic Medicine,* 1967, *29,* 598-605.

Giles, H. P., and Powesland, P. F. *Speech style and social evaluation.* London: Academic Press, 1975.

Giles, H., and Smith, P. M. Accommodation theory: Optimal levels of convergence. In H. Giles and R. St. Clair (Eds.), *Language and social psychology.* Baltimore: University Park Press, 1979.

Goldband, S. Imposed latencies, interruptions and dyadic interaction: Physiological response and interpersonal attraction. *Journal of Research in Personality,* 1981, *15,* 221-232.

Gottman, J. M. Detecting cyclicity in social interaction. *Psychological Bulletin,* 1979, *86,* 338-348.

Gottman, J. M. *Time series analysis.* New York: Cambridge University Press, 1981.

Gough, H. G., and Heilbrun, A. B. Jr. *The Adjective Check List manual.* Palo Alto, CA: Consulting Psychologists Press, 1965.

Greenbaum, P., and Rosenfeld, H. M. Patterns of avoidance in response to interpersonal staring and proximity: Effects of bystanders on drivers at a traffic intersection. *Journal of Personality and Social Psychology,* 1978, *36,* 575-587.

Griffith, W., and Veitch, R. Hot and crowded: Influences of population density and temperature on interpersonal affective behavior. *Journal of Personality and Social Psychology,* 1971, *17,* 92-98.

Haber, R. N. Discrepancy from adaptation level as a source of affect. *Journal of Experimental Psychology*, 1958, *56*, 370-375.

Harper, R. G., Wiens, A. N., and Matarazzo, J. D. *Nonverbal communication.* New York: John Wiley, 1978.

Hastie, R., and Carlston, D. E. Theoretical issues in person memory. In R. Hastie, T. M. Ostrom, E. B. Ebbesen, R. S. Wyer, D. L. Hamilton, and D. E. Carlston (Eds.), *Person memory: The cognitive basis of social perception.* Hillsdale, NJ: Lawrence Erlbaum, 1980.

Hayes, D. P., and Meltzer, L. *Interpersonal evaluation and participation.* Unpublished manuscript, 1978. (Available from Department of Psychology, Cornell University, Ithaca, New York.)

Hayes, D. P., and Sievers, S. A sociolinguistic investigation of the "dimensions" of interpersonal behavior. *Journal of Personality and Social Psychology*, 1972, *24*, 254-261.

Henkin, R. E. The prediction of behavior response patterns to music. *Journal of Psychology*, 1957, *44*, 111-127.

Heska, S., and Nelson, Y. Interpersonal speaking distance as a function of age, sex, and relationship. *Sociometry*, 1972, *35*, 491-495.

Hopkins, J. R., Zelanko, P. R., Jacobson, S. W., and Kagan, T. Infant reactivity to stimulus discrepancy. *Genetic Psychology Monographs*, 1976, *93*, 27-62.

Hutt, C., and Ounstedt, C. The biological significance of gaze aversion with particular reference to the syndrome of infantile autism. *Behavioral Science*, 1966, *11*, 346-356.

Jurich, A. P., and Jurich, A. P. Correlations among nonverbal expressions of anxiety. *Psychological Reports*, 1974, *34*, 199-204.

Kaplan, H., Burch, N. R., and Bloom, S. W. Physiological covariation and sociometric relationships in small peer groups. In P. H. Leiderman and D. Shapiro (Eds.), *Psychological approaches to social behavior.* Stanford, CA: Stanford University Press, 1964.

Kaplan, H., Burch, N. R., Blood, S. W., and Edelberg, R. Affective orientation and physiological activity (GSR) in small peer groups. *Psychosomatic Medicine*, 1963, *25*, 245-252.

Kelley, H. H. The warm-cold variable in first impressions of persons. *Journal of Personality*, 1950, *18*, 431-439.

Kelly, F. D. Communicative significance of therapist proximity cues. *Journal of Consulting and Clinical Psychology*, 1972, *39*, 345.

Kleinke, C. L., and Pohlen, P. D. Affective and emotional responses as a function of other person's gaze and cooperativeness in a two-person game. *Journal of Personality and Social Psychology*, 1971, *17*, 308-313.

Lacey, J. I. Psychological approaches to the evaluation of the psychotherapeutic process and outcome. In E. A. Rubenstein and M. B. Perloff (Eds.), *Research in psychotherapy.* Washington, DC: American Psychological Association, 1959.

Lynch, J. J., Thomas, S. A., Paskewitz, D. A., Katcher, A. H., and Weir, L. O. Human contact and cardiac arhythmia in a coronary care unit. *Psychosomatic Medicine*, 1977, *39*, 188-191.

Maddi, S. R. Affective tone during environmental regularity and change. *Journal of Abnormal and Social Psychology*, 1961, *62*, 338-345.

Malmo, R., Boag, T. J., and Smith, A. A. Physiological study of personal interaction. *Psychosomatic Medicine*, 1957, *19*, 105-119.

Matarazzo, J. D., and Wiens, A. N. *The interview: Research on its anatomy and structure.* Chicago: Aldine, 1972.

Matarazzo, J. D., Wiens, A. N., Matarazzo, R. G., and Saslow, G. Speech and silence behavior in clinical psychotherapy and its laboratory correlates. In J. Schlien, H. Hunt, J. D. Matarazzo, and C. Savage (Eds.), *Research in psychotherapy* (Vol. 3). Washington, DC: American Psychological Association, 1968.

McBride, G., King, M. G., and James, J. W. Social proximity effects of galvanic skin responses in adult humans. *Journal of Psychology,* 1965, *61,* 153-157.

McCall, R. B. Smiling and vocalization in infants as indices of perceptual-cognitive processes. *Merrill-Palmer Quarterly,* 1977, *18,* 341-347.

McCall, R. B., and Kennedy, C. G. Subject uncertainty, variability of experience and the infant's response to discrepancies. *Child Development,* 1980, *5,* 285-287.

McClelland, D. C., Atkinson, J. W., Clark, R. A., and Lowell, E. L. *The achievement motive.* New York: Appleton-Century-Crofts, 1953.

McDowall, J. J. Interactional synchrony: A reappraisal. *Journal of Personality and Social Psychology,* 1978, *36,* 963-975.

Mehrabian, A. Inference of attitudes from the posture, orientation, and distance of a communicator. *Journal of Consulting and Clinical Psychology,* 1968, *32,* 296-308. (a)

Mehrabian, A. Relationship of attitude to seated posture, orientation, and distance. *Journal of Personality and Social Psychology,* 1968, *10,* 26-30. (b)

Mehrabian, A. *Nonverbal communication.* Chicago: Aldine, 1972.

Mehrabian, A., and Friar, J. T. Encoding of attitude by a seated communicator via posture and position cues. *Journal of Consulting and Clinical Psychology,* 1969, *33,* 330-336.

Nesbitt, P. D., and Steven, G. Personal space and stimulus intensity at a Southern California amusement park. *Sociometry,* 1974, *37,* 105-115.

Nichols, I. A., and Champness, B. G. Eye gaze and the GSR. *Journal of Experimental Social Psychology,* 1971, *7,* 623-626.

Noller, P. Gaze in married couples. *Journal of Nonverbal Behavior,* 1980, *5,* 115-129.

Norton, R. Foundation of a communicator style construct. *Human Communication Research,* 1978, *4,* 99-112.

Nowlin, J., Eisdorfer, C., Bogdornoff, M. D., and Nichols, C. R. Physiological response to active and passive participation in a two person interaction. *Psychosomatic Medicine,* 1968, *30,* 87-94.

Patterson, M. L. Stability of nonverbal immediacy behaviors. *Journal of Experimental Social Psychology,* 1973, *9,* 97-109.

Patterson, M. L. An arousal model of interpersonal intimacy. *Psychological Review,* 1976, *83,* 235-245.

Patterson, M. L. The role of space in social interaction. In A. W. Siegman and S. Feldstein (Eds.), *Nonverbal behavior and communication.* Hillsdale, NJ: Lawrence Erlbaum, 1978.

Patterson, M. L. A multi-stage functional model of nonverbal exchange. *Psychological Review,* forthcoming.

Patterson, M. L., Jordan, A., Hogan, M. B. and Frerkar, D. Effects of nonverbal intimacy on arousal and behavioral adjustment. *Journal of Nonverbal Behavior,* 1981, *5,* 184-198.

Patterson, M. L., and Sechrest, L. B. Interpersonal distance and impression formation. *Journal of Personality,* 1970, *38,* 161-166.

Pavitt, C., and Haight, L. *Implicit theories of communicative competence: 2. The semantics of social behavior.* Unpublished manuscript, 1982. (Available from Department of Communication Arts, University of Wisconsin, Madison, Wisconsin.)

Putman, W. B., and Street, R. L. The conception and perception of noncontent speech performance: Implications for Speech Accommodation Theory. *International Journal of the Sociology of Language,* forthcoming.

Rosenthal, M. K. Attachment and mother-infant interaction: Some research impasses and a suggested change in orientation. *Journal of Child Psychology and Psychiatry,* 1973, *14,* 201-208.

Rubin, Z. Measurement of romantic love. *Journal of Personality and Social Psychology,* 1970, *16,* 265-273.

Russell, J. A. circumplex model of affect. *Journal of Personality and Social Psychology,* 1980, *39,* 1161-1178.

Sainsbury, P. Gestural movement during psychiatric interview. *Psychosomatic Medicine,* 1955, *17,* 458-469.

Schaeffer, G. H., and Patterson, M. L. Intimacy, arousal, and small group crowding. *Journal of Personality and Social Psychology,* 1980, *38,* 283-290.

Schaeffer, H. R. Acquiring the concept of the dialogue. In M. H. Bornstein and W. Kessen (Eds.), *Psychological development from infancy.* Hillsdale, NJ: Lawrence Erlbaum, 1979.

Scherer, K. *The effect of stress on the fundamental frequency of the voice.* Unpublished manuscript, 1977. (Available from Department of Psychology, University of Giessen, Giessen, West Germany.)

Schiffenbauer, A., and Schiavo, R. S. Physical distance and attraction: An intensification effect. *Journal of Experimental Social Psychology,* 1976, *13,* 274-282.

Schneider, F. W., and Hansvick, C. L. Gaze and distance as a function of changes in interpersonal gaze. *Social Behavior and Personality,* 1977, *5,* 49-53.

Schneirla, T. C. An evolutionary and developmental theory of biphasic processes underlying approach and withdrawal. In M. R. Jones (Ed.), *Nebraska Symposium on Motivation* (Vol. 7). Lincoln: University of Nebraska Press, 1959.

Schneirla, T. C. Aspects of stimulation and organization in approach-withdrawal processes underlying vertebrate behavioral development. In D. L. Lehrman, R. Hinde, and E. Shaw (Eds.), *Advances in the study of behavior.* New York: Academic Press, 1965.

Shrout, P. E., and Fiske, D. W. Nonverbal behaviors and social evaluation. *Journal of Personality,* 1981, *49,* 115-128.

Siegman, A. W. The telltale voice: Nonverbal messages of verbal communication. In A. W. Siegman and S. Feldstein (Eds.), *Nonverbal communication.* Hillsdale, NJ: Lawrence Erlbaum, 1978.

Siegman, A. W. The voice of attraction: Vocal correlates of interpersonal attraction in the interview. In A. W. Siegman and S. Feldstein (Eds.), *Of speech and time.* Hillsdale, NJ: Lawrence Erlbaum, 1979.

Skotko, V. P., and Langmeyer, D. The effects of interaction distance and gender on self-disclosure in the dyad. *Sociometry,* 1977, *40,* 178-182.

Smith, A. A., Malmo, R. B., and Shagass, C. An electromyography study of listening and talking. *Canadian Journal of Psychiatry,* 1954, *8,* 219-227.

Smith, B., Brown, B., Strong, W., and Rencher, A. Effects of speech rate on personality perception. *Language and Speech,* 1975, *18,* 145-152.

Snyder, M., Tanke, E. D., and Berscheid, E. Social perception and interpersonal behavior: On the self-fulfilling nature of social stereotypes. *Journal of Personality and Social Psychology,* 1977, *35,* 656-666.

Sodikoff, C. L., Firestone, I. J., and Kaplan, K. J. Distance matching and distance equilibrium in the interview dyad. *Personality and Social Psychology Bulletin,* 1974, *1,* 243-246.

Sokolov, E. N. *Perception and the conditioned reflex.* New York: Pergamon Press, 1964.

Sroufe, L. A., and Waters, E. The ontogenesis of smiling and laughter. *Psychological Review,* 1976, *83,* 173-189.

Stechler, G., and Carpenter, G. A viewpoint on early affective development. In J. Hellmuth (Ed.), *The exceptional infant* (Vol. 1). Seattle: Special Child Publications, 1967.

Stern, D. Mother and infant at play: The dyadic interaction involving facial, vocal and gaze behavior. In M. Lewis and L. A. Rosenblum (Eds.), *The effect of the infant on its caregiver.* New York: John Wiley, 1974.

Stern, D., Beebe, B., Jaffe, J., and Bennett, S. The infant's stimulus world during social interaction: A study of caregiver behavior with particular reference to repetition and timing. In H. R. Schaffer (Ed.), *Studies in mother-infant interaction.* New York: Academic Press, 1977.

Stone, G. L., and Morden, C. J. Effect of distance on verbal productivity. *Journal of Counseling Psychology,* 1976, *23,* 486-488.

Street, R. L. Evaluation of noncontent speech accommodation. *Language and Communication,* 1982, *2,* 13-31.

Street, R. L., and Giles, H. Speech Accommodation Theory: A social cognitive approach to language and speech behavior. In M. Roloff and C. Berger (Eds.), *Social cognition and communication.* Beverly Hills, CA: Sage, 1982.

Street, R. L., Street, N. J., and Van Kleeck, A. Noncontent speech convergence among talkative and reticent three year-olds. Unpublished manuscript, Department of Communication Arts, University of Wisconsin-Madison, 1981. (Available from Department of Speech, Texas Tech University, Lubbock, Texas.)

Sundstrom, E., and Sundstrom, M. G. Personal space invasions: What happens when the invader asks permission? *Environmental Psychology and Nonverbal Behavior,* 1977, *2,* 76-82.

Thompson, D. E., Aiello, J. R., and Epstein, Y. M. Interpersonal distance preferences. *Journal of Nonverbal Behavior,* 1979, *4,* 113-118.

Triandis, H. C. *Interpersonal behavior.* Monterey, CA: Brooks/Cole, 1977.

Walden, T. A., and Forsyth, D. R. Close encounters of the stressful kind: Affective, physiological, and behavioral reactions to the experience of crowding. *Journal of Nonverbal Behavior,* 1981, *6,* 46-64.

Wallerstein, H. An electromyograph study of attentive listening. *Canadian Journal of Psychology,* 1954, *8,* 228-238.

Warner, R. Activity pattern, personality, and social interaction. Unpublished manuscript, 1979. (Available from Department of Psychology, University of Miami, Coral Gables, Florida.)

Warner, R. M., Kenny, D. A., and Stoto, M. A new round robin analysis of variance for social interaction data. *Journal of Personality and Social Psychology,* 1979, *37,* 1742-1757.

Welkowitz, J., and Feldstein, S. Dyadic interaction and induced differences in perceived similarity. *Proceedings of the 77th Annual Convention of the American Psychological Association*, 1969, *4*, 343-344.

Whitcher, S. J., and Fisher, J. D. Multidimensional reaction to therapeutic touch in a hospital setting. *Journal of Personality and Social Psychology*, 1979, *37*, 87-96.

Willis, F. N. Initial speaking distance as a function of the speakers' relationship. *Psychonomic Science*, 1966, *5*, 221-222.

Wish, M., D'Andrade, and Goodnow, J. E. Dimensions of interpersonal communication: Correspondence between structures for speech acts and bipolar scales. *Journal of Personality and Social Psychology*, 1980, *39*, 848-860.

Wish, M., Deutsch, M., and Kaplan, S. J. Perceived dimensions of interpersonal relations. *Journal of Personality and Social Psychology*, 1976, *33*, 409-420.

Wish, M., and Kaplan, S. Toward an implicit theory of interpersonal communication. *Sociometry*, 1977, *40*, 234-236.

Worchel, S., and Teddlie, C. The experience of crowding: A two factor theory. *Journal of Personality and Social Psychology*, 1976, *34*, 30-40.

Wundt, W. *Grundzuge der physiologischen psychologie.* Lerig: Engelman, 1874.

Zelazo, P. Smiling and vocalizing: A cognitive emphasis. *Merrill-Palmer Quarterly*, 1972, *18*, 349-365.

Zimny, G. H., and Weidenfeller, E. W. Effects of music upon GSR and heart rate. *Journal of Psychology*, 1963, *76*, 311-314.

Chapter 5

SPEAKING TURNS
Studies of Structure and Individual Differences

Starkey Duncan, Jr.

SPEAKING TURNS may not deserve extended consideration in their own right. After all, turns are a fairly mechanical aspect of conversation—the structural skeleton supporting the rich significances of relationship and meaning. Turn taking may be necessary—by definition—for conversation, but it is, nevertheless, the bare minimum. If turns were the only aspect of conversation that an interactant had mastered, that unfortunate individual would be more than a little socially inept, not to mention incapable of carrying out a conversation.

It may seem ironic that these remarks come from me. I have spent as much time as anyone else focusing on conversations in general and on turns in particular. But for me turns have been strictly a means to an end, a vehicle for developing methods for working on the structure and strategy of interaction. The aim has been to develop a set of methods and a conceptual framework that might be useful for studying interactions of any sort. Although the turn phenomena themselves may have some substantive interest, the research was always intended to point beyond itself. Substantively, the research was intended to provide an example of the sorts of things that structural research might come up with. (Other investigators, such as Kendon [1977] and those in Kendon et al. [1975], have provided more than a few other examples. Goffman's wide-ranging insights provide structural investigators with enough material to keep them busy for decades.) The methods used were designed to be applicable to studying interaction structure in general, not just the turn-taking phenomena examined. Moreover, the description of the turn system was

AUTHOR'S NOTE: This research was supported in part by National Science Foundation grant BNS-8004433 to Sarkey Duncan, Jr., and Donald W. Fiske.

carefully elaborated to suggest various elements that may be important in describing interaction structure. (It was also hoped that the strength of results obtained on turn phenomena might suggest to other investigators some of the rewards of structural research.)

Thus, it is with some chagrin that I find the results have been more interesting to many investigators than the methods, and that an apparent effect of the work on turns has been to heighten interest in turns per se, typically without regard to the notion of rules, rather than to encourage the investigation of a wide set of interactions from a structural point of view, using a relatively standard conceptual framework and set of methods. As far as I am concerned, the real potential of the turn research to date will be lost if researchers are tempted to perseverate on the subject of turns, to the neglect of all other critical aspects of conversation, not to mention all other kinds of interaction.

It is from this perspective that I undertake in this chapter a consideration of turn taking in conversations. There will be some necessary account of phenomena, but the focus will be on the rationale of the research and methodological issues in structural research in particular and "nonverbal communication" research in general.

TURN-SYSTEM OUTLINE

For starters, and to clear the decks for more important discussion, let me briefly outline the hypothesized "turn system." More extended discussion of research rationale and evidence supporting the hypotheses may be found later in this chapter and in Duncan and Fiske (1977).

A primary purpose of structural research is to discover major "units" into which the stream of interaction may be divided. These units presumably provide participants with building blocks of various sizes to be used in the construction of interactions. Two different units were hypothesized in Duncan and Fiske, one nested within the other.

The larger unit was the turn itself. It was hypothesized that the exchange of a speaking turn—that is, drawing the boundary of a turn unit—was properly accomplished in the conversations we studied through a coordinated, three-step action sequence involving both speaker and auditor: (1) the speaker activates a speaker turn signal and does not concurrently activate the gesticulation signal (these signals will be described below); (2) the auditor becomes the new speaker, beginning a new speaking turn and concurrently activating the speaker-state signal; and (3) the erstwhile speaker yields the turn, that is, does not continue the original turn and shifts to the auditor state.

Another unit of conversational interaction was hypothesized that operated, where it occurred, to break speaking turns into smaller units, termed "within-turn units." As in the turn unit, the boundary of a within-turn unit was created through a coordinated, three-step action sequence involving both speaker and auditor: (1) the speaker activates a within-turn signal; (2) the auditor displays a back-channel signal; (3) the speaker activates the speaker continuation signal. The turn system provides for some variation on this sequence, but this simplified description should suffice here.

I shall briefly sketch the major behavioral elements of these signals. More detailed description of the signals and their accompanying rules, including such aspects as location restrictions for signal actions and the differentiation of signal display from signal activation, as well as consideration of other elements necessary to the description of the turn system as a whole, may be found in Duncan and Fiske.

A speaker turn signal is said to be displayed upon the occurrence of any one of its six constituent cues: (1) a certain pattern of intonation at the end of phonemic clauses (Trager and Smith, 1957); (2) a sociocentric sequence (Bernstein, 1962) such as "you know"; (3) the completion of a syntactic clause; (4) a paralinguistic drawl (Trager, 1958) on the final syllable or the stressed syllable of a phonemic clause; (5) termination of a hand gesticulation or relaxation of a tensed hand position, such as a fist; and (6) decrease of paralinguistic pitch or loudness on a sociocentric sequence.

The hypothesized relation between the turn signal and the exchange of speaking turns was this: "The auditor may claim the speaking turn during the active period of the turn signal, subject to [certain] verbal-overlap restrictions. . . . In proper operation of the turn system, if the auditor so claims the turn in response to the signal, the speaker is obliged to relinquish immediately his claim to the turn. When the turn signal is not active, auditor claims of the turn are inappropriate within the context of the system, leading in most cases to simultaneous turns" (Duncan and Fiske, 1977: 185).

A speaker gesticulation signal was simply any gesticulation by one or both hands or a tensed hand position, such as a fist. Gesticulations were differentiated from "self-adaptors" (Ekman and Friesen, 1969): movements in which the hand comes in contact with the body or apparel, often with the appearance of grooming. Also excluded from the definition of gesticulations were object-adaptors, defined similarly to self-adaptors. The effect of a gesticulation signal was to turn off, or to inhibit, a concurrently activated turn signal.

The speaker-state signal was defined as the display of either one of two constituent cues: (1) a shift in head direction away from the partner, and

(2) the beginning of a gesticulation. There was a strong tendency for the speaker-state signal to accompany the beginnings of speaking turns, but not auditor back channels.

A speaker within-turn signal was also composed of two cues, either one of which constituted a display of the signal: (1) a shift of head direction toward the auditor, and (2) the completion of a syntactic clause.

There were five broad types of actions classified as "back channels": (1) m-hm: a group of expressions such as "m-hm," "yeah," and "right";(2) sentence completions: a completion of the speaker's sentence by the auditor, after which the speaker would continue the turn;(3) requests for clarification; (4) brief restatements of the speaker's preceding utterance; and (5) head nods and shakes. On the basis of further research (Brunner, 1979), auditor smiles were added as a sixth type of auditor back channel. Within the turn system, auditor back channels were not considered to be speaking turns or requests for speaking turns. That is, back channels did not alter the current speaker/auditor state of the two participants. Evidence on differences in the distributions of auditor back channels and speaking-turn beginnings in the stream of interaction, as well as on the differential occurrence of the speaker-state signal with respect to auditor back channels and turn beginnings, is presented in Duncan and Fiske.

A speaker continuation signal was composed of a single cue: the turning of the head away from the auditor.

STRUCTURAL RESEARCH AND INDIVIDUAL DIFFERENCES

Armed with this cursory review of the turn system, let us consider some basic notions of structural research. I am well aware that most investigators of nonverbal communication are not primarily interested in the structure of interaction per se, but rather in the use of various nonverbal actions as correlates or indices of external variables of psychological interest, such as those relating to individual differences. I do not wish to disparage that interest. I believe that nonverbal variables have been and will continue to be fruitful for this sort of inquiry. I do wish to argue as strongly as possible that, apart from strictly genetically based actions that are also not extensively subject to "display rules" (Ekman et al., 1972), the pursuit of individual-difference studies will be most productive when carried out within a structural framework. Two main considerations lie behind this assertion.

First, as increased information on interaction structure is developed, individual-difference studies may become more focused on the specific actions and aspects of actions that comprise the optimal indices for the individual-difference characteristic in question. This heightened focus may permit both greater specificity with respect to variables and inclusion of a wider range of relevant, rule-based actions as appropriate. Second, the structure of interaction rules within which an action occurs provides a strong and unified explanatory basis for individual-difference results that are obtained.

As an example, let us take a possible individual-difference relationship for which, to my knowledge, no results exist: a relationship between gesticulating in conversations and dominance. Such a relationship is at least suggested by Duncan and Fiske's finding that in most cases, while the speaker is gesticulating, the auditor is effectively deterred from acting to take the turn. Further, the hypothesized rules for this phenomenon lead to the inference that total duration is not the critical aspect of gestures that is most likely to be relevant to something like dominance. Rather, the critical aspect is the presence of the gesture at those points (specified by the rules) at which the auditor may appropriately act to take the turn. Thus, rather than a general measure of gestural extent, such as total duration, a more effective variable might contain information on the relative prevalence of gesturing at those structurally defined points at which the auditor might otherwise appropriately take the turn. It is at least theoretically possible that a given speaker might gesture extensively, but rarely at points at which the auditor may take the turn, or, conversely, might gesture relatively little, but unerringly at those points. In this way, structural hypotheses may both refine the definition of variables to be used as indices and provide a rationale for the potential relationship.

Beyond the specific examples, the message of structural research to investigators with individual-difference concerns is that it is important not only *that* an action occurs, but also *what aspects* of the action occur *where* in the stream of interaction; and the key to choosing the action and defining the *aspects* and the *where* lies in information on interaction structure.

The problem with this general state of affairs is that the structural research must precede the individual-difference research, and most investigators do not appear inclined to launch into major structural projects. This fact is not surprising in that the initial phase of structural research is always exploratory, and it appears that exploratory research seems rather foreign, if not downright unnatural, to investigators trained in experimental methods—the experimental social psychologists most active in nonverbal communication research. This perception seems unfortunate because it may constitute a significant obstacle to the development of the field as a whole.

More pragmatically, it may be noted that the results from structural research are gratifyingly strong—much stronger that those typically obtained in individual-difference research. This is because the operation of rules in interactions introduces strong regularities in the actions of the participants. Furthermore, although in exploratory research there is an inherent risk that one will simply not find anything, this has not been the case with investigators who have ventured into the area. Briefly, one might cite the research programs of Duncan and Fiske (1977) and Kendon (1977), and recently published studies by students, such as Brunner (1979), Kubicek (1980), and Martini (1980). (The latter two studies are concerned with interaction far removed from adult conversations.)

STRUCTURAL RESEARCH

All of this leads us to a consideration of the basic principles of structural research. This discussion will be couched in the broadest possible terms and will primarily emphasize points not appearing in Duncan and Fiske (where more detailed discussion may be found).

The basic tenet of the structural approach is that interaction, like language and other aspects of social life, is rule-governed. The task of structural research is to discover the meaningful elements of social action and how they are combined to form strings of appropriate social action. In the linguistic study of phonology, one seeks to discover the basic sound elements of the language system—the phonemes—and how these elements combine to form syllables appropriate to the language. In a roughly analogous manner, a series of speaker turn cues, for example, was defined, and the manner of their combination described, along with the relation of their occurrence to the response of the auditor. In structural research on interaction, the crucial aspect of this descriptive process is the interactive one: how the actions of one participant relate to the actions of the other participant, that is, the construction of appropriate interaction sequence. This emphasis contrasts with the linguistic emphasis on patterns of occurrence within messages of a single participant.

OPTIONAL AND OBLIGATORY SEQUENCES

For the purposes of research on interaction sequences, it has been important to distinguish between two broad types of rule-governed sequences: obligatory sequences and optional sequences. In an obligatory sequence, at some specified point(s) in the stream of interaction, a given participant must (or must not) appropriately take some action. A convenient example of an obligatory situation is the traffic light. Motorists must stop when it is red and must go when it is green. Within the rules hypothesized for the turn system, the speaker gesticulation acts as a sort of red light; the auditor must not act to take the turn in response to a turn signal while the speaker is gesticulating. Signals of this sort may be termed "obligatory signals." In an obligatory sequence involving two actions, the first action should always be followed by the second, and the second should always be preceded by the first.

Distinguished from the obligatory action sequence is the optional sequence. In an optional sequence, at some specified point(s) in the stream of interaction, a given participant may appropriately take some action. Thus, the participant has, at those points, the option of whether or not to take the action. However, the action may be appropriately taken only at those designated points. Within the turn system the speaker turn signal indicated points at which the auditor may appropriately act to take the turn. At some proportion of the turn-signal displays (typically 20%-25%), the auditor chose to exercise the option of taking the turn. Such attempts, when the turn signal was active, typically resulted in the smooth exchange of the speaking turn. That is, there was no overlap in the respective turns. When the auditor attempted to take the turn when the turn signal was not active, the result was typically the occurrence of "simultaneous turns," characterized by an overlap in the respective turns. In a properly operating optional sequence, the second action is always preceded by the first, but the first is followed by the second to a lesser and unspecified extent.

For ease of discussion, let us consider action sequences in terms of signals and subsequent actions. For our present purposes, the important property of signals is that they indicate points in the stream of interaction at which some action either must or may be taken by a participant. Framed in this way, part of the process of evaluating the relation between a potential signal and some other action, such as taking the turn, involves a certain amount of looking backward. We have to know not only if the signal was followed by the action, but also if the action was preceded by the signal. Interestingly, this second type of information, though present in all data on interaction sequences, is rarely used in interaction research. This is unfortunate because such information is essential for structural research. The source of regularity in this "backwards" sequence is the operation of rules in interaction. Research on the turn system in conversations suggests that striking regularities, not at all hard to find, occur in such backwards sequences.

We may be more explicit about the connection between the two types of rules and the information contained in interaction sequences. Stated another way, what sort of sequential information is appropriate as evidence to substantiate a claim of finding either an optional or an obligatory signal operating in an interaction? Let A represent an action (or signal) by one participant, and let B represent some subsequent action by the partner. Given a body of data on interaction sequences, two sequential probabilities are always available: the probability of a consequent (the probability of B following an occurrence of A) and the probability of an antecedent (the probability of A preceding an occurrence of B).

In the case of an obligatory signal, ideally both the probability of a consequent and the probability of an antecedent would be 1.00. That is, each A is followed by a B, and each B is preceded by an A. In the case of an optional signal, the probability of an antecedent would ideally be 1.00, while the probability of a consequent is not directly specified but is appreciably lower than 1.00. Here, each B is preceded by an A, but As are followed by Bs at a rate that is the result of the partner's inclination to exercise the available option.

It is apparent that the effect of obligatory signals should be strong enough to be virtually unmissable (though obligatory signals indicating points at which one must *not* do something may be somewhat more subtle). However, it is also apparent that most optional signals would be virtually undetectable by investigators focusing exclusively on the probability of a consequent. To take a simple but not unrepresentative example, let us say that there are 50 As in a data corpus and only 5 Bs; but each of these Bs occurs immediately after an A. The probability of a consequent B, given A, is only .10; but the probability of an antecedent A, given B, is 1.00. Here is a real lead that might be pursued in data from other interactions, but it would be noticed only by those bothering to calculate the probability of the antecedent of B.

Put in these terms, the process of exploratory structural research may not seem so mysterious. Both the obligatory and the optional signal require a substantial probability of an antecedent. Thus, the search often begins there. One needs only become accustomed to working one's way backward through the data sequences, listing recurrent actions and the like and subsequently testing and refining the definition of potential relationships. Investigators looking at probabilities of antecedents for the first time may be surprised at the regularities to be found in action sequences.

It should be clear from the discussion that the definition of both obligatory and optional signals (or, more generally, action sequences) requires simultaneous consideration of both the probability of a consequent and the probability of an antecedent. This principle underlay the analyses presented in Duncan and Fiske, but it was never stated explicitly.

FURTHER CRITERIA

In addition to the criteria associated with the consequent and ante-cedent probabilities, investigators will typically apply other criteria to their analyses. For example, the speaker turn signal was tested for the extent to which it preceded smooth exchanges of the turn and was absent prior to instances of simultaneous turns; and the speaker-state signal was tested for its appearance at the beginnings of speaking turns as opposed to auditor back channels. In cases of alternative hypotheses competing as candidates for describing a relationship, investigators may also invoke parsimony.

STRATEGY SIGNALS

It is entirely possible that a potential signal in interaction fails one or more of the criteria established for it as a structural signal yet still shows a significant interaction effect. A simple example would be speaker head direction toward the auditor as a potential part of the turn signal. (Speaker head direction is used here instead of speaker gaze because the resolution on some of our videotapes does not permit clear differentiation of speaker gaze. However, the phenomena discussed with respect to speaker head direction are assumed to be attributable to gaze.) Speaker head direction was rejected as a turn cue, in part because it failed to differentiate smooth exchanges of the turn from instances of simultaneous turns—one of the criteria established for the turn signal. In one of our data sets there were 26 occurrences of simultaneous turns. Of these, 19 (73%) were instances in which the auditor attempted to take the turn in the presence of speaker gaze but in the absence of any of the hypothesized turn cues. Because the turn signal was defined in terms of the occurrence of any one of its constituent cues, it may be seen that speaker head direction does not function well as a turn cue. In the data set mentioned, almost three-fourths of instances of simultaneous turns resulted when the auditor attempted to take the turn in response to speaker head direction alone.

Nevertheless, there is a striking effect associated with the speaker's head being toward the auditor. In our data, the speaker's head toward the auditor is associated with a substantial increase in the probability of the auditor's taking a turn. This increase was observed in each of the sixteen participants studied in Duncan et al. (1979).

When this general sort of result was obtained, we proposed the hypoth-esis of a new sort of signal: the strategy signal. We proposed four criteria for hypothesizing a strategy signal: "(a) that the strategy-signal action not meet criteria for hypothesizing it as an element in the relevant part of the organization of the interaction(s) studied; (b) that the action have an effect on the probability of occurrence of a subsequent action; (c) that this effect be highly consistent across the participants for which it is hypothesized; and (c) that the effect apply to action sequences involving legitimate alternatives—that the signal not be invariably followed by the subsequent action in question" (Duncan et al., 1979: 309).

In Duncan et al. (1979), two other strategy signals were hypothesized. The number of turn cues conjointly displayed by a speaker was found to be positively related to the probability of a smooth exchange of the turn (when the speaker gesticulation signal was not concurrently being displayed). Recall that number of turn cues displayed (in excess of one) was not a part of the definition of the turn signal. A single turn cue was sufficient to constitute a display of the signal as a whole. In addition, speaker smiling in conjunction with a speaker within-turn signal was said to increase the probability of a subsequent auditor smile.

One reason for distinguishing between structure signals and strategy signals is that structure signals have a built-in strategy effect. In the case of the turn signal, imagine that in a set of 100 smooth exchanges of the turn, 99 are preceded by the turn signal, and the auditor responds to 25% of the turn-signal displays by taking the turn. In terms of the probability of a consequent, the probability of a smooth exchange jumps from essentially zero when the turn signal is not displayed to 25% when it is displayed. But this is a direct consequence of the antecedent-probability criterion required of the structure signal. A similar sort of strategy effect may be observed for any established structure signal. Thus, when an action is observed to have a definite effect on the probability of some subsequent action, this effect may be resulting from the operation of a structure signal. If the action is investigated in terms of structure-signal criteria and is found to fail those criteria, it is still possible to hypothesize the action as a strategy signal if it meets the four strategy-signal criteria outlined above.

STUDIES OF SPEAKING-TURN PHENOMENA

In terms of the pattern of evidence proposed for structural studies of action sequences, it becomes difficult to evaluate many recent studies of speaking-turn phenomena. I know of no such study that has provided information on the probabilities of both a consequent and an antecedent. Some examples may illustrate this contention. They are drawn somewhat at random from the literature but represent thoughtful and carefully executed studies.

In a paper highly relevant to the turn system, Beattie (1978: 13) examined the hypothesis that "gaze plays a role in floor apportionment, and facilitates speaker switches." He analyzed sections of rather long academic examinations and discussions between British participants. His primary interest was in whether or not the length of "switching pauses" was affected by the presence or absence of speaker gaze toward the auditor. He found no such effect. More to the point of this discussion, Beattie also noted whether or not the turn signal (Duncan and Fiske, 1977) was present at the ends of turns. Of particular interest here is that he provides data on the probability of speaker gaze preceding a speaker switch, given the presence of the turn signal. In this situation, 46% of speaker switches were preceded by speaker gaze and the turn signal, while the balance was preceded by the turn signal alone. This information on the probability of events antecedent to speaker switches is most valuable. Unfortunately, it is difficult to evaluate from a structural point of view because information is lacking on the more typically reported consequent probabilities: the probability of a speaker switch following the turn signal with and without speaker gaze. In other words, does speaker gaze affect the probability of a speaker switch following the turn signal? Also relevant to the hypothesized turn system would be information on smooth exchanges of the turn and instances of simultaneous turns in association with speaker gaze and the turn signal in Beattie's conversations. I shall return to this interesting study in a later section.

LaFrance and Mayo (1976) studied speaker and auditor gaze by black and white participants in conversations. They report two studies: a careful, fine-grained exploratory study of two conversations, followed by a hypothesis-testing study involving 126 dyads. For the purposes of this discussion, it will suffice to consider only the first, more detailed study. The first five minutes of each of two ten-minute conversations were examined. Both conversations involved a black graduate student in library science. One conversation was with a white corporation executive; the other was with a black institutional administrator. The investigators carried out a frame-by-frame transcription of gaze from the films of these interactions. They report on the mean gaze per fifty frames for each participant as speaker and as auditor. The results indicate that the black participants in the conversations gazed more as speakers and less as auditors and that the white participant exhibited the opposite pattern, gazing more as auditor and less as speaker. (The pattern for the white participant has also been obtained in a number of other studies, including our own.)

The results reported by LaFrance and Mayo certainly suggest some sort of difference between the black and white interactants. But what is the nature of the pattern? Neither antecedent nor consequent probabilities are reported—only average amount of gazing by speaker and auditor. We need information on where in the stream of interaction the gazes are occurring.

This is frustrating because, given the work already invested in their microtranscription, the additional transcription required to provide the necessary data on the turn signal and other elements would not have been great. As it is, we do not have the information necessary to formulate hypotheses concerning the source of the observed differences in gross amount of gazing.

Beyond issues involved with obtaining full information on interaction sequences, there are other issues concerned with the distinctions made in defining phenomena. These distinctions—or the lack thereof—have the potential for significantly affecting results. Use of standardized definitions is not extensive in the literature, although studies that are part of a larger program of research are typically consistent in their definitions. When the phenomena under investigation are defined differently in different studies, it obviously becomes difficult to evaluate results. Could an observed difference in pattern reflect merely a difference in definition? I believe that interaction is sufficiently subtle and sensitive that this could often be the case. Here are some examples of definitional issues. Other investigators will have their own candidates. For the most part I do not cite references for these examples because I have not kept a complete list of studies using a given definition.

Turn Exchanges and Back Channels. Most studies differentiate smooth exchanges from instances of simultaneous turns, although many studies will focus entirely on one phenomenon or the other. In some cases, when the study is concerned with "speaker switches," it is not specified whether or not these include instances of simultaneous turns. In the case of simultaneous turns, only a few studies keep track of which participant emerges with the turn. A number of studies, primarily those using some form of automated speech processing such as the AVTA system (Jaffe and Feldstein, 1970), consider all utterances by a participant to be equivalent, thus combining turns and back channels. Structural research (Duncan and Fiske, 1977) has produced evidence for the different distributional characteristics of turn beginnings and auditor back channels, as well as different patterns for these two types of utterances in response to speaker actions. The distinction, scarcely originated by us, is typically used by investigators using less automated approaches to behavior transcription. Studies ignoring the turn-beginning/auditor-back-channel distinction, however, are typically concerned with temporal parameters of interaction. The issue, then, is whether or not the temporal properties of turn beginnings are different from those of auditor back channels. If so, then collapsing the distinction introduces distortion in the results. To my knowledge this issue has not been directly addressed. We are currently carrying out an initial study of this issue. At this writing, data analysis is not completed.

When simultaneous turns are included in a study, they may not be defined explicitly. Many studies appear to leave this definition to the observers, who simply indicate when instances of simultaneous turns occur. This may not introduce serious distortion in the data, but one is left wondering just what the criteria were, and if they were consistent across raters. In particular, it would be of interest to know if a distinction was made between simultaneous turns and simultaneous talking (Duncan and Fiske, 1977). Examples of simultaneous talking not considered in Duncan and Fiske to be simultaneous turns would be auditor back channels overlapping with the speaker's utterances and turn beginnings overlapping with the speaker's sociocentric sequences, such as "you know." Inclusion of either of these phenomena in the definition of simultaneous turns would certainly inflate the rate of simultaneous turns and would possibly affect the pattern of action observed in connection with simultaneous turns.

Pause Phenomena. A number of interesting studies have been carried out on patterns of speech and silence within and between utterances by participants in conversations. Some of these have used the AVTA system, while others have timed pauses by other sorts of instruments or by hand. Apart from the turn-beginning/back-channel distinction just mentioned, other issues arise in research of this sort. Some studies are concerned with pauses in interaction. In this case, issues arise concerning the minimum silence to be used as a pause (200 msec is often the threshold), and the differentiation of (1) different types of pauses in the speech stream (such as filled and unfilled), and (2) different locations in the speech stream (such as Boomer and Dittmann's [1962] distinction between juncture and hesitation pauses). Finally, an important technical issue concerns the length of the time period, if any, over which pauses and other speech variables (such as talk time) are sampled. That is, what is the resolution of one's temporal data? For example, the AVTA system samples speech at a rate of 300 msec. Each participant is checked every 300 msec in terms of whether or not he or she is speaking. While this is in some senses a rather short period of time, it may not be considered particularly short for interaction. Jaffe and Feldstein (1970) report pauses within a subject's speech to average from .567 to .783 seconds, depending on conditions (Table D-2) and, similarly, switching pauses to average from .773 to 1.341 seconds (Table D-3). (These means are affected by the AVTA feature that eliminates pauses shorter than about 200 msec.) Thus, the sampling interval is a considerable fraction of the mean pause length.

Short Turns and Questions. Finally on this list of definitional (or operational) issues is the matter of differentiating types of utterances. Data we are currently analyzing suggest that a number of parameters are relevant to the operation of the turn system. It appears that very short turns (one or two units of analysis long) are handled somewhat differently from longer turns (Duncan and Fiske, 1977). That is, the speaker appears to mark very short turns as such at the beginning of the turn, differentiating them from longer turns. Similarly, the exchange of turns in conjunction with questions, or at least certain types of questions, seems to be handled differently from discursive utterances. In this regard, the type of question may make a significant difference. In Beattie's (1978) study, the questions involved presumably demanded academic discussion; in the conversations we have been analyzing, the questions are what Beekman (1973) called "social questions," those involved in simple get-acquainted sorts of conversations. It seems that that the explication of conversational phenomena may well depend increasingly on distinctions of this sort.

LIMITATIONS TO GENERALITY

Returning to the Beattie (1978) and LaFrance and Mayo (1976) papers as examples, let us assume that each of these studies yielded results on turn-taking phenomena substantially different from those reported by Duncan and Fiske. LaFrance and Mayo found significant black-white differences in the use of gaze by speakers and auditors. Let us say that Beattie found that in the discussions between British subjects, the role of speaker gaze was substantially different from that reported by Duncan et al. (1979). What might be the source of these observed differences, apart from the possibly critical issues of definition just discussed?

From the structural point of view, a major source of observed regularity in interactions is the operation of conventions or social practices. To say that actions are "rule-governed" is another way of referring to the operation of conventions. While there is always the possibility that some aspects of interaction are true human universals, it seems more likely in most cases that observed regularities stem from conventions. Until proven otherwise, we assume that the regularities we have observed in connection with turns, back channels, and related phenomena are convention-based. This applies to both structural signals as reported in Duncan and Fiske and strategy signals (Duncan et al., 1979).

When two studies obtain different results for a given aspect of interaction, such as turn taking, it is at least possible that neither study is actually "wrong" or faulty in its execution. The use of social practices in interaction is too complex to permit such an immediate, direct interpretation of the discrepancy. Let us consider several possible sources of differences in results.

An obvious source of difference is the possibility that the two groups of participants are using different conventions. This might come about for two reasons: different cultures or subcultures, and different definitions of the situation. Participants belonging to different cultures or subcultures may simply have different ways of handling the aspects of the interaction (such as greeting or turn taking) under study; for example, they may have different languages or use different dialects. Even when the two sets of participants belong to the same subculture and therefore have access to the same repertoire of conventions, something about the way the studies were set up may have led the two sets of participants to define the situation differently and therefore to use different sets of conventions. The significance of a change in the definition of the situation is that there is at least some change in the conventions considered appropriate for use. That change may have affected the particular conventions under study.

Once a convention is hypothesized to be operating in an observed interaction, the extent to which it is used in other interactions is simply an empirical issue. I know of no way to define the extent of use of a convention on a theoretical basis.

The hypothesized convention may prove to be used in all situations by every member of the relevant culture; on the other extreme, it may be unique to the participants in the observed interaction, and only in a highly specific situation at that. More likely, of course, the observed convention occupies some intermediate position and is used in some situations and not others; as are many familiar greetings, for example.

Major differences in results may occur even when the conventions used by the participants in the two studies are quite the same. The participants may be differing in the strategies used within the applicable conventions. For example, the gesticulation signal or speaker gazing may be used more or less, some auditors may choose to interrupt more than others, and so on.

These considerations may be applied to the Beattie (1978) and LaFrance and Mayo (1976) studies already discussed. Because Beattie used English subjects, one cannot be sure a priori whether or not there are some cultural differences in the conventions under study. Even when there are no such differences, there may be differences in definition of the situation. The participants in status-marked academic examinations may choose to use different conventions for turn taking from those in get-acquainted conversations between peers. Finally, there may be differences not in convention but in strategy. Beattie's auditors may have been using and responding to speaker gaze in the same manner as the auditors in the Duncan et al. (1979) study, but his speakers may simply be using it less.

We need not remain in the dark concerning which, if any, of these possibilities is leading to differences in results. The methods and criteria sketched above are designed to permit definite identification of behavior patterns as elements of interaction structure (including strategy signals) or as strategies taken within that structure. At the same time, investigators need to be sensitive to differences in behavioral definition or research procedure that may lead to different results. Through detailed description of procedure and systematic analysis of results, information on major sources of influence on interaction process can be accumulated.

VARIABLES IN INTERACTION RESEARCH

From the overall rationale for structural research, let us turn our consideration to issues related to the use of variables in interaction research. These issues are, I believe, relevant to any study dealing with interaction, regardless of the conceptual framework used. I must admit that the complexities of variables in interaction research have caused us in this laboratory more than one unpleasant surprise. Our first such surprise concerned "simple-rate" variables.

SIMPLE-RATE VARIABLES

Some years ago, Susan Beekman (now Susan Frances), Donald Fiske, and I undertook a large-scale external-variable study. (This study is reported in detail in Duncan and Fiske, 1977.) There were 88 participants, each of whom was in two conversations, yielding 88 conversations. Sixteen different actions were counted or timed, including turns, back channels, filled pauses, gazes, gestures, self-adapters, smiles, laughing, foot movements, and posture shifts.

The various actions were converted into three basic types of variables: rate, extent, and mean length. These types may be illustrated using speaker gaze as an example. A participant's rate of gazing while speaking would be calculated by dividing his or her total number of speaker gazes by his or her duration of speaking. Extent would involve dividing the total duration of speaker gazes by the total duration of speaking. For mean length the total duration of speaker gazes would be divided by the total number of speaker gazes. These are basic rate variables, familiar in most types of psychological research, including nonverbal communication. At first glance, one would find their use in interaction research to be unexceptional. For the purposes of this discussion, let us term this a "simple-rate" variable. A simple-rate variable is generated by counting or timing the occurrence of an action and dividing that number by some broader count or timing representing the frequency or total time that it could have occurred in the interaction. The defining characteristic of simple-rate variables is that they do not contain information on the sequences in which the actions occur in interaction.

After a large-scale transcription effort, followed by a similarly large-scale analysis of the many factors involved in the research design as well as of the many correlations obtaining between the variables, Fiske and I were going over the analyses, looking for the major trends. (Beekman had finished her dissertation and taken an academic position.) To our great surprise and chagrin, it dawned on us that the results from the simple-rate variables did not contain the information necessary to draw useful inferences concerning the interaction processes they represent. As a result of this consideration, we came to the conclusion, and recommended in Duncan and Fiske (1977), that studies using simple-rate variables be abandoned in nonverbal communication research. This conclusion has been misunderstood about as widely as it has been ignored. Let me say that at the very least it was not a "holier than thou" sort of position but stemmed from our own painful experience with a major research project.

Our argument against simple-rate variables was not, as some have alleged, based on sour grapes because we failed to obtain an impressive number of significant results in our study. Nor did we argue that simple-rate variables, while useful, should be replaced by another sort of variable (to be described later) because the simple-rate variable contained relatively less information than the alternative variable.

Rather than resentment or degree of usefulness, the argument against simple-rate variables was based on principle. The argument goes like this: The essence of face-to-face interaction is interpersonal sequences of actions. Interaction is not composed of a collection of well-formed utterances and actions by each of the participants, but by appropriate sequences of actions between the participants. We propose that such interpersonal sequences are the appropriate basis for describing face-to-face interaction. But simple-rate variables contain no information on such interpersonal sequences. For this reason, results based on analyses of simple-rate variables cannot be interpreted in terms of interaction processes. Therefore, simple-rate variables in interaction studies do not contain sufficient information to permit adequate interpretation of results based on them.

An example of the problem would be finding a high correlation between the simple rate of smiling by one participant and that by the partner, based on observation of a number of interactions. The obvious, intuitive interpretation is that there is a strong tendency toward mutual smiling in the observed dyads. But this, of course, is an invalid inference from the simple-rate data because there is no information on smiling sequences in the variables. The same correlation could have been obtained if all of one participant's smiling was during the first half of the interaction, all of the partner's smiling was during the second half, and the amount of these respective smilings was consistently proportional for the two participants in each interaction.

ACTION-SEQUENCE VARIABLES

In Duncan and Fiske (1977: 319ff.) we proposed action-sequence variables as an alternative to simple-rate variables. In their most common form, action-sequence variables contain information on a participant's action (for example, turn signal) and some subsequent action by the partner (such as acting to take the turn). In addition, action-sequence variables may also contain information on sequences within a participant's actions. For example, the turn signal itself is defined in terms of actions occurring at certain locations within the speaker's message.

Action-sequence variables are described in terms of (1) the participants involved, (2) the aspects of actions relevant to the variable (such as onset, offset, or duration of an action), (3) the type of linkage between the sequential actions (temporal or event-based), and (4) the identification of actions as either independent or dependent. An independent action is one that must occur in order for the variable to be observed (placed in the denominator when rates are calculated), and a dependent action is one that may or may not occur, forming the numerator. Thus, in counting the number of smooth exchanges of the speaking turn following speaker display of a turn signal, the turn signal is the independent action, and the smooth exchange is the dependent action.

(Dependent and independent actions, while useful in defining action-sequence variables, are also the elements used in calculating the antecedent and consequent probabilities mentioned above. For smooth exchanges and the turn signal, the probability of a consequent in the observed interaction(s) would be the number of smooth exchanges following speaker display of the turn signal, divided by the number of displays of the turn signal. The corresponding probability of an antecedent would be the number of smooth exchanges preceded by the turn signal, divided by the total number of smooth exchanges.)

A special case of action-sequence variables is the "cryptosequential" variable, often encountered in studies predominantly using simple-rate variables. A cryptosequential variable is an action-sequence variable that is "incompletely specified, observed, and rationalized" (Duncan and Fiske, 1977: 321). Examples would be "rate of interruptions" and "mutual gaze." Such variables contain information on sequences, but not enough for a thoroughgoing interpretation of results. We do not know, for example, what speaker actions preceded the interruptions or which participant initiated or terminated a mutual gaze. Thus, these variables, typically indiscriminately mixed with simple-rate variables, remain too cryptic for adequate interpretation.

There can be little doubt that action-sequence variables possess a major advantage over simple-rate variables for interaction research: all action-sequence variables permit interpretation in terms of interaction. It would appear that a number of other investigators have also realized the potential in action sequences. There have been a number of publications concerned with issues of analyzing these sequences, such as Cairns (1979), Gottman (1979), Kraemer and Jacklin (1979), and Lamb et al. (1979).

RUN-SEQUENCE VARIABLES

It now appears that action-sequence variables can be improved upon. Significant additional information can be included in action-sequence variables, affording further differentiation of research questions and interpretations and therefore greater analytic power and precision. When the stream of interaction is divided into units of analysis, such as seconds, syntactic clauses, or the more complex units described in Duncan and Fiske, it is possible to describe the duration of a given action. We use the term "run" to denote the stretch of interaction, measured in units, over which a single action occurs. For example, a given gesticulation might constitute a run of three units. By recording the length of each run of a given type, one can obtain a distribution of run lengths for the action in the observed interaction; this distribution would provide the basis for subsequent data analysis.

The value of run-length information is obvious. An action may occur many times in very short runs or only once in a very long run; both of these cases might yield the same total number of units for an action-sequence variable. Omission of information on run length thus obscures the manner in which an action was actually used. Consideration of run length permits analysis of subtle changes in a participant's actions within or between interactions, as well as broad distinctions between participants.

As first suggested by Hartmut Mokros in our laboratory, the distribution of run lengths seems to provide a much more differentiated picture of the interactional behavior in question than, for example, a summary figure such as average duration or total time of the action, both of which obscure the frequency of the action and the manner in which the lengths were distributed. In fact, in view of the highly skewed run-length distributions we have obtained for participants in our conversations, it appears that an average-duration figure is relatively deceptive.

The notion of run length provides a flexible approach to the analysis of interactions. Taking speaker gaze as an example, one can obtain a distribution not only of the run lengths of speaker gaze, but also of the run lengths of the absence of speaker gaze. Obviously, one can ask questions about runs combined with action sequences. Runs of speaker gaze ended by the speaker (the speaker gazes away) can be differentiated from those ended by the auditor (the auditor takes the speaking turn). In this case, for each action two run-length distributions are produced: speaker-ended runs and auditor-ended runs.

But it becomes immediately apparent that one can further specify the variable in terms of other actions that precede or follow the run in question. For example, speaker gazes that begin speaking turns can be differentiated from those that occur at some point after the turn has begun. We may become interested in runs of speaker gaze that end in instances of speaker gaze plus a speaker turn signal, once again differentiating the runs into those that are speaker- or auditor-ended at the point of the simultaneous display of gaze plus turn signal. One can then add specifications as to the antecedents of the speaker-gaze runs—for example, those that were preceded by no speaker gaze as opposed to those that were preceded by an instance of speaker gaze plus the turn signal. At this point, we might be charting the distribution of runs of speaker gaze that were (1) preceded by speaker gaze plus turn signal, (2) ended by speaker gaze plus turn signal, and (3) were followed by the auditor taking the turn after the second instance of speaker gaze plus turn signal.

Table 5.1 shows some simplified data on the distribution of run lengths for two pairs of run-sequence variables. For a given variable the table shows how many runs were one unit long, two units long, and so forth, where "unit" is defined as in Duncan and Fiske (1977). The first pair of variables has to do with speaker head direction (presumably gaze). The variables represent runs of the speaker's head being either toward or away from the auditor. Eliminated from these data are runs occurring at the beginnings of speaking turns. In addition, the runs are speaker-ended; that is, they are ended by the speaker's shifting head direction rather than by auditor attempts to take the speaking turn. Thus, the "head direction toward" variable represents runs of that action that are both preceded and followed by head direction away, so that the variable represents the following three-run sequence: away-toward-away, where the length of the "toward" run is being measured. Similarly, the "head direction away" variable represents away runs that are both preceded and followed by head direction toward: toward-away-toward.

The distribution of run lengths for head toward and for head away runs are remarkably similar. Subject to further analyses, the data suggest the possibility of a fairly regular cycling of toward and away, with the toward

TABLE 5.1 Distributions of Selected Run-Sequence Variables

				Duration in Units					
	1	*2*	*3*	*4*	*5*	*6*	*7*	*>7*	Σ
		Speaker Head Direction Toward Auditor (Speaker Ended)							
N	165	121	78	49	26	11	12	15	477
P	.35	.25	.16	.10	.05	.02	.03	.03	
Cum.	.35	.60	.76	.87	.92	.94	.97	1.00	
		Speaker Head Direction Away from Auditor (Speaker Ended)							
N	172	147	77	53	27	14	6	17	513
P	.33	.29	.15	.10	.05	.03	.01	.03	
Cum.	.33	.62	.77	.87	.93	.95	.97	1.00	
		Nonreciprocated Smiles							
N	48	31	20	15	6	1	2	3	126
P	.38	.25	.16	.12	.05	.01	.02	.02	
Cum.	.38	.63	.79	.90	.95	.96	.98	1.00	
		Reciprocated Smiles							
N	12	26	29	21	20	16	6	57	187
P	.06	.14	.16	.11	.11	.09	.30	.03	
Cum.	.06	.20	.36	.47	.58	.66	.70	1.00	

phase similar in length to the away phase. For both toward and away, the modal length is one unit; about 60% of the runs are only one or two units long, and the curves are near asymptote at four units. Thus, the distribution is heavily skewed to the left, bringing into question the usefulness of representing these data in terms of average length.

Each smile variable includes both speaker and auditor smiling. "Non-reciprocated smiles" are those smiles to which there is no smiling in return by the partner. "Reciprocated smiles" are those to which there is a smile in response. It may be seen immediately that unreciprocated smiles do not tend to last long; their distribution of run lengths is very similar to the distributions for head direction toward and away. Once again, the modal length is one unit, and over 60% of the runs are one or two units long.

In contrast, reciprocated smiles are much longer: 30% are seven units or more. The distribution might be considered bimodal. In any event, it is sharply skewed to the right, calling into question a calculation of average length. Thus, the data on a participant's initiation of smiling are sharply affected by sequential information on whether or not the partner smiles in response.

While these data demonstrate nothing, they may suggest the sort of information that can be obtained from run-sequence variables. At present, the run-sequence variable, elaborated in terms of both antecedents to the run and the manner of run termination, is the most differentiated description we can achieve in our variables. There is no reason to expect, however, that further improvements will not eventually be developed.

PSEUDO-UNILATERALITY

One of the intriguing aspects of working with interaction is that there continue to be surprises and unexpected complications when standard psychological research procedures are applied to interaction data. One surprise was just described: the inability of simple-rate variables to capture information necessary for the interpretation of results in terms of interactional processes. However, this criticism may seem irrelevant to many researchers in the area. Much nonverbal communication research is directed not at explicating interaction processes, but rather at using nonverbal behaviors as indices of individual differences. Now it seems there are serious complications in using standard procedures for studying individual differences using nonverbal behaviors.

It appears that simple-rate variables are subject to extensive potential error when results from such variables are interpreted in terms of individual behavior in interaction. This problem is not at all confined to simple-rate variables. It applies equally to certain forms of the higher-powered action-sequence variables and run-sequence variables just discussed, as well as to every other sort of variable currently used in interaction research. I term this general interpretive error "pseudo-unilaterality." Readers will perhaps forgive the unaesthetic but inevitable acronym PU.

While the problem is a general one, for simplicity's sake I shall begin discussing it in terms of simple-rate variables. Simple-rate variables are often taken as direct indices of a participant's behavior in interaction. A typical use of such variables would be to contrast the actions of different groups of subjects, such as observing the use of speaker gaze by females, as contrasted with that of males, in conversations. Obtaining, for example, a greater extent of gaze by females in conversations would be interpreted as the females tending to gaze more while speaking than do the males. One might also use simple-rate variables to study change in the actions of the same subjects in different situations or interactions. Change in the simple-rate variables for a subject would be interpreted as change in the subject between the two interactions; conversely, lack of change in the variable would be interpreted as lack of change in the subject. I wish to argue that, when natural or uncontrolled interactions are involved, these interpretations are not necessarily justified.

As mentioned above, in a simple-rate variable the numerator is the action with which the variables are concerned, such as number or duration of gazes or gestures. The denominator is a broader, encompassing action, such as time with the speaking turn or number of turns.

The basic problem is that, depending on the actions involved, the numerator, the denominator, or both may reflect the actions not only of the participant in question but also of the partner. It becomes entirely possible, then, to analyze and interpret a variable as a product strictly of the actions of one participant when it is in fact deeply influenced by the actions of both participants. In such cases the variable reflects a property of the interaction as a whole rather than the pattern of action of a single participant. Interpretation of results strictly in terms of the participant's action is the error of pseudo-unilaterality. Examples may help clarify the manner in which the partner's action may directly affect either the participant's action in question (the numerator), or the action used as the denominator of the rate variable.

Numerator Affected. Let us consider gaze. For the sake of example, let us say that the participant has an entirely rigid gaze pattern while speaking: an alternation of three seconds gazing away from the partner, followed by three seconds gazing toward the partner. (Such a rigid pattern is not, of course, necessary for the PU effect to occur; it does simplify the example.) The variable of interest might be extent of gaze while speaking: number of seconds gazing at the partner while speaking, divided by number of seconds speaking, summed over the interaction. Let us say that we are interested in the degree of change in this variable for a participant from one interaction to another. In the first interaction it happens that the partner typically takes the speaking turn during the first gaze cycle, after the third second of gaze toward the partner, that is, just before the speaker would have begun the second gaze-away cycle. In this case gaze extent would be approximately .50. In the second interaction the partner typically takes the speaking turn during the first cycle no more than one second after gaze toward the partner begins. Here gaze extent would be approximately .25. In each case the partner's taking the speaking turn directly affects the length of the participant's gaze as speaker. In this example there has been no change in the participant's response. Still, the results in this situation would typically be interpreted as reflecting a major unilateral change in the participant from one interaction to the next.

More subtle actions than the partner's taking the turn may affect the duration of the participant's actions. Staying with the example of gaze extent while speaking, imagine that there is an interaction pattern in which, during the speaker's gaze, there is a tendency for the gaze to be turned away after an auditor back channel. Once again, different rates of auditor back channels in different interactions will affect measures of speaker gaze duration.

Taken together, these two examples using gaze suggest the possibility that a given action by the participant may be affected by more than one action by the partner, making the total effect much more complex.

Denominator Affected. Let us say that we wish to measure the degree of stability of a certain speaker's gestures from one interaction to another. Our variable will be extent of gesturing: duration of gesturing divided by duration of speaking. For simplicity, imagine that our speaker has a completely rigid and unchanging pattern of gesturing. At the beginning of each speaking turn he gestures for five seconds and then stops, having no further gestures for the remainder of the turn. This pattern is unaltered both during each interaction and between interactions. In the first interaction the auditor always waits for five seconds after the end of the gesture and then takes the turn, resulting in an extent of gesturing for the speaker of .50. In the second interaction the auditor is more active, taking the turn one second after the end of each gesture. In this case the extent is .83. The data suggest a 66% increase in extent of gesturing on the part of the speaker, but his gesturing pattern—and total number of seconds gesturing—have remained completely constant. The change is entirely due to the difference in the auditor's responses.

While the examples are artificially simple, the principle should be clear. Speaking turns (or speaking time), number of turns, and an undetermined number of specific actions by a participant are interactively determined. A variable in which turns or any of these actions are involved cannot be said to "belong" exclusively to one participant but is a product of the joint action of both participants in a way that cannot be determined on the basis of the variable alone. Variables based on such interactively determined elements cannot legitimately be used as an index of unilateral individual performance. Calculating rates with speaking time as a denominator, it would be entirely possible both for a participant to appear to change from one interaction to the next when there was little or no such change, and for a participant to appear to remain relatively constant when there actually was substantial behavioral change. Of course, using other interactively determined actions in the denominator incurs the same problems.

The case of total time (or units) speaking was a particularly devastating one to me because it indicated that a prime denominator to beware of is that most obvious, most natural, and most common of denominators. Total time speaking is one of the most interactive of measures. As such, it seems entirely subversive of accurate information on individual differences. In Fiske's and my early research on interaction strategy, this denominator had been used extensively, as well as in the external-variable study (Duncan and Fiske, 1977). Realization of the effect of total speaking time as a denominator required broad-reaching retooling of our current research.

The interpretation of many results in the literature may be subject to the PU error. A prominent example would be the early and frequently replicated finding that female speakers in conversations gaze more at the partner than do male speakers. (For reviews of many of these studies, see Argyle and Cook, 1976, and Harper et al., 1978.) On the basis of the data available for natural interactions, one cannot be sure whether the females are gazing for longer periods, the partners of the males are taking the turn sooner after the onset of the males' gazing, the males have longer periods between gazing (that is, longer runs of nongazing), or some combination of these is occurring. It is at least possible that the entire effect has nothing at all to do with actual gaze patterns by males and females, but rather with differential patterns of turn taking in response to gaze by partners of males, as opposed to females.

It is clear that this issue was completely overlooked in the external-variable study reported in Duncan and Fiske (1977: Part II). One example is our finding a remarkably low stability of variables from the first conversation to the second. First-to-second conversation correlations for variables ranged from .80 to .00, with a median of .40—not a substantial proportion of the variance attributable to the individual participant. What we did not realize was that these results might reflect not only the different reactions of a participant to a new partner, but also the different actions of the partner. More than likely, the low consistencies reflected the contributions of both interactants.

The error of PU is not restricted to any single type of variable. Strictly speaking, it is not a problem of the variable itself but of its appropriate interpretation. Simple-rate variables, action-sequence variables, run-sequence variables, raw count or duration variables for time-series analyses—all of these may be susceptible to the PU error.

These considerations do not, of course, necessarily imply that any given set of results based on interactively influenced variables is "wrong." The implication is, rather, that we simply cannot know, apart from independent analyses, whether or not the results are misleading when interpreted in a unilateral manner. Such variables may be constructively used when interpreted as reflecting a property of the interaction as a whole rather than the action pattern of a single participant. However, variables such a simple-rate variables and raw counts and timings do not permit the differentiation of the participant's contribution to the results from that of the partner.

Given the error involved in a pseudo-unilateral interpretation of the data, how may it be avoided? First of all, the issue of PU does not arise when the study is concerned with interactional processes. As a case in point, the pattern of evidence outlined above for structural studies seems unproblematic in its interpretation. The analysis explicitly includes and differentiates speaker and auditor actions, and results are interpreted in terms of interactional processes, as opposed to characteristics of a single participant. (For example, when B is consistently preceded by A, but A is relatively infrequently followed by B, A is interpreted as a structural signal for the optional occurrence of B.)

But are we forced to abandon the study of individual consistency, or lack thereof, between interactions? Are we prohibited from investigating individual differences using interaction data? Perhaps when we are dealing with "inter-action," it is wrongheaded to attempt to consider the characteristics of individual participants. I, for one, would be extremely reluctant to reach these conclusions. Both Fiske and I have high hopes for the productiveness of interaction data in contributing to the study of individual differences. It seems very important to try to find ways of gaining insight into how a participant chooses to pursue a given interaction.

We must expect both that a partner's actions will affect the participant's actions and that the partner's action will affect the calculation of variables related to the participant's actions. At this writing I do not know how one might achieve results in interaction research that would permit a directly unilateral interpretation; but it may be possible to tease apart some strands of evidence in order to reach some reasonable indirect inferences about individual performance.

In the first place, investigators seem most liable to the PU error when variables are defined in a unilateral manner. This appears to be most frequently the case with speaker variables (such as rate of gaze or rate of gesticulation). Such variables appear to reflect properties of the speaker, independent of the actions of the auditor.

In contrast, it seems natural to define auditor variables so as to indicate that they are contingent on the speaker's action (such as rate of attempts to take the turn, given a speaker turn signal). Variables of this sort appear to be interpretable as an interactional property of the auditor, given an action by the speaker.

It seems possible to define speaker variables in a similar way. An example might be speaker's rate of averting gaze after (1) a within-turn signal and (2) a subsequent auditor back channel. The rate of averting gaze in this situation can be contrasted with that rate after (1) a within-turn signal and (2) no subsequent auditor back channel, or other such sequences. These speaker variables are action-sequence variables. They define the target action as contingent on both preceding speaker and auditor actions. And they both avoid using a denominator such as "total time speaking," which is an indeterminate mixture of both speaker and auditor actions.

A related but distinguishable approach to the problem would be through run-sequence variables. In their simplest form, these variables can describe the distribution of durations of a given action, such as gaze, differentiating those gazes that are ended by the speaker's gazing away from those that are ended by the auditor's taking the turn. More complex run-sequence variables may specify any number of antecedent and concurrent actions, in addition to consequent actions.

Strictly speaking, differentiating speaker-ended from auditor-ended runs of a given action does not permit unequivocal description of the individual characteristics of the participants in an interaction. After all, the auditor is limited in response to those displays provided by the speaker; in a sense, the speaker-ended runs are only those left over when the auditor-ended runs are removed; and we cannot know how long the speaker might have continued a run if the auditor had not intervened. What the analysis of runs does provide, I believe, is much more differentiated information on the characteristics of each participant's action in the context of the interaction in which they are engaged. Thus, we are still speaking of interactional characteristics, but in a more differentiated way. Data on run sequences permit us to ask more specific questions in our analyses.

In general, then, it appears that the strategy for minimizing the PU error involves making the relevant antecedent speaker and auditor actions explicit. The effects of presence and absence of these relevant antecedent actions can be directly investigated. When rate variables are used, the denominator should include these relevant antecedent actions. Of course, I would hold that a major way of identifying relevant antecedent actions is through exploratory structural studies.

DISCUSSION

Rather than attempting to review all the research that has been done on turn taking and conversation, I have considered some research issues in the area that I believe to be particularly salient. While it appears unlikely that there will be broad consensus on many of these points, it seems appropriate that the issues be raised and debated.

In itself, the notion of rule-governed interaction does not seem particularly unusual or unfamiliar. By this time, the literature on structure may be large enough that the research process does not seem particularly unusual, either. Research procedures need not be a black box that mysteriously produces results. I have attempted to suggest that reasonably straightforward criteria may be used for evaluating structural hypotheses. I would reiterate that the regularities that may be found in the probability of antecedent actions are often quite strong—an investigator's delight. This in itself may induce some to venture on the foreign shores of exploratory structural research. In any event, I do suggest that the notion of rule-governed action provides a powerful framework for research on face-to-face interaction. Mere concurrence with this position will benefit the field very little; the real payoff lies in productive research.

It may seem incongruous that a discussion on conversation structure devote considerable attention to individual differences. It should be clear, however, that structure is seen as precisely the element of interaction that imparts meaning to individual differences. Without the presence of interaction structure, individual differences would be mere random variation, apart from any actions that have universal significance. For this reason, even those investigators primarily concerned with individual differences must be mindful of structure. Given the relation of structure to individual differences, it may be argued that the most effective and precise description of individual differences is one that is carefully derived from interaction structure. This, in turn, lends further importance to more diversified efforts to discover elements of structure in many types of interaction.

The problem of pseudo-unilaterality was a surprising one for us in this laboratory, though it was, perhaps, a problem that we should have recognized earlier. While the necessity of viewing an individual's actions as representing the individual-in-interaction has been widely accepted as a general principle, the connection to the contamination of actual variables was not made. It was startling to realize that standard psychological variables for studying individual differences were capable of delivering misleading results. I suppose the lesson is that, in interaction research, nothing can be taken for granted. Interaction seems to require some significant adjustments of traditional psychological thinking and research methods. We are still considering the ways of dealing constructively with this issue.

REFERENCES

Argyle, M., and Cook, M. *Gaze and mutual gaze.* Cambridge: Cambridge University Press, 1976.

Beattie, G. W. Floor appointment and gaze in conversational dyads. *British Journal of Social and Clinical Psychology*, 1978, *17*, 7-15.

Beekman, S. J. *Nonverbal behavior in dyadic conversations in relation to subject sex and partner sex.* Unpublished doctoral dissertation, University of Chicago, 1973.

Bernstein, B. Social class, linguistic codes, and grammatical elements. *Language and Speech*, 1962, *5*, 221-240.

Boomer, D. S., and Dittmann, A. T. Hesitation pauses and juncture pauses in speech. *Language and Speech*, 1962, *5*, 215-220.

Brunner, L. J. Smiles can be back channels. *Journal of Personality and Social Psychology*, 1979, *37*, 728-734.

Cairns, R. B. (Ed.). *The analysis of social interactions: Methods, issues and illustrations.* Hillsdale, NJ: Lawrence Erlbaum, 1979.

Duncan, S. D., Jr., Brunner, L. J., and Fiske, D. W. Strategy signals in face-to-face interaction. *Journal of Personality and Social Psychology*, 1979, *37*, 301-313.

Duncan, S. D., Jr., and Fiske, D. W. *Face-to-face interaction: Research, methods, and theory.* Hillsdale, NJ: Lawrence Erlbaum, 1977.

Ekman, P., and Friesen, W. V. The repertoire of nonverbal behavior: Categories, origins, usage, and coding. *Semiotica*, 1969, *1*, 49-98.

Ekman, P., Friesen, W. V., and Ellsworth, P. *Emotion in the human face: Guidelines for research and an integration of findings.* New York: Pergamon Press, 1972.

Gottman, J. M. Detecting cyclicity in social interaction. *Psychological Bulletin*, 1979, *86*, 338-348.

Harper, R. G., Wiens, A. N., and Matarazzo, J.D. *Nonverbal communication: The state of the art.* New York: John Wiley, 1978.

Jaffe, J., and Feldstein, S. *Rhythms of dialogue.* New York: Academic Press, 1970.

Kendon, A. *Studies in the behavior of social interaction.* Bloomington: Indiana University Press, 1977.

Kendon, A., Harris, R. M., and Key, M. R. (Eds.). *The organization of behavior in face-to-face interaction.* The Hague: Mouton, 1975.

Kraemer, H. C., and Jacklin, C. N. Statistical analysis of dyadic social behavior. *Psychological Bulletin*, 1979, *86*, 217-224.

Kubicek, L. Organization in two mother-infant interactions involving a normal infant and his fraternal twin brother who was later diagnosed autistic. In T. M. Field, S. Goldberg, D. Stern, and A. Sostek (Eds.), *High-risk infants and children: Adult and peer interactions.* New York: Academic Press, 1980.

LaFrance, M., and Mayo, C. Racial differences in gaze behavior during conversations: Two systematic observational studies. *Journal of Personality and Social Psychology,* 1976, *33,* 547-552.

Lamb, M. E., Suomi, S. J., and Stephenson, G. R. (Eds.). *Social interaction analysis: Methodological issues.* Madison: University of Wisconsin Press, 1979.

Martini, M. Structures of interaction between two autistic children. In T. M. Field, S. Goldberg, D. Stern, and A. Sostek (Eds.), *High-risk infants and children: Adult and peer interactions.* New York: Academic Press, 1980.

Trager, G. L. Paralanguage: A first approximation. *Studies in Linguistics,* 1958, *13,* 1-12.

Trager, G. L., and Smith, H. L., Jr. *An outline of English structure.* Washington, DC: American Council of Learned Societies, 1957.

Chapter 6

DYADIC RELATIONSHIP DEVELOPMENT

Mark L. Knapp

Sometimes these [nonverbal] statements are made singularly;
sometimes opposing ones are mixed together; sometimes they
are made aloud or visible; sometimes they exist only as a
potential based on the memory that, having been made at least
once previously, they can be made again.

Murray S. Davis
Intimate Relations, p. 91

THE ESSENCE of our relationships with other people is derived from *ongoing* personal and societal expectations that influence, and are influenced by, our overt communication behavior. Although the subject of human communication in the process of relationship development has received a considerable amount of scholarly attention in recent years (Altman and Taylor, 1973; Berger and Calabrese, 1975; Bochner, forthcoming; Knapp, 1978; Miller, 1976; Phillips and Metzger, 1976), this chapter focuses on a decidedly limited part of this process: the manifestation of nonverbal behavior during fluctuations in the degree of closeness or intimacy felt by the relationship partners.

As a first step toward gaining a greater understanding of these nonverbal messages as they occur in a variety of close and distant relationships, let's examine the published writings and research on the subject. Even though the titles of nonverbal communication studies commonly use terms like "intimacy," "liking and disliking," "quasi-courtship behavior," "attraction," "involvement," "affection," and "affiliation," most of what we currently know about nonverbal communication in developing relationships is derived from single observations or single conversations between two previously unacquainted students whose laboratory behavior is individually quantified. Although the knowledge we can derive from these studies is valuable, the knowledge we are unable to obtain due to conceptual and methodological limitations is also valuable in providing guidelines for continuing advances in theory and research. Within this perspective, then, previous writing and research is discussed according to (1) the conceptualization of relationships and (2) the identification of nonverbal behaviors.

THE CONCEPTUALIZATION OF RELATIONSHIPS

Sometimes we discuss a person's relationship with another in the context of a specific conversation at a specific point in time—for example, "I could tell she didn't like me when she said . . ." But we also use the term "relationship" to refer to a qualitative summary of several conversations and/or observations over a period of time. The behavior associated with intimacy, then, may refer to a specific type of behavior in the context of a specific conversation, or it may refer to a state of general closeness (or distance) in an ongoing relationship which may or may not manifest behavior reflecting that state at any given point in time. This distinction has important implications for the conceptualization and conduct of future research focusing on nonverbal communication in developing relationships, as well as for the interpretation of previous research.

Up to the present time, nonverbal studies have almost exclusively focused on one-time observations of previously unacquainted individuals during their initial meeting. Thus, references to "intimacy" and "intimate behavior" normally do not address established relationships that have an interaction history. Even seminal contributions like "intimate distance" (Hall, 1966), "intimacy-equilibrium" (Argyle and Dean, 1965), and "immediacy" (Mehrabian, 1972) were largely spawned within and later applied to situations involving people in relationships with relatively low levels of intimacy. While the influence of these concepts for relationships of this type has been profound, their contribution to our understanding of developing and ongoing relationships is still unknown.

A few studies have examined the nonverbal behavior of people whose relationships were designated by a label commonly associated with a more advanced stage of intimacy—for example, friends and spouses. Even these studies have been limited primarily to one-time conversations or observations, and the operational definitions for these relationship terms are sufficiently different from study to study to make generalizations most difficult. Can we, with confidence, generalize about the nonverbal behavior of "friends" by combining the findings from studies in which friends are defined as "pairs who have known each other for three months" (Sundstrom, 1978), "a person you address or greet by name" (Willis,

1966), "all pairs who reported themselves to be either acquaintances, friends or close friends" (Baker and Shaw, 1980), or "your closest friend on campus" (Coutts and Schneider, 1976)?

To illustrate further the difficulties involved in synthesizing this research, we are faced with the finding that friends do not sit significantly closer to each other than do strangers (Coutts and Schneider, 1976), but newlyweds who report few disagreements do (Beier and Sternberg, 1977). Friends, in one study, gazed at each other significantly more than did strangers (Coutts and Schneider, 1976), while another study found that nonadjusted spouses were the ones who gazed at each other significantly more than adjusted ones (Noller, 1980). Willis (1966) found that women stood closer to close friends at the beginning of a conversation than did men, but further away from "just friends." He also observed that parents initiated conversations with their children at a distance similar to that used by two strangers.

In some instances, the type of relationship is based on information obtained from both partners, but sometimes only one partner defined the relationship. Even when relationship partners agree on a label that characterizes their relationship, the perceived intimacy levels should be independently verified. The term, "spouses," for example, may represent a wide range of intimacy levels. Some studies of spouses do distinguish between "adjusted" (or nondistressed) and "nonadjusted" (or distressed) couples (Birchler, 1972; Gottman, 1979; Noller, 1980).

Presumably, nonadjusted spouses will be less intimate than adjusted ones. Some important conceptual distinctions between different types of relationships have been made, however. Fitzpatrick (1977, 1979) has identified four common marital relationship types. Rubin (1973) noted that there may be several types of liking—liking based on respect, affection, or both. If the liking relationship we examine is one based on respect but not affection, we would expect different nonverbal behaviors—perhaps less touching. Other scholars have tried to make useful distinctions among different types of love relationships (Bersheld and Walster, 1974; Lee, 1976). We can expect the nonverbal language of love to manifest several styles.

Due to the small number of studies that have examined the nonverbal behavior of people with established relationships, the variety of ways used to select the research participants in these studies, and the lack of multiple observations over time, generalizations about specific behavior characterizing a relationship at a particular level of intimacy should await further research.

In addition, generalizations applicable to everyday interaction must also consider the sources of perceptual information. In some cases, observers make judgments about unknown people whose behavior is viewed on a television monitor. This, of course, provides a large number of observer judgments and a reasonably consistent stimulus. Thayer and Schiff (1974) used this procedure when they asked students to estimate the duration of a relationship between a man and a woman who were seated and reading at desks and who glanced at each other in different ways. Longer looks and the mutual gaze, as expected, elicited responses from viewers that were associated with estimates of greater relationship duration. In another study, of actors portraying client-therapist interviews, Trout and Rosenfeld (1980) found that congruent limbs and forward-leaning postures were perceived as significant contributors to rapport by student viewers.

Although the way we perceive the behavior of unknown others is not unrelated to how we perceive our own behavior or how we perceive the behavior of a known relationship partner, the extent of the overlap is often unclear. The motivation and perceptual involvement of observers who view videotaped actors and actresses in a low-information environment would seem to be different in some important ways from the motivation and involvement of people who make judgments about their own behavior or that of an interaction partner in face-to-face, high-information contexts. This should make us extremely cautious about applying the findings from one context to the other. The forward lean of a single, isolated, and unknown person on a TV screen may be judged more "intimate" than not (especially if those are the only response options provided by the researcher), but a similar lean by a loved one in a shared context may be intimate, irritating, or humorous. Fretz et al. (1979), for instance, found that perceptions of "warm" and "cold" counselors (established by manipulating their nonverbal behavior) were significantly different when the counselors were viewed on a videotape, but when the same counselors were observed in a field setting, the observer ratings were not significantly different. Still another view may have resulted if the observers had actually interacted with the counselors.

While observers and researchers are usually preoccupied with behaviors that are shown, participants in a relationship may be primarily concerned with behaviors *not* shown. Feelings of intimacy may depend as much on the absence of nonintimate or unpleasant behaviors (such as nose picking or staying in the bathroom too long) as on the revelation of intimate ones. Similarly, some intimate behaviors, once performed, need not become common fare, so intimate feelings often rest on a behavioral potential that may be only infrequently or intermittently realized. Although relationship partners process such information, observers cannot. The perceptions of relationship participants and outside observers are both needed and worthwhile perspectives, but without empirical verification it seems inappropriate to base our expectations of behavior in developing relationships too strongly on findings derived solely from observations of videotaped sequences of unknown others.

Finally, most of the studies that provide some information about nonverbal behavior in human relationships do not adopt a developmental perspective. The analysis of behavioral sequences over time is extraordinarily difficult, but it is necessary in order (1) to establish baselines for interpreting frequency and duration data, and (2) to identify the differential impact of behaviors that occur at different points in the chronology of the relationship or within the development of a specific conversation.

The frequency and duration of behavior are likely to vary considerably at different points in relationship time. Perceptions of physical attractiveness may be frequent and of central importance to a relationship at some developmental points but not at others. The frequency (per time unit, not total frequency for the life of the relationship) and duration of hugs and kisses may need to be higher to establish a close heterosexual relationship than to maintain it. Dominance behavior often follows this sequence too. Frequent staring, shouting, and displays of physical strength may be necessary to establish dominance over someone, but such behavior may occur infrequently once dominance has been established and accepted.

Ironically, then, during any given period of time, the most intimate relationship may manifest less total immediacy or affection behavior than occurred during some earlier periods of the relationship. The quality of the behavior display (perceived sincerity, magnitude of expression, perfect timing, and so on) at such times is, for the participants, often a sufficient replacement for quantity. Some behaviors necessary for establishing a close relationship may even disappear completely as other behaviors become accepted substitutes. When intimacy is threatened, we would expect to observe an increase in the behaviors used to establish the relationship. When frequency and duration of behaviors do not increase during relationship-threatening conditions, we might expect an eventual decline in the established intimacy. Sometimes, once the decline begins, even extremely high frequencies and durations of behavior will not be sufficient to restore stability. It should be noted that even though the general pattern of these behavioral changes may be similar across relationships, the baselines and magnitude of the changes may vary considerably from one relationship to another.

Timing and location of a particular behavior or cluster of behaviors may be especially important during periods when the relationship is not well defined by frequency and duration measures. Averaging frequency and duration over a period of time may hide behavior effects which are due to the location in a sequence of signals. For example, the extended hand by one partner in an intimate relationship following a particularly vicious fight, and the eventual joining of hands may provide more information about a couple's intimacy level than the number of times they hold hands. Similarly, the refusal of one partner to join hands when one is proffered is likely to be a powerful indication of momentary feelings and may, in addition, reflect an overall orientation toward the relationship.

Although some efforts have been made to develop methodologies for describing changing influence patterns over time in uncontrolled interactions (Gottman, 1979; Cappella, this volume), our knowledge of communicative effects due to sequencing and timing is severely limited. Clore and his colleagues (1975a, 1975b) found that the sequencing of nonverbal behavior was influential in changing observer perceptions. Viewers were exposed to a videotape of a man and woman interacting. The woman initially engaged in "warm" behaviors (looked into the man's eyes, smiled frequently, moved toward him, and so on), then turned "cold" (moved away, looked at the ceiling, frowned, and the like). In another version of the videotape, the sequence was reversed, cold behaviors preceding warm ones. Still other versions portrayed warm or cold behavior throughout. People judged that the man on the videotape would be more attracted to the woman who was cold at first and warm later than he would to the woman who was warm for the entire interaction. Furthermore, viewers felt that the woman whose behavior turned from warm to cold was less attractive to the man than the woman who was cold during the entire interaction. Whether the interactants themselves would have similar perceptions is not known. Noller (1980), in another study which illustrates the utility of knowing when certain behaviors occur, found gaze behavior differed for "high adjustment" and "low adjustment" married couples. Low adjustment couples tended to gaze at their partner more during negative messages and more while speaking than listening. This, says, Noller, may suggest greater competitiveness in low adjustment couples or a greater felt need to monitor their partners' behavior at certain times.

In summary, the framework for studying nonverbal behavior in developing relationships has, to date, the following characteristics: (1) interactants generally have no relationship history; (2) interactants who do have a relationship history (as friends, for example) are identified in so many different ways that synthesis of these findings is injudicious; (3) the nature of the relationship is normally assessed at a single point in time; (4) perceptions of noninteracting observers provide the basis for most of our inferences about how interactants are likely to behave; (5) our understanding of nonverbal behavior in developing relationships is primarily recorded in quantitative terms (that is, duration and frequency); and (6) there is very little descriptive work available to guide our experimental studies. Although this pioneering work has provided valuable insights into the low intimacy relationship that probably comprises most of our contacts with people, future research in this area should also consider the value of longitudinal, qualitative, and participant-based perceptions of interactants with relationship histories.

THE IDENTIFICATION OF NONVERBAL BEHAVIORS

Many studies of nonverbal communication have attempted to identify behaviors associated with warmth, liking, and attraction. Typically, these behaviors are derived from the analysis of a single individual's behavior (with the other interactant's behavior "controlled") during an initial meeting. They represent only those behaviors that exhibit statistically significant contrasts with opposite states—for example, coldness, dislike, and lack of attraction. Mehrabian (1976: 68), summarizing his own research, presents a list of behaviors commonly found in nonverbal studies and associated with greater "closeness" or "intimacy":

> Some important indicators of positive feeling are physical immediacy cues such as a close position to another, leaning toward him, touching, and orienting the body and head so as to be facing toward rather than away from him. Positive feeling is also indexed by declarative statement rate (how much we say to the other person), how much eye contact we have during conversation, the positiveness in the contents of what we say, the rate of head nodding, and the rate of hand and arm gestures.

In addition, positive facial signals, usually operationalized as smiling (Reece and Whitman, 1962), and positive vocal signals (Rutter and Brown, 1966; Weitz, 1972) are also allied with positive attitudes and feelings toward another person.

These behavioral indices of intimacy, then, present a rather commonsensical and stereotypical picture of nonverbal signals associated with intimacy. A similar picture emerges for the so-called nonintimate behavior as well. Hinde (1979: 58) acknowledges this view of previous research results and speculates on its origin and application:

> Perhaps as an inevitable consequence of the use of the scientific method, the signals that have been most studied are the stereotyped and culturally accepted ones. These are, perhaps, of special importance in the early stages of a relationship or in interactions between individuals who are not specially intimate with each other.

Although established relationships can be examined scientifically, Hinde is probably correct if he is suggesting that scientific control is easier to exert on people with no relationship history. In addition, although new acquaintances are likely to manifest a higher ratio of stereotyped and culturally accepted behavior to idiosyncratic or unique behavior than are people in relationships with a longer history, such behavior does occur in established relationships. That a relationship is labeled "intimate" does not mean that all the behavior exhibited is also classifiable as intimate. Intimate, nonintimate, positive, negative, stereotyped and unique behavior coexist in relationships we label intimate. Two very different behaviors can be enacted simultaneously.

In addition to the early phases of a developing relationship, when would we expect to observe behavior reflecting more sterotyped cultural norms? While there may be other situations, two seem to be good possibilities: First, during times when message clarity is perceived as critical, a person may be more likely to rely on behavioral stereotypes. Thus, transitions in the development of a relationship may elicit more stereotyped behaviors. Initiating a relationship can be described as a transition, but so can the termination of one. Other transitions may include those times when a relationship partner seeks sharply to escalate or deescalate the existing level of relationship intimacy. Also, transitions occur within a given state of intimacy and are associated with the normal ebb and flow of positive and negative forces. For example, stereotyped intimacy behaviors may be perceived as the clearest way of communicating one's caring for his or her partner and concern for the relationship following a fight that has scarred the relationship and left each partner with considerable pain. The relationship is particularly vulnerable during this transition, and the nonverbal behaviors used to signal a return to intimacy should not be too ambiguous. At this juncture, then, we might find the expression of affection following a stereotyped pattern of lower pitch, slower rate, softer volume, and somewhat slurred enunciation (Davitz, 1964: 63). But at other times, perhaps most of the time, the expression of affection may not be closely associated with this vocal pattern.

Second, stereotypical nonverbal behaviors are also likely to occur in situations deemed formal or public by the participants. Parties and other public gatherings are often used to show others how close or distant a relationship is, and the signals others understand best are the cultural stereotypes. Research laboratories may also be sufficiently formal and public to facilitate the appearance and accentuate the intensity of stereotypical signals—even among those who normally exhibit more idiosyncratic behavior. Gottman's (1979) research, for example, showed marital interaction in a research laboratory to be much more positive than that practiced at home. Also, distressed couples did not manifest the lengthy negative reciprocity in the lab that they did at home. Intimates may gaze at each other more in a university research setting than they do at home; although the amount of touching between a husband and wife in the laboratory may far exceed that of two strangers, the same husband and wife may show very different behavior in a private setting. The stereotyped behavior may camouflage an increased amount *or* a decreased amount of touching that characterizes their private interaction.

Although stereotyped intimacy behaviors do occur in relationships ranging from new acquaintances to long-established intimates, overall the newly acquainted tend to rely on them the most. Increasing intimacy is brought about by, and brings about, the use of a broader spectrum of nonverbal messages. Many stereotyped nonverbal messages that were crucial in the establishment of a close relationship lose their effectiveness if performed too often, so they appear less frequently than we might imagine in more intimate relationships. The stereotyped phrase, "I love you," may be very effective in expressing affection, but, like any behavior, overuse can drain its impact. Consequently, intimates often devise a variety of messages to communicate the same idea. If we are to learn more about the nonverbal behavior found in relationships characterized by a level of intimacy beyond that of new acquaintances, we must examine *both* stereotyped and unique behavior.

MEANING AND BEHAVIOR

One of the frequent difficulties associated with research that identifies nonverbal behavior associated with various approach or avoidance forces is that, for some, these behaviors seem to take on a permanent meaning of their own; that is, mutual gaze, close proximity, and touching may seem always to "mean" greater intimacy, or smiling may be perceived to "mean" relaxation and enjoyment. No. In any given situation, mutual gaze may mean tension and hostility; smiling may reflect a person's anxiety; silence accompanies distant relationships as well as close ones; similar clothes may make people feel proud or hostile. Even sexual intercourse, which many regard as the most intimate behavior available to us, may be practiced by two people who barely know each other, care very little for each other, and do not desire to continue their relationship. Reduced gaze for couples who were role-playing conflict assumed several different meanings—for example, disapproval, less power, and a reduction of intimacy to compensate for accompanying increases in the other person's approval behaviors (Lochman and Allen, 1981). Nonverbal signals often mean several things at once. Tightly gripping a child's shoulder during a reprimand may mean "pay attention," "remember this," "I care about you," "I am angry," or "I am capable of physically hurting you if you don't obey." In fact, enmity and intimacy are commonly found together in intimate communications. A lover who roughly grabs his partner's arm, stares menacingly at her and threatens, "I could kill you for saying that" may also accompany his message with a smile. This may be interpreted by both parties as a sign that the relationship is so close it can withstand this kind of potential hostility. In addition, it may be perceived as a signal that the closeness is not entirely stable and each should be alert to prevent the possibility of less amiable hostility erupting.

Although some behaviors may be more likely to characterize relationships in which the participants feel greater or lesser intimacy, meanings associated with intimacy (or anything else) are not inherent in the behaviors. The same behaviors that inspired passion during the birth of a romance may inspire poison when the relationship is threatened. Since the same behaviors are likely to be found in many types of relationships, it is important to understand how they occur, when they occur, the behavioral, environmental, and psychological context within which they occur, and so forth. The meaning associated with a specified behavior is most productively viewed within the historical, sociological, and interpersonal contexts that frame the behavior.

The meanings researchers derive from observations of behavior are also linked to the detail and precision of measurement. Important information may be lost in excessively broad coding categories. Coders who measure the duration of gaze, for instance, may conclude that intimates have more "extended gaze" than acquaintances. But hidden within the measure of gaze duration may be cold stares, warm gazes, and other varieties of gaze. Such distinctions could be made by examining eyebrow, lower-eyelid, and mouth configurations. Gottman (1979) did not distinguish among expressions of anger, sadness, and boredom. Instead, all of these expressions were categorized as "negative affect"; hence the specific type of negative affect distressed couples tend to reciprocate awaits further research. For some studies, microscopic distinctions may be unnecessary, but some refinements are crucial for accurate interpretation of the behavior studied. Smiling and nodding, like gaze, are often discussed as if they have a common behavioral referent. Smiles come in many sizes and shapes, and listener nods have at least two very different manifestations: (1) the slow, regular nods that occur at natural junctures of the speaker's speech and communicate, "I like what you're saying; continue"; and (2) the rapid-fire, staccato nods that occur without much regard for placement in the stream of speech and communicate, "Hurry up and finish so I can talk (or leave)."

Thus, our conclusions about the function or meaning of a particular nonverbal signal may depend greatly on how precisely we measure it.

INTERACTION OF BEHAVIORS

Today, a great deal of the literature bearing on the development of nonverbal signals in human relationships is not interaction-based. Behavioral interaction may be viewed individually or jointly. To observe the interaction of behaviors within a given individual's repertoire requires that we move beyond research designs that "control" all signals except the one being studied. Single signals are, no doubt, important keys for understanding on some occasions, but the more important and difficult breakthroughs require analysis of how several behaviors combine and act together. I sometimes conduct a class exercise in which two students are asked to engage each other in a standing conversation. Each student is given separate instructions. One is told to invade the personal space of the other slowly—to try to move the other person back without that person realizing it. In order to make the invader's task easier, I give the other person a distracting task. This task requires the person slowly to make it clear that his or her opinions are in total disagreement and to watch the other person's gestures when this occurs. I soon learned that this instruction was far from irrelevant. It seems that many of the people whose verbal disagreements are expressed strongly also tend to be less susceptible to the spatial invasion. They have literally and figuratively "taken a stand." The verbal and nonverbal systems are working in concert with one another. In this same exercise, it is not unusual to notice that while the invader is making feet and body intrusions, there are analogous intrusions into the other's speech in the form of interruptions and simultaneous talking. Few would argue that an understanding of nonverbal signals in developing relationships should examine multisignal configurations. Although some research is moving in this direction, too much of our current information about nonverbal signals in relationships of varying degrees of intimacy are based on the analysis of single cues.

Our past research has also been heavily dependent on studies of nonverbal behavior as manifested by a single individual. In the interest of experimental control, a common methodological approach trains a confederate to behave in a "standardized" manner. Often the possibility of creating an unreal interaction situation, which makes generalizing to everyday interaction problematic, is greatly increased under such conditions. A confederate may display a "neutral" face in order to avoid showing positive or negative evaluations, but the "neutral" facial expression *is* an evaluation because it may suggest disinterest and/or lack of involvement. In one study a confederate was instructed to gaze at her male interaction partners 100%, 50%, or none of the time (Kleinke et al., 1975). These unusual behavioral extremes make interpretation of the findings—that the subjects' liking for the confederate was unrelated to gaze—hazardous at best.

The quantification of individual behavior is commonly found in studies that do not use confederates as well. From Beier and Sternberg (1977) we learn that married couples who reported the most disagreement tended to touch themselves more, while those reporting the least disagreement tended to touch each other more. Bauchner (1978) found that friends were more accurate in detecting deception than were married people. As interesting as these findings are, it may be even more instructive to find out how these actions manifest themselves in the give and take of interaction. At what point in the interaction, where and how do these married couples touch themselves or their partners? And, given the opportunity to cross-examine their friends or spouses (the reality we wish to make generalizations about), are spouses still less likely to detect deception? Some research has examined patterns of interaction. Gottman (1979), for instance, found that reciprocity patterns among married couples were more consistent across situations than were frequencies of behavior and that the exchange of negative affect was more consistent than the exchange of positive affect. Behaviors associated with the exchange of negative affect discriminated the distressed from the satisfied couples, although positive exchanges did not. The distressed couples reciprocated negative behaviors even on low conflict tasks. Birchler (1972) also identified this pattern. These patterns of exchange, argues Gottman, generalize across age, years married, degree of marital satisfaction, type of task, and setting.

Other studies, like those of Gottman, have attempted to provide an understanding of how nonverbal behaviors mutually influence each other during interaction. Most of these studies focus on the extent to which there is reciprocal or compensatory influence. Since most of this research has been undertaken in the context of studying nonverbal behaviors associated with increases or decreases in intimacy (Argyle and Dean, 1965; Patterson, 1973, 1976; Stern, 1974), they are pertinent to our understanding of signals used in relationship development. After a detailed and comprehensive review of the mutual influence research, Cappella (1981) concluded that increased proximity and, to a lesser extent, question intimacy follow a compensatory pattern of mutual influence. Reciprocal or matching patterns were strongest for "noncontent" phenomena (pauses, latency, and intensity), verbal self-disclosures, and, to a lesser extent, gaze. Cappella is quick to point out, however, that these general tendencies are subject to modification and reversal depending on each person's expected and preferred level of involvement and the extent to which the other behaves according to those expectations and preferences.

We are most likely, then, to compensate when we perceive behaviors that violate our expectations and preferences and reciprocate those that are more congruent. Most of the reciprocation and compensation patterns for nonverbal behavior are limited to the same general time frame—for example, occasionally one marital partner may mirror the other's facial expression within one or two seconds of its occurrence (Gottman, 1979). Other manifestations of mirroring or compensation may manifest longer delays and involve conscious planning. We might even predict that intimates would be more likely to tolerate longer delays with a greater variety of behavior than people who have relationships with less intimacy. In addition, reciprocity and compensation patterns for intimates may be more difficult to identify because these partners typically exchange a greater variety of behaviors with idiosyncratic meanings. Furthermore, intimates who have negotiated the relative value of different resources (which acquaintances have not) would be expected to have a greater range of behavior options for reciprocating or compensating. They may exchange the same or similar behavior, but the scope and use of "equivalent" behaviors is likely to be much greater for more intimate pairs.

In summary, the identification of nonverbal behaviors associated with developing relationships is, to date, primarily characterized by (1) clusters of dichotomous and stereotypical behavior most characteristic of new acquaintances but which may occur in more established and intimate relationships when clarity, formality, or public situations dictate more stereotypical behavior; (2) general rather than detailed behavior coding procedures; (3) an underrepresentation of the influence of context on the meaning of nonverbal behavior; (4) an overemphasis on the analysis of single nonverbal behaviors; and (5) an underemphasis on the analysis of nonverbal signals as they occur in response to naturally occurring signals from another person. This assessment is not meant to be critical—only to provide possible guidelines for future study. The work to date has brought us far, but if we are to learn more about nonverbal signals in developing relationships we will need to move beyond the stereotypical intimacy signals, analyze behavior in greater microscopic detail, and study the effects of more complex behavioral configurations as they occur in actual interaction.

EXAMINING NONVERBAL COMMUNICATION IN DEVELOPING AND DETERIORATING RELATIONSHIPS: A CONCEPTUAL FRAMEWORK

In 1973, Altman and Taylor proposed eight "generic . . . overlapping 'dimensions' of nonverbal, environmental and verbal behaviors" (p. 129) that they felt described "behavioral changes which occur as relationships develop" (p. 135). In 1978, I (Knapp, 1978: 14-17) discussed a modified version of these dimensions in the context of changing patterns of communication during the growth and decay of relationships (see Table 6.1). A recent statement by Bochner (forthcoming) provides additional testimony concerning the salience of these dimensions for developing relationships: "More individualized relationships should be characterized by more efficient communication, more diversity in the modes of communication used, more synchrony in the duration of speeches among the parties, more positively valenced reciprocity, and more idiosyncratic symbols." Intimacy, in the context of the model presented in Table 6.1, refers to variations in knowledge of and/or commitment to one's relationship partner. With changes in intimacy we would expect corresponding changes in a dyad's communication behavior, which could be plotted along the eight dimensions shown in the table. Although the direction of movement should be similar across couples, the rate of development, the extent of development, and the overall profile of behavior may vary considerably from relationship to relationship. Human communication in developing relationships probably varies along dimensions other than those shown in Table 6.1, but analyses based on these dimensions should provide a useful initial framework for understanding the process. The dimensions represent the content, diversity, quality, patterning, and interpretation of messages and interactions. Before we examine the utility of this model further, let's consider the role of nonverbal behavior in the context of these eight dimensions.

NARROW-BROAD

This dimension refers to the variety of messages communicated. As intimacy increases, we would expect the participants to have an expanding number of ideas and feelings to communicate. We would also expect greater refinements of ideas and feelings previously communicated in a more general way. In order to communicate this expanding number of messages, intimates are expected to rely on a broader range of verbal and nonverbal behaviors. New acquaintances will probably have a narrower range of message needs. Decreasing intimacy in an established relationship

TABLE 6.1   General Dimensions of Communication Associated with Relationship Development

Toward More Intimacy ⟶

⟵ Toward Less Intimacy

Narrow	Broad
Stylized	Unique
Difficult	Efficient
Rigid	Flexible
Awkward	Smooth
Public	Personal
Hesitant	Spontaneous
Overt Judgment	Overt Judgment
Suspended	Given

should bring about a decrease in the number of ideas and feelings the participants wish to communicate.

Increased breadth of nonverbal behavior may include such things as (1) a greater number of facial blends used to communicate a wider range of emotional states; (2) a greater number of vocal nuances and blends for communicating a wider range of messages; (3) less sharply dichotomous behavior—for example, "This is my territory sometimes, but at other times you can use it"; and (4) a greater amount of time spent together, which may mean more messages exchanged.

We would not expect the breadth of nonverbal behavior to increase continuously. Once the relationship is established, many messages assume an implicit status and do not need to be acted out. Thus, breadth, like all the other dimensions, will eventually stabilize at a level that is lower than the highest level achieved or achievable.

Although it is not the usual case, sometimes people who feel very little intimacy will manifest a lot of breadth. For example, two people who have a broad range of overlapping experiences and activities may initially show more breadth than other partners at their intimacy level. Still, we would expect increasing breadth from each couple as intimacy increases. Similarly, some intimates may show a relatively narrow pattern, but in the history of their relationship it should be much broader than when they first encountered one another.

STYLIZED-UNIQUE

When we first come into contact with people, our nonverbal behavior will most likely be characterized by stylized conventions that are widely understood. Our message adaptations are based on cultural or sociological information rather than personal information specific to a given individual. Gradually, however, we obtain more information about how this person is similar to or different from others we have met. Thus, uniqueness of nonverbal communication involves the adoption of a more idiosyncratic communication system adapted to the peculiar nature of the interactants.

We would expect less intimate relationships, then, to manifest the most common emblems, the most stereotyped facial expressions, and so on. Intimates, on the other hand, should develop more specialized and unique communication patterns adapted to the particular characteristics of their personalities and the relationship. A couple may, for instance, accept low gaze frequency and duration as a part of their relationship that they consider very intimate. The handshake in greetings and partings is an example of a stylized behavior that may change as a friendship becomes more intimate. These changes may occur in any of the following ways: (1) The handshake may disappear completely. (2) The handshake itself may change. For example, it may change from a longer, firm grip to a brief, casual clasp or a slap. Close friends may also accompany a handshake with a hug. (3) The handshakes of friends may, indeed, show very little behavioral change when compared with earlier stages of intimacy but be infused with new meaning by the friends. Intimates have the option of using stylized behaviors employed earlier in the relationship and maintaining the old meaning or associating new meaning with an earlier behavior. As Davis (1973: 71) said: "Intimates respond to the face value, but also to the added value for the relationship." (4) Seemingly nonintimate hand- shakes or "false starts" may also occur with intimates when absence has made their intimacy level ambiguous or when the formality of the situa- tion dictates more stylized behavior.

Thus, even though intimate relationships should manifest more unique nonverbal behavior than less intimate ones, we should not be surprised to find some stylized expressions also used by intimates. Similarly, we would expect relationships moving toward less intimacy to manifest an increasing amount of stylized nonverbal behavior, even though some aspects of uniqueness are also apparent. It may be that one of the very difficult communication tasks for long-time intimates during the disengagement process is divesting unique meanings from ordinary behavior.

Some specific nonverbal messages that illustrate the uniqueness I have been discussing were uncovered in our study of couples' personal idioms (Hopper et al., 1981). About 28% of the 495 private expressions and gestures reported to us by married and cohabiting couples involved non- verbal behavior. Eight categories of personal idioms were identified, but nonverbal behavior was most evident in "expressions of affection." For example, twitching of the nose was used to say "You're special" to one's partner; pulling the right ear lobe and a forward movement of the hand with the thumb, first and fourth fingers extended and the second and third curled down, both meant, "I love you." One couple agreed that a twist of the wedding ring was a signal to the other that meant, "Don't you dare say (or do) that." This was categorized with other "requests and routines." Other nonverbal expressions were categorized as "confrontations," "sexual invitations," "names for others outside the relationship," and "teasing insults"—although the latter two were primarily represented by verbal expressions. Two other categories were devoid of any nonverbal expressions in this study: "sexual references and euphemisms" and "partner nicknames." Although most of these nonverbal behaviors were emblematic, communicative uniqueness may also occur with other nonverbal signals as well—illustrators and regulators, for example. This study also suggests that expressions of affection may be particularly appropriate for individual nonverbal messages.

DIFFICULT-EFFICIENT

With increased opportunities for interaction and feedback and a high motivation to communicate effectively as feelings of intimacy increase, we would predict a gradual increase in accuracy, speed, and efficiency of communication as intimacy increases. Difficulty in communication is not absent in intimate relationships, but we would predict that new acquaintances and relationship partners experiencing a decrease in intimacy would experience the most difficulty. Kahn (1970: 455), for example, found that "dissatisfied husbands and wives are particularly prone to misinterpreting each other's nonverbal signals." In this study, the dissatisfied husbands were much more likely to interpret their wives' attempts to communicate affection, happiness, and playfulness in a negative manner.

A few studies provide support for greater accuracy and efficiency accompanying greater intimacy. Honeycutt et al. (forthcoming) tested people at three levels of intimacy on a cloze procedure task with nonverbal signals present. The test words had been edited out of a videotape made of the interactants. Generally, partners who were more intimate were better able to reconstruct each other's speech. Low intimacy couples, however, were less accurate when nonverbal signals were provided than when they were not. These nonverbal cues may be a barrier for new acquaintances on this kind of predictive accuracy task. On a password task, nonverbal cues increased accuracy for more intimate couples, but the trend was not statistically significant. Zuckerman and Przewuzman (1979) found parents able to decode the facial expressions of their own children better than those of their children's classmates, and German biologists Margret Schleidt and Barbara Hold are reported to have shown that blindfolded men and women can identify the perspiration odors of their spouses (Time, 1981). Seventy-five couples in West Germany, Japan, and Italy wore cotton T-shirts to bed for a week and avoided using deodorants or perfumes. Generally, those tested were able to sniff out the shirts worn by their mates.

Just as a familiarity with visual, olfactory, and auditory responses of one's partner will often make communication more efficient for intimates, it may occasionally engender an overconfidence that leads to periods of difficulty—periods when old assumptions are no longer valid. Similary, we can expect occasions when people with little intimacy will be strikingly efficient communicators compared to others at this point, but we would also expect this efficiency to increase as intimacy develops.

RIGID-FLEXIBLE

As relationship partners come to know each other better, they should be able to communicate the same idea or feeling in several different ways. New acquaintances and people in relationships that are close to termination are likely to have fewer channels of communication and to maintain more consistent ways of communicating any given message.

Some of the increased options available to people in closer relationships are associated with the negotiation of signals that are unique to the relationship pair, but we also learn interchangeable signals for certain messages as a result of experiencing interaction with another person in a variety of contexts using a variety of channels. Nonverbal signals, then, provide an important reservoir of additional communication channels to use as message substitutes or equivalents. Hence, a signal for approval may expand from multiple nods accompanied by an affirmative verbal confirmation ("Yes, I agree") to any of the following: (1) a smile, (2) a single nod, (3) a silence that signals approval due to the absence of any negative verbalization, (4) raising eyebrows and smiling during an other-directed gaze, (5) a vocalized "mm" or "mmm-hmmm," (6) a movement of the head to one side similar to the gesture people use to signal a person to "go ahead," (7) an extended hug following an action that could be evaluated negatively, (8) disapproval stated verbally and vocally in an exaggerated manner and followed by a smile, and so on.

Even though intimates have the opportunity to be more flexible in their communication behavior, they may not practice as much message flexibility with some messages as with others.

AWKWARD-SMOOTH

Although some interaction partners adapt to one another's styles more quickly than others, new acquaintances are likely to display less interpersonal meshing or synchrony than they will as their relationship becomes more intimate. Intimates have an inclination toward fusion—psychologically and behaviorally. When established relationships become less intimate, we would expect the smoothness characteristic of a blending of interpersonal styles to become more awkward and less synchronized.

Nonverbal displays of relationship meshing may be consciously used in an effort to promote greater smoothness of interaction (see Cappella, this volume, for more on this). For example, similarities of dress and ornamentation may enhance feelings of closeness and facilitate the appearance of other coordinated activity. This synchronized activity may be in one or more areas, such as posture, body movements, or speech. Both Kendon (1970) and LaFrance (1979) have linked kinesic synchronization with attention and rapport. Scheflen (1974: 60) suggests extraordinary possibilities for body synchronization in more intimate relationships:

> In fact, members of an affiliated established relationship may retain isomorphic postures and move in synchrony even when they have actively dissociated by walking away from each other and joining separate groups. One can often observe marital partners or siblings at opposite sides of a large room sitting in the same posture and changing their postures synchronously even though they are not side by side or even talking to the same *others*. Sometimes these partners will even unconsciously extend their hands and legs toward each other or hold their hands out as if they were holding hands. And later, when these partners compare notes, they are sometimes surprised to find that they were talking about the same things to different listeners.

Speech patterns may also reveal an increasing convergence with intimacy. Giles and Powesland (1975) indicate that people sometimes accommodate their speech styles to those of others in order to enhance perceptions of similarity and to increase attraction. Feldstein and Welkowitz (1978) reviewed research related to conversational congruence (the occurrence of similar intensity, frequency, and/or duration values for temporal patterning in speech). They make the following observations, which may have some utility for understanding developing relationships: (1) The extent to which the conversational participants become congruent depends on their perceived enjoyment of the contacts they have with their partners. (2) Temporal congruence was found to be positively related to observers' ratings of warmth, genuineness, and empathy of the participants. Altman and Taylor (1973: 122) cite several sources that have identified a positive relationship between the speech lengths of friends and spouses.

In some cases, the predicted smoothness of interaction associated with increased intimacy between two people may be a result of daily accommodations over an extended period of time in close proximity. These people may gradually pick up each other's linguistic and kinesic habits. The use of facial muscles for laughing and worrying over the same things may, over time, even make others think the two intimates look physically similar.

Although there is no shortage of speculation and anecdotal evidence concerning the development of greater behavioral synchrony in conjunction with increased relationship closeness, the research to date is not definitive. Before adequate observations can be made of interaction synchrony in relationships that differ in intimacy, some basic conceptual and measurement issues must be resolved (Rosenfeld, 1981). It is not clear from the research in this area to date exactly what behaviors of one person we would expect to by synchronized with what behaviors of the other and how this manifests itself (Cappella, 1981). The methods of measurement and the reliability of these measurement strategies have also been questioned (Gatewood and Rosenwein, 1981).

Despite the current difficulties in conceptualizing and measuring the smoothness of interaction, common sense tells us that intimates do rely on nonverbal signals for interaction smoothness. When intimates must communicate over the telephone or through letters, the extent of this reliance is sometimes dramatic when communications become somewhat awkward again.

Some people may have a relatively low degree of intimacy and a high amount of smoothness or synchrony on certain limited topics. Intimates should have greater smoothness across all types of interaction. Some types of relationships may have more synchrony than others—for example, same-sex relationships may show more than opposite-sex relationships—but in each type of relationship we would expect more synchrony as the intimacy increases. Smoothness, like the other dimensions, generally stabilizes within a range that is below the peak of smoothness behavior achieved or achievable.

PUBLIC-PERSONAL

At first we reveal our public selves to others. Gradually, more and more of our personal or private selves is made available to our relationship partners. When relationships lose intimacy, we would expect behaviors representing our public selves to increase. Some intimate relationships will manifest a great deal of personalized communication before stabilizing; others will experience less depth of revelation before stabilization. In each relationship, some aspects of our more private selves remain unknown to our relationship partners.

How are nonverbal behaviors associated with more personalized communication? Just as verbal self-disclosures provide information to others about our most personal thoughts, feelings, and beliefs, nonverbal behavior can also be used to open ourselves to others and to reveal previously unknown behavior. And, like verbalizations, these nonverbal revelations make us vulnerable. First, we can show our availability and permeability to another person by providing greater access to ourselves and our possessions. Access to another may take several forms: (1) increased proximity, (2) more bodily touching in general, (3) touching certain body parts inaccessible to others, (4) looking into the other's eyes for extended periods—which Rubin (1970) found to be common among engaged couples, (5) looking at another's body or specific body parts, (6) relaxation of any body tension that may suggest a "guarded" approach, and so on. (Some of these behaviors may also be found in rapidly developing sexual relationships designed to provide momentary access to certain body parts while keeping other personalized revelations under wraps.) Second, personalized communication is also manifested by the revelation of previously unknown behaviors. With increased exposure to another, we are more likely to observe behaviors that have been deliberately hidden or controlled. These may include such things as crying, picking one's toenails or nose, or eye behavior manifested only in relation to certain topics. Although adaptors and regulators generally receive little feedback in conversations with less intimate others, we might expect more verbalized feedback as intimacy increases—for example, "Why don't you ever look at me when I talk to you?!" or "Must you always pick your nose?!"

HESITANT-SPONTANEOUS

Communication with less predictable others (new acquaintances and former intimates) is likely to be cautious. Thus, the behavior we observe should show a greater degree of hesitancy. Increased intimacy, however, should bring with it increased spontaniety—a lack of observable planning.

The explicitness of a person's hesitancy or spontaniety may vary, but some possible nonverbal manifestations may include the following: (1) Whereas spontaneous gestures and movements are free-flowing, hesitancy is characterized by gestures that stop in mid-air (for example, a movement to cover the mouth with the hand, aborted at the chest) and repeatedly incomplete "stuttering" gestures, like "false start" handshakes or vocal hesitations. (2) The speed of movement is also likely to differentiate hesitant and spontaneous behavior. Hesitancy may reveal slow, deliberate movement, but sometimes this slowness is accompaned by extreme quickness, which gives the complete gesture what can best be described as a "jerky" motion. For example, a hesitancy to touch another person may involve a slow, deliberate approach and a rapid withdrawal much like touching a hot stove. (3) We might also expect hesitant behavior to show more consistency—fewer changes or shifts. This would be especially true for difficult transitions, such as moving from serious, affectionate behavior to kidding. (4) Hesitancy may also be revealed by more low intensity communication (gestures closer to the body, less vocal loudness, and fewer behavioral extremes in general). (5) Body tenseness, rather than relaxation, would also seem to be characteristic of hesitant communication. (6) We might also predict that during the course of the interaction, communicators who manifest more hesitancy will also be more sensitive to intimacy violations in the areas of space, eye behavior, and touching.

Although hesitancy is less characteristic of more intimate relationships, intimates will be hesitant during the discussion of certain topics or on certain occasions. On the other hand, people who have very little intimacy associated with their relationships may be extremely spontaneous— especially if they are not very concerned about the development of the relationship.

OVERT EVALUATION SUSPENDED-OVERT EVALUATION GIVEN

We probably make a number of covert evaluations about people during the first stages of acquaintanceship, but our uncertainty about how the other will respond and the limited scope of these conversations tends to depress the number of overt evaluations. Too much or inappropriate praise may be perceived as insincere; too much or inappropriate criticism may provoke immediate dislike. Evaluations that occur during the formative period of a relationship are more likely to be general and positive when they do occur. In one study, both distressed and satisfied married couples provided more negative evaluations of each other than they did when interacting with unknown others (Birchler, 1972). Although positive and negative feedback are probably much less inhibited in more intimate relationships, suspended judgments are likely to return as intimacy decreases. With decreasing intimacy the motivation for giving positive feedback is decreased and the participants may eventually want to avoid the inevitable conflict brought on by negative evaluations, so, in time, those are avoided as well.

The nonverbal behaviors associated with this dimension are those that signal approval or disapproval. In new relationships, the nonverbal signals of evaluation will be stereotypical liking and disliking cues; relationships with a longer history not only will be able to use stereotypical signals, but will also have other evaluative signals. These evaluative signals for intimates are also likely to have a higher evaluative potential—more is at stake.

The maintenance of close proximity provides intimates with a never-ending list of microscopic behavioral details of daily life to evaluate; it also makes immediate reactions to the evaluation (positive or negative) subject to further evaluation. Almost any nonverbal signal associated with dramatic shifts in the intimacy level of established relationships will be interpreted as evaluative. A "neutral" facial expression may be perceived as "cold," "uninvolved," or "uncaring" during a period of distress for a relationship that was previously perceived as very close. Even stereotypical signals of liking—for example, "Don't give me that feigned interest approach!"—may be perceived negatively during periods of decreasing intimacy. In time, participants who feel intimacy decreasing will even avoid commentary on such behavior in order to avoid the predictable argument over whether the expression was feigned or genuine.

Naturally, intimates do not offer overt evaluations about all that they could. Evaluations are normally avoided in what are known to be emotionally sensitive areas. In some areas, overt evaluations are absent because the evaluation has become implicit for the relationship partners (for example, "You don't need to laugh at all my witty remarks, because I know you evaluate me positively in that area"). Eventually, the relationship partners will operate within an acceptable range of overt evaluations that will be less than the highest level achieved or achievable.

PERCEPTIONS OF COMMUNICATION AND RELATIONSHIP DEVELOPMENT

Although the preceding dimensions are intended to represent patterns of actual communication behavior, I was also interested in the extent to which people believed relationships varying in intimacy changed along these dimensions.

Knapp et al. (1980) obtained ratings of thirty statements of verbal and nonverbal communication behavior for six types of relationships (acquaintance, colleague, pal, friend, best friend, and lover) from over 1,000 people between the ages of 12 and 90 in eight different locations across the United States. Factor analysis produced three factors that we called Personalized Communication, Synchronized Communication, and Difficult Communication.

Our respondents perceived Personalized Communication to increase as the intimacy of the relationship increased. Personalized Communication included (1) telling another person things one does not tell most people—

feelings, secrets, personal information—but not indiscriminately giving opinions about their behavior; (2) relying on a greater variety of channels for sending and receiving messages, including subtle nonverbal channels that may have been considered a specialized or a personal domain; and (3) cultivating and using messages that were more personal to the interacting pair only. Thus, Personalized Communication was perceived to encompass some elements of the dimensions public-personal, stylized-unique, rigid-flexible, and overt judgment suspended-overt judgment given.

Synchronized Communication was also perceived to increase steadily as the relationship became more intimate. This factor included conversations that were smooth-flowing, effortless, spontaneous, relaxed, informal, and well-coordinated. Synchronized Communication, then, was composed of some elements of our difficult-efficient, awkward-smooth, and hesitant-spontaneous dimensions.

Difficult Communication also characterized communication in relationship development, but it was not perceived to vary systematically across relationship types from less intimate to more intimate. Difficult Communication for these respondents reflected a general strain, difficulty, and awkwardness of interaction—even though it did not necessarily follow that this contributed to greater inaccuracy in communicating. The dimensions of difficult-efficient and awkward-smooth were represented in this factor.

Since the eight dimensions were originally conceptualized as overlapping and interdependent, it was not surprising that our respondents' perceptions collapsed around three dimensions rather than eight. Although it was interesting that all dimensions except narrow-broad were part of these perceptions, it should also be noted that these responses neither confirm nor deny the hypothesized patterns for *actual* communication in developing relationships.

PATTERNS OF COMMUNICATION DEVELOPMENT
WITHIN RELATIONSHIPS

Throughout the preceding discussion of the eight dimensions listed in Table 6.1, assumptions about various patterns of development were also made. These and other assumptions are reiterated here in order to suggest possible patterns of movement (toward and away from intimacy) along each of the dimensions.

(1) It is believed that communication behavior along each dimension will continue to move in the direction of greater intimacy until an optimum level (as determined by the interacting pair) is achieved. Once this level is achieved, communication patterns can then stabilize within a range below this maximum. Even though it may be possible during the life

of a long-term relationship to establish a new maximum, communication at the extreme ends of any dimension is not likely to be tolerated too long.

(2) Fluctuations along each dimension will be common and sometimes sizable (arguments and makeups), but the average variation along any dimension in long-term relationships should show a fairly stable range of responses. During shifts in overall intimacy levels and during severe relationship crises we will probably see more extreme fluctuations. Each party to the relationship may be communicating at a different point on each dimension, but if the manner of communication is too divergent (out of the acceptable range), relationship strain is likely to be felt.

(3) Since the dimensions are interdependent, we would expect changes on one dimension to bring about changes on others; for example, if my nonverbal expression of affection for my partner is fairly hesitant, it may mean I have a tendency to suspend overt judgments in that area, to have difficulty communicating in that area, and so on. This does not mean that development will be parallel along each dimension—only that we would normally expect most to be within the same general range. But the range within which stabilization takes place may not be exactly the same from couple to couple, even though the expressed and perceived knowledge of the other and commitment to the other are similar.

(4) As intimacy increases, the variety of possible communication patterns also increases. Movement along any dimension toward greater intimacy does not mean patterns used at less intimate stages cannot still be used. Similarly, people who have experienced an intimate relationship may still manifest some of the patterns developed during that time, even though their relationship is now much less intimate.

(5) Communication along the eight dimensions can be thought of in both quantitative and qualitative terms. The quantity of any given behavior is likely to be most important for increasing perceptions of intimacy during the formation of the relationship, when new areas are explored in an established relationship, and when intimacy in an established relationship is threatened. The quality of a behavior (perceived sincerity, magnitude of expression, perfect timing, and the like) is apt to be more important for maintaining perceptions of intimacy in an established relationship—particularly in areas previously experienced.

CONCLUSION

To be honest, I think one of the reasons I wanted to write this chapter was that its topic, I sense, is one few people know much about. My survey of the extant literature provided some confirmation of my belief. It revealed a fairly restricted body of knowledge concerning nonverbal behavior in developing relationships. Most of the work available has conformed to accepted experimental designs and has examined unacquainted students during their initial meeting. Sometimes their individual, laboratory behavior is then quantified at a single point in time; more often, the perceptions of student observers of portrayals of behavioral extremes (warm-cold, positive-negative) is quantified. While this body of information provides some useful and important beginnings, there is a paucity of basic theoretical and descriptive work for understanding both verbal and nonverbal communication in relationships at various stages of intimacy. As a result, I have proposed a framework for viewing changes in nonverbal behavior that may accompany changes in intimacy.

Breaking relatively new ground is exciting and challenging, but it is also frustrating. It was my intent to provide enough speculation to provoke further thought. I do not pretend to have all the answers to this extremely complex subject. I am well aware of the important questions I have left unanswered (When do we measure the quantity of behavior and when do we measure the quality? How do we measure the quality? How do we operationalize each dimension for observational purposes?) I also realize how far some of these ideas are from being empirically testable. It is my hope, however, that these ideas will stimulate further thought directed toward a greater understanding of this area.

As important as nonverbal communication is for understanding the way people communicate at different stages of relationship development, a full understanding of the process must also examine verbal behavior. It is often the case that nonverbal signals are best understood in a context in which the verbal behavior is also known. Although many of our verbal and nonverbal behaviors are influenced by the nature of our relationships with other people, overlapping factors—such as age, cultural background, gender and situation will surely exert their influence as well. Nevertheless, there is considerable satisfaction derived from the process of trying to connect a few pieces within this complex communication mosaic.

REFERENCES

Altman, L., and Taylor, D. *Social penetration: The development of interpersonal relationships.* New York: Holt, Rinehart & Winston, 1973.

Argyle, M., and Dean, J. Eye contact, distance and affiliation. *Sociometry,* 1965, *28,* 289-304.

Baker, E., and Shaw, M. E. Reactions to interpersonal distance and topic intimacy: A comparison of strangers and friends. *Journal of Nonverbal Behavior,* 1980, *5,* 80-91.

Bauchner, J. E. *Accuracy in detecting deception as a function of level of relationship and communication history*. Unpublished doctoral dissertation, Michigan State University, 1978.

Beier, E. G., and Sternberg, D. P. Subtle cues between newlyweds. *Journal of Communication,* 1977, *27,* 92-103.

Berger, C. R., and Calabrese, R. J. Some explorations in initial interactions and beyond: Toward a developmental theory of interpersonal communication. *Human Communication Research,* 1975, *1,* 99-112.

Bersheid, E., and Walster, E. A little bit about love. In T. L. Huston (Ed.), *Foundations of interpersonal attraction.* New York: Academic Press, 1974.

Birchler, G. R. *Differential patterns of instrumental affiliative behavior as a function of degree of marital distress and level of intimacy.* Unpublished doctoral dissertation, University of Oregon, 1972.

Bochner, A. Functions of communication in interpersonal bonding. In C. Arnold and J. W. Bowers (Eds.), *Handbook of rhetoric and communication.* Boston: Allyn & Bacon, forthcoming.

Cappella, J. N. Mutual influence in expressive behavior: Adult-adult and infant-adult dyadic interaction. *Psychological Bulletin,* 1981, *89,* 101-132.

Clore, G. L., Wiggins, N. H., and Itkin, S. Gain and loss in attraction: Attributions from nonverbal behavior. *Journal of Personality and Social Psychology,* 1975, *31,* 706-712. (a)

Clore, G. L., Wiggins, N. H., and Itkin, S. Judging attraction from nonverbal behavior: The gain phenomenon. *Journal of Consulting and Clinical Psychology,* 1975, *43,* 491-497. (b)

Coutts, L. M., and Schneider, F. W. Affiliative conflict theory: An investigation of the intimacy equilibrium and compensation hypothesis. *Journal of Personality and Social Psychology,* 1976, *34,* 1135-1142.

Davis, M. S. *Intimate relations.* New York: Free Press, 1973.

Davitz, J. R. *The communication of emotional meaning.* New York: McGraw-Hill, 1964.

Feldstein, S., and Welkowitz, J. A chronography of conversation: In defense of an objective approach. In A. W. Siegman and S. Feldstein (Eds.), *Nonverbal behavior and communication.* Hillsdale, NJ: Lawrence Erlbaum, 1978.

Fitzpatrick, M. A. A typological approach to communication in relationships. In B. Ruben (Ed.), *Communication Yearbook 1.* New Brunswick, NJ: Transaction, 1977.

Fitzpatrick, M. A. Dyadic adjustment in relational types: Consensus, cohesion, affectional expression, and satisfaction in enduring relationships. *Communication Monographs,* 1979, *47,* 167-178.

Fretz, B. R., Corn, R., Tuemmler, J. M., and Bellet, W. Counselor nonverbal behaviors and client evaluations. *Journal of Counseling Psychology,* 1979, *26,* 304-311.

Gatewood, J. B. and Rosenwein, R. Interaction synchrony: Genuine or spurious? A critique of recent research. *Journal of Nonverbal Behavior,* 1981, *6,* 12-29.

Giles, H., and Powesland, P. F. *Speech style and social evaluation.* New York: Academic Press, 1975.

Gottman, J. M. *Marital interaction: Experimental investigations.* New York: Academic Press, 1979.

Hall, E. T. *The hidden dimension.* Garden City, NY: Doubleday, 1966.

Hinde, R. A. *Towards understanding relationships.* New York: Academic Press, 1979.

Honeycutt, J. M., Knapp, M. L., and Powers, W. G. On knowing others and predicting what they say. *Western Journal of Speech Communication* (in press).

Hopper, R., Knapp, M. L., and Scott, L. Couples' personal idioms: Exploring intimate talk. *Journal of Communication,* 1981, *31,* 23-33.

Kahn, M. Non-verbal communication and marital satisfaction. *Family Process,* 1970 *9,* 449-456.

Kendon, A. Movement coordination in social interaction: Some examples described. *Acta Psychologica,* 1970, *32,* 100-125.

Kleinke, C. L., Staneski, R. A., and Berger, D. E. Evaluation of an interviewer as a function of interviewer gaze, reinforcement of subject gaze, and interviewer attractiveness. *Journal of Personality and Social Psychology,* 1975, *31,* 115-122.

Knapp, M. L. *Social intercourse: From greeting to goodbye.* Boston: Allyn & Bacon, 1978.

Knapp, M. L., Ellis, D. G., and Williams, B. A. Perceptions of communication behavior associated with relationship terms. *Communication Monographs,* 1980, *47,* 262-278.

LaFrance, M. Nonverbal synchrony and rapport: Analysis by the cross-lag panel technique. *Social Psychology Quarterly,* 1979, *42,* 66-70.

Lee, J. A. *The colors of love.* Englewood Cliffs, NJ: Prentice-Hall, 1976.

Lochman, J. E., and Allen, G. Nonverbal communication of couples in conflict. *Journal of Research in Personality,* 1981, *15,* 253-269.

Mehrabian, A. *Nonverbal communication.* Chicago: Aldine, 1972.

Mehrabian, A. *Public places and private spaces.* New York: Basic Books, 1976.

Miller, G. R. (Ed.). *Explorations in interpersonal communication.* Beverly Hills, CA: Sage, 1976.

Noller, P. Gaze in married couples. *Journal of Nonverbal Behavior,* 1980, *5,* 115-129.

Patterson, M. L. Compensation in nonverbal immediacy behaviors: A review. *Sociometry,* 1973, *36,* 237-252.

Patterson, M. L. An arousal model of interpersonal intimacy. *Psychological Review,* 1976, *83,* 235-245.

Phillips, G. M., and Metzger, N. J. *Intimate communication.* Boston: Allyn & Bacon, 1976.

Reece, M., and Whitman, R. Expressive movements, warmth, and verbal reinforcement. *Journal of Abnormal and Social Psychology,* 1962, *64,* 234-236.

Rosenfeld, H. M. Whither interactional synchrony? In K. Bloom (Ed.), *Prospective issues in infant research.* Hillsdale, NJ: Lawrence Erlbaum, 1981.

Rubin, Z. The measurement of romantic love. *Journal of Personality and Social Psychology,* 1970, *16,* 265-272.

Rubin, Z. *Liking and loving.* New York: Holt, Rinehart & Winston, 1973.

Rutter, M., and Brown, G. W. The reliability and validity of measures of family life and relationships in families containing a psychiatric patient. *Social Psychiatry,* 1966, *1,* 38-53.

Scheflen, A. E. *How behavior means.* Garden City, NY: Doubleday, 1974.

Stern, D. N. Mother and infant at play: The dyadic interactions involving facial, vocal, and gaze behavior. In M. Lewis and L. A. Rosenblum (Eds.), *The effect of the infant on its caregiver.* New York: John Wiley, 1974.

Sundstrom, E. A test of equilibrium theory: Effects of topic intimacy and proximity on verbal and nonverbal behavior in pairs of friends and strangers. *Environmental Psychology and Nonverbal Behavior,* 1978, *3,* 3-16.

Thayer, S., and Schiff, W. Observer judgment of social interaction: Eye contact and relationship inferences. *Journal of Personality and Social Psychology,* 1974, *30,* 110-114.

Time. Nose knows more ways than one. November 30, 1981, p. 87.

Trout, D. L., and Rosenfeld, H. M. The effect of postural lean and body congruence on the judgment of psychotherapeutic rapport. *Journal of Nonverbal Behavior,* 1980, *4,* 176-190.

Weitz, S. Attitude, voice and behavior: A repressed affect model of interracial interaction. *Journal of Personality and Social Psychology,* 1972, *24,* 14-21.

Willis, F. N. Initial speaking distance as a function of the speaker's relationship. *Psychonomic Science,* 1966, *5,* 221-222.

Zuckerman, M., and Przewuzman, S. J. Decoding and encoding facial expressions in preschool-age children. *Environmental Psychology and Nonverbal Behavior,* 1979, *3,* 147-163.

Chapter 7

NONVERBAL RECEIVING ABILITY

Ross Buck

ONE OF THE MOST enduring concepts in psychology is the notion that the ability accurately to gain information from others is a critical skill in social relations. This skill has gone under many names, including "empathy," "accuracy in person perception," and "social sensitivity," and it has been the subject of empirical social science research virtually since such research began. A major reason for this continuing interest is that questions regarding the nature of this skill—how it develops, whether and how it may be learned, whether some are more skillful than others—have clear practical implications. Unfortunately, attempts to measure this skill have been, on the whole, unsuccessful, and a coherent conception of it has never emerged from the multitude of empirical studies.

With the increasing interest in nonverbal communication, there have been attempts to reconceptualize this skill in terms of nonverbal receiving ability—the ability accurately to read or "decode" nonverbal cues in others. Unfortunately, attempts to measure nonverbal receiving ability have likewise proved disappointing in many respects. In particular, no measure has been demonstrated usefully to assess nonverbal receiving ability in all of its complex aspects. My goal in this chapter is to discuss the problems apparent in recent attempts to measure nonverbal receiving ability and to explore some of the reasons for these problems. In doing so, I suggest the nature of some of the hidden complexities of the deceptively simple-sounding concept of nonverbal receiving ability.

AUTHOR'S NOTE: The author is grateful to Reuben Baron, Albert Dreyer, David Kenny, Barbara Montgomery, and Ronald Sabatelli for their contributions to the ideas presented in this chapter and their useful suggestions in reading it, and to the University of Connecticut Research Foundation for its support of research reported here.

NONVERBAL COMMUNICATION ABILITIES
AS TRANS-SITUATIONAL ATTRIBUTES

SENDING ACCURACY

Nonverbal sending accuracy involves the tendency to express affect in such a way that it can be accurately received by others. It has been easy to defend the notion that nonverbal sending accuracy can usefully be regarded as a relatively stable attribute of the individual that appears across a reasonably wide variety of situations. First, sending accuracy has been found to be associated with one of the most durable of individual difference distinctions: that between tendencies toward internal and external expression. This distinction appears in the work of an extremely heterogeneous group of investigators. For example, Jung (1939) discussed the concept of introversion/extraversion as one of the major cornerstones of personality; Pavlov (1927) described the strength of the nervous system in dogs, which has been associated with introversion/extraversion by Eysenck (1967) and Gray (1972) and has stimulated much research in the Soviet Union; H. E. Jones (1950, 1960) described externalizing and internalizing patterns of response in his studies of the development of emotional expression. Many of these investigators have suggested that these externalizing/internalizing response modes have a biological basis.

In my own research, nonverbal sending accuracy has been operationalized as communication accuracy in a slide-viewing paradigm that was developed from Miller's Co-operative Conditioning Procedure, used to measure the communication of affect in rhesus monkeys (see Buck, 1978, 1979b). Briefly, "senders" view a series of emotionally loaded color slides and verbally describe their emotional reactions while, unknown to them, their facial/gestural responses to the slides are videotaped. Later, groups of "receivers" view the videotapes without audio and attempt to guess what kind of slide the sender viewed and how pleasant or unpleasant the sender's emotional response was on each trial. The result is a communication accuracy score that reflects both "sending accuracy"—the degree to which the sender's facial/gestural responses accurately portray the type of slide viewed—and "receiving ability"—the ability of the receiver to attend to the appropriate responses and to decode them accurately. If a group of receivers views senders, the resulting scores may be taken to reflect sending accuracy; if receivers view a group of senders, the resulting scores may be taken to reflect receiving ability.

Studies employing this measure have suggested that sending accuracy is a relatively stable and unidimensional individual attribute. Large and consistent sex differences have been found in adults, females being more expressive of the feelings evoked by the slides than males (Buck et al., 1972, 1974). In preschool children, this sex difference appears to be much smaller, and sending accuracy is negatively correlated with age among boys but not among girls (Buck, 1975, 1977).

Substantial correlations have been found between different measures of sending accuracy, and sending accuracy has been related to such personality measures as extraversion, self-esteem, and cognitive style (Buck et al., 1974; Sabatelli et al., 1979). Sending accuracy has been found to be negatively correlated with the electrodermal and heart rate responses to the affective slides (Buck, 1979a). Perhaps most convincing, large individual differences have been found in the sending accuracy of preschool children, and these differences have been found to be related to teachers' ratings on the Affect Expression Rating Scale (AERS), which involves a variety of qualities that Jones (1950, 1960), Block (1957), and others have found to be associated with externalizing/internalizing response tendencies (Buck, 1977). Also, sending accuracy has been found to be higher in patients with brain damage in the left cerebral hemisphere and in non-brain-damaged patients than it is in right-hemisphere-damaged patients and patients with Parkinson's disease, supporting the notion of a biological basis for sending accuracy and suggesting that the right cerebral hemisphere may be involved (Buck and Duffy, 1980; Buck, 1983).

Taking these findings together, I have suggested that sending accuracy may be grounded in biologically based systems of "temperament," which in turn may be influenced by social learning. One may be born with a given tendency toward an internalizing or externalizing response mode, but social experience can alter these tendencies in situationally specific ways (Buck, 1979a). Thus, a male who tends toward an externalizing response mode may be expressive in most situations but learn in our culture to inhibit emotional response. A female with a similar expressive temperament may learn to "control herself" in aggressive and achievement situations but remain relatively free in emotional situations. Presumably, the initial temperament or disposition is based on innate biological systems that are alterable by learning. The exact nature of these systems is not yet clear, although there are clues that they may involve reward/punishment systems that are particularly associated with right-hemisphere processing (see Olds and Fobes, 1981; Tucker, 1981).

RECEIVING ABILITY

In contrast to the experience with nonverbal sending accuracy, evidence that receiving ability can be usefully considered to be an individual attribute has been exceedingly scanty. As noted above, the measurement of receiving ability from the slide-viewing technique is straightforward: One simply presents different receivers with a standard group of senders and notes the accuracy with which they "decode" the senders. This was done systematically in the construction of the Communication of Affect Receiving Ability Test (CARAT). The CARAT was first shown in 1972 at the Anthropological and Documentary Film Conference at Temple University (Buck and Miller, 1972). In the same year I became aware of the efforts of Robert Rosenthal to develop a similar instrument: the Profile of Nonverbal Sensitivity (PONS). Although designed to measure the same conceptual variable, PONS was constructed from a different point of view from CARAT, and their potential strengths and weaknesses appeared to be complementary. PONS employed a single sender posing expressions, while CARAT used a variety of senders responding spontaneously; PONS sampled a variety of channels, while CARAT in its initial form showed only facial/gestural responses; different sorts of affects were sampled by PONS and CARAT. Thus, with some anticipation, John Carroll and I in 1974 compared the PONS and CARAT scores in group of college students. The result, however, was not encouraging: a correlation of .04.

It has become increasingly clear that receiving ability does not explain the magnitude of variance in nonverbal communication accuracy that sending accuracy appears to do. In the succeeding sections of this chapter, I review a number of techniques designed in recent years to assess nonverbal receiving ability, discuss the problems associated with these techniques, and suggest the nature of the complexities in nonverbal receiving ability that cause these problems. I then suggest ways these complexities might be addressed in a new conceptualization of the nature of nonverbal receiving ability.

APPROACHES TO NONVERBAL
RECEIVING ABILITY

MEASURING TECHNIQUES

A number of techniques designed to measure nonverbal receiving ability have been advanced in recent years. All of these are based on the same general notion: that nonverbal receiving ability involves the ability to decode the states of others via nonverbal cues, and that a reasonable way to approach the measurement of nonverbal receiving ability is to present judges with samples of nonverbal behavior, ask them questions about it, and assess the accuracy of their replies.

The Affective Sensitivity Test. The Affective Sensitivity (AS) scale was developed by Kagan and his colleagues (Campbell et al., 1971; Kagan, 1977). The original version showed brief videotaped excerpts of client-counselor interactions. For each excerpt, the subject was asked to indicate what the client was feeling given three alternatives, one of which was considered correct. The criteria for the accuracy involved the client's recall of his or her actual feelings during the interaction, and the judgments of expert observers.

A more recent version of the test shows thirty excerpts of interactions between a variety of professionals and their clients, including teachers and pupils, therapists and clients, and physicians and patients. Following each excerpt, the subject answers questions about the thoughts and feelings of the interactants. In each case, the subject is given five alternatives. One is considered most correct, receiving two points; another is considered incorrect, receiving no points; and three are considered partially correct, each receiving one point. The points are summed for a total score and for thirteen subscores involving logically similar types of items (that is, those involving males versus those involving females).

The AS instrument has high face validity, particularly since a major area of potential application involves the ability of professionals to decode the nonverbal behavior of their clients. The early version was demonstrated to distinguish between effective and ineffective counselors (Campbell et al., 1971). It was discovered with some dismay, however, that scores on the later version of the test do not correlate significantly with scores on the original version (r = .06; Kagan, 1978). Apparently the two versions are measuring different things, the nature of which is not clear.

The Brief Affect Recognition Test. BART (Ekman and Friesen, 1974a) includes seventy black and white slides showing seven types of posed facial expressions, six of which were selected to represent the primary affects (happiness, sadness, fear, anger, surprise, and disgust), plus a neutral expression. These slides are presented for 1/30 second via a tachistoscope, with the justification that the short exposure is similar to the brevity of spontaneously emitted facial cues. The task is to judge the expression; accuracy criteria are based on Ekman and Friesen's studies of judgments of posed expressions. Seven scores are derived from BART: one for overall accuracy and one for each of the six primary affects.

An advantage of BART is that it measures sensitivity to different specific emotions. One of the major disadvantages is that it has not proved amenable to group administration, since a tachistoscopic presentation has been found to be necessary. Also, tachistoscopic proficiency has been found to be a major factor in the accuracy scores, necessitating the use of another test, the Facial Interpretation Test (FIT), to partial out the effects of tachistoscopic proficiency from the BART scores (O'Sullivan and Hagar, 1980). The FIT consists of slides of faces with the mouth and eyes in stages of being open or closed. The subject's task is to judge whether the eyes and/or mouth are open or closed.

The Communication of Affect Receiving Ability Test. CARAT was assembled by performing a standard item analysis using as items 23-second videotaped sequences taken via the slide-viewing technique (Buck, 1976). The task of the subject is to guess which kind of slide the sender viewed on each trial; the criterion of accuracy is the actual slide viewed. The instrument has thirty-two items involving four kinds of slides: sexual, scenic, unpleasant, and unusual. Twenty-five different stimulus persons are included.

The item-analysis process by which CARAT was constructed should theoretically lead to the construction of an internally homogeneous test. This did not, however, prove to be the case. The 600 items originally available were reduced to 108 items in an initial selection and further refined into two 40-item test forms. These were shown to large groups of subjects, and an item analysis was performed in which those items showing the highest correlations with the total score were retained. The internal consistency of a 20-item operational test derived from this procedure, as indexed by coefficient alpha, was estimated to be .57. The 47 "best" items from these two 40-item forms were then given to a new sample, and a 32-item final form was derived which, with minor modifications, remains the final form of CARAT. Unfortunately, the internal consistency of the instrument was not improved; the coefficient alpha of the final version is estimated to be .56. The test-retest reliability of CARAT, on the other hand, has been found to be satisfactory ($r = .79$ and .80 in two samples).

Two additional versions of CARAT have been developed: CARAT-C was constructed by Alper (1978) for measuring receiving ability in preschool children. It consists of relatively easily decoded facial responses of preschoolers to slides of familiar persons, unpleasant scenes, and unusual scenes. CARAT-CF was recently constructed by Blanck and myself. It involves the original CARAT items but includes a content-filtered voice channel. The resulting items are presented in audio-only, video-only, and audio-video format.

CARAT has several advantages in that it is the only test of nonverbal receiving ability that employs videotapes of the spontaneous response to emotional stimuli. It employs a number of stimulus persons and a variety of emotions, the criterion of accuracy is straightforward, and the task is easily understood by the subjects (see Buck, 1976). However, the failure to improve coefficient alpha with item analysis, coupled with the problems that Kagan (1977) found in correlating the first and second versions of the AS test, raise questions about whether it is in fact possible to construct an internally homogeneous test of nonverbal receiving ability in instruments like these. This lack of homogeneity suggests that nonverbal receiving ability may be a complex, multidimensional attribute and that a requirement for homogeneity may therefore be inappropriate.

The Profile of Nonverbal Sensitivity. PONS, developed by Rosenthal et al. (1979), involves twenty emotional situations that are posed by a single individual. The situations were designed to vary along dominance-submission and positive-negative dimensions. Each of these situations is presented eleven times in all possible combinations of three video forms (face only, body only, face plus body) and two audio forms (content-filtered voice and ramdomized spliced voice). This results in 220 stimulus scenes, each of which lasts two seconds. The subject is given a choice between two situations on each trial, one of which is "correct." The instrument yields a total score and also a "profile" of scores reflecting a person's relative sensitivity to, for example, facial versus body versus tone-of-voice cues.

Several versions of PONS have been developed for particular purposes and have been used in research that has shed considerable light on the phenomenon of nonverbal receiving ability. For example, there is a short form of PONS that includes only facial and bodily cues; a "brief expo-sure" PONS tests sensitivity to brief presentations of visual cues with a median exposure of 250 milliseconds (Rosenthal et al., 1979); the Non-verbal Discrepancy Test (NDT) shows facial and bodily enactments paired with altered-voice enactments that are entirely consistent, moderately discrepant, or completely discrepant with one another (DePaulo et al., 1978); the Measure of Verbal and Nonverbal Sensitivity (MOVANS) shows visual and altered-voice enactments paired with verbal transcripts, the whole of which are discrepant or nondiscrepant to different extents (Blanck and Rosenthal, 1981, 1982). The task of the subject in the latter two procedures is to rate the stimulus in the degree of discrepancy, as well as positiveness and dominance, with the goal of determining skill at recognizing discrepancy and which channels are used to judge positiveness and dominance when discrepancy exists.

PONS and its derivatives have been subjected to much more study than any of the other measures of nonverbal receiving ability, and these studies have done much to further our understanding in this area. For example, it seems clear that abilities to decode via visual channels are not related to abilities to decode via audio cues, a fact that again speaks to the lack of unity of the phenomenon of receiving ability. However, there are problems with PONS as well. For example, it uses the posed expressions of only one individual as its stimuli. Also, in the full PONS, each different stimulus is presented eleven times in various forms (face only, face plus body, and so on), and it is possible that subjects might recall cues from one presentation to another.

The Situations Interpretation Task. SIT (Archer and Akert, 1977) involves twenty brief videotaped segments showing naturally occurring situations that, although the participants were aware of the camera, were otherwise unposed. For example, one scene shows a person talking on the telephone; another shows two persons talking while an infant plays nearby. Audio as well as visual cues are present. For each segment, the subject is asked a question that has a definitely correct answer: for example, "Is the person on the telephone talking to a man or a woman?" "Which of the two women is the mother of the infant?"

SIT uses an inventive methodology, and it points out the complexity of the information that is present in nonverbal behavior. For instance, there is *something* in the behavior of the interactant on the telephone that allows the receiver to guess whether the other party is male or female at a level above chance. Unfortunately, there has not yet been sufficient research using SIT to determine what these cues might be or to allow a final conclusion on the value of the technique as a measure of receiving ability.

RELATIONSHIPS BETWEEN MEASURES

We have considered a number of potential measures of nonverbal receiving ability and have seen that several have problems with internal consistency—the new version of the AS test does not correlate significantly with the old, coefficient alpha of the CARAT was not improved by items analysis, abilities on different channels of the PONS are often inconsistent, and so forth. Studies of the relationships between these measures have been similarly disappointing. As noted above, Buck and Carroll (1974) found a .04 correlation between CARAT and the long form of PONS. More recently, Klaiman (1979) found a significant correlation between CARAT and the face score of the PONS short form for females (r [109] = .24, p < .01) but not for males (r [97] = .09). Fields and O'Sullivan (1976) report a disappointing pattern of correlations between BART, PONS, and SIT. Blanck and I have recently found a similarly disappointing pattern of correlations between CARAT-CF and MOVANS, with an average r (98) of .09.

Each of these instruments appears to have its own strengths and weaknesses; hence they should be considered to be alternative and complementary, rather than competing, approaches to the measurement of nonverbal receiving ability. Apparently these instruments are sensitive to different aspects of receiving ability, or, to put it another way, nonverbal receiving ability is not a unidimensional construct but instead involves a number of different "abilities."

CONCLUSIONS

Different measures of sending accuracy relate to one another in coherent ways; measures of receiving ability do not. Apparently the empirical approach of presenting people with samples of nonverbal behavior and measuring their ability to decode it is not sufficient to capture the complexities of receiving ability. In the next section, we shall examine some of the factors that might underlie the different abilities nonverbal receiving ability appears to involve, specifically: (1) learned "decoding rules," which may cause a person's nonverbal receiving ability to vary in different situations and with different nonverbal cues; (2) the related factor of the "education of attention" to nonverbal cues; (3) "specific nonverbal receiving ability," which involves the investigation of receiving ability in the context of a specific dyadic relationship; and (4) the relationship of receiving ability and nonverbal sending accuracy during interaction.

DECODING RULES AND THE
EDUCATION OF ATTENTION

DEFINITIONS

"Decoding rules" are cultural rules or expectations about the attention to, and interpretation of, nonverbal displays. They are analogous to display rules in the analysis of sending accuracy (see Ekman and Friesen, 1975). Thus, a person may learn to pay close attention to the interpretation of certain nonverbal cues but may not learn (or *learn not*) to attend to others. This learning may be situationally specific, so that one may learn to attend to the interpretation of cue complex A in some situations, ignoring cue complex B, while in other situations one may learn to attend to B and ignore A.

The concept of decoding rules involves the separate but related aspects of *attention* and *interpretation,* where attention is a necessary but not always sufficient condition for interpretation. If one does not attend to cue complex A, one certainly cannot interpret it; if one does attend, the interpretation may or may not be accurate. Presumably, one will become more accurate in the interpretation of a given cue complex if one has much experience in attending to and interpreting such displays in the past, although the extent to which such accuracy is learned or may be based on innate factors is not yet understood. I term the learning of patterns of attention to nonverbal cues the *education of attention.*

All of the measures of nonverbal receiving ability considered in the preceding discussion ignore whether subjects spontaneously attend or do not attend to nonverbal displays, in that they specifically direct attention to such displays in their instructions. They therefore assess the ability of the individual to interpret nonverbal displays once attention has been specifically directed to them. We shall examine the problem of attention later. For the moment, let us consider differences in the ability to interpret different constellations of nonverbal cues when attention is directed to the display. Most of this research has been directed toward the decoding of deception, and the nonverbal cue constellations have thus been conceptualized in terms of their "leakiness," or the extent to which they reveal the sender's "true feelings."

LEAKAGE AND THE DETECTION OF DECEPTION

Sex Differences in Accommodation. A great deal of work has been done in this area by Rosenthal and his colleagues, using derivatives of the PONS. It is commonly found that women score higher than men in tests of nonverbal receiving ability (Hall, 1978). DePaulo and Rosenthal (1979a) have suggested that this effect may be restricted to more obvious, less "leaky," nonverbal cues that the sender is not attempting to conceal. They suggest, following Ekman and Friesen (1969, 1974b), that different nonverbal channels can be ordered according to their leakiness, the face being the most controlled and least leaky, the body being more leaky than the face, tone of voice being more leaky than the body, very brief exposures of "micromomentary" facial/bodily cues being still more leaky, and discrepancies between different channels being the most difficult to control and therefore the most leaky of all. DePaulo and Rosenthal (1979a) present evidence that, as nonverbal cues become less controlled and more leaky, women progressively lose their advantage over men in their nonverbal receiving ability scores. They hypothesize that women do not learn, or *learn not,* to "eavesdrop" on the leaky nonverbal cues of others. Women see only what the other wishes them to see; in effect, they are more polite and accommodating in their interactions with others. DePaulo and Rosenthal present evidence that women who are not so nonverbally accommodating are judged by others as having less successful interpersonal outcomes, and that sex differences in accommodation are greater in cultures in which women are less liberated and in women who are socially and personally more vulnerable.

Development of Decoding Rules. Blanck and Rosenthal (1982) have recently reviewed studies analyzing the development of strategies for decoding discrepant multichannel messages. They suggest, for example, that nonverbal sensitivity becomes increasingly differentiated with age (DePaulo and Rosenthal, 1979b; Zuckerman et al., 1980) and that children learn to rely more heavily on leakier, less controllable channels when discrepancies are perceived in a message, apparently because they learn that these channels express the true, underlying meaning of the message (Blanck et al., forthcoming a). Also, Blanck et al., (1980) have found evidence of sibling similarity in nonverbal skill and style on the Nonverbal Discrepancies Test.

There are sex differences in the development of decoding rules that are consistent with the DePaulo and Rosenthal (1979a) analysis. Blanck (forthcoming b) have found that as young girls grow older, they progressively lose more of their advantage over males on leakier channels, while they gain more of an advantage on less leaky channels. This apparently reflects sex differences in learning about when it is and is not socially appropriate to decode different constellations of nonverbal cues.

DEVELOPMENTAL STUDIES OF
NONVERBAL RECEIVING ABILITY

Other investigators have studied the course of the development of nonverbal receiving ability using paradigms that do not involve the detection of deception (see the recent review by Field and Walden, 1982). These studies are relevant to the question of the extent to which receiving ability may be based on innate factors as opposed to learned decoding rules or skills. For example, several studies have demonstrated significant discrimination of facial expression by infants (Field and Walden, 1982; LaBarbera et al., 1976; Nelson et al., 1979; Young-Browne et al., 1977). In older children, a number of studies have assessed the ability correctly to recognize or categorize photographs of basic facial expressions (Borke, 1973; Ekman and Friesen, 1971; Feshbach and Roe, 1968; Gitter et al., 1971; Izard, 1971; Kalliopuska, 1981). These studies have not demonstrated cultural differences in recognition ability (black American versus white American, French versus American, Chinese versus American), but consistent age trends have been found showing recognition improving up to age 6 (Field and Walden, 1982).

Of the studies that investigated sex differences, Borke (1973) found that girls were more accurate in both Chinese and American samples, and Feshbach and Roe (1968) found an overall effect favoring girls but an interaction in which girls were more accurate at judging girls while boys were more accurate at judging boys. Kalliopuska (1981) found among preschool girls that firstborn and only children were more accurate than were later-born children. Field and Walden (1982 and forthcoming) reported positive relationships between the ability to decode posed expressions, the ability to encode such expressions, and teachers' ratings of extraversion. Several studies have suggested that happy expressions are reliably discriminated earlier than sad expressions and that discrimination of fearful and angry expressions appears later, although this finding is not universal.

Other studies have used more dynamic stimuli in the analysis of the development of nonverbal receiving ability. For example, Abramovich and Daly (1979) have shown that preschool children use immediacy cues in determining whether two persons shown on a videotape know one another. Also, Daly et al. (1980) found that children whose mothers are good senders tend to be good receivers, and Pendleton and Snyder (1980) have studied the development of the ability to articulate a decoding strategy in children attempting to decode the preferences of a videotaped child for a hidden toy.

ATTENTION TO NONVERBAL CUES

As noted previously, most of these studies have specifically directed the attention of the receiver to nonverbal cues. This is another problem with existing measures of nonverbal receiving ability, for there is no assurance that a person who attends to nonverbal cues while taking a test will also do so in "real life." Thus, the receiving ability score obtained may bear little or no relationship to the person's actual tendency to attend to, and receive information from, the nonverbal behavior of others.

The Education of Attention. The education of attention is a concept from Gibson's (1966, 1977) theory of perception, which is discussed in more detail below. It involves the perceptual selection of information from oneself and the environment. There may be cultural and individual differences in this selection: One can learn to attend to information that others ignore.

This concept is critical to the analysis of nonverbal receiving ability. A person skilled in nonverbal receiving ability may differ from a less skilled receiver not only in the ability to decode a nonverbal display once it is perceived, but also in the tendency to attend to nonverbal displays at all. Also, a "poor receiver" who ignores the nonverbal displays of others may conceivably be successful when instructed to attend to such displays in a test situation. The ability appropriately to direct one's attention in the face of complex cues in a real-life situation is an extremely important basis for individual differences in receiving ability.

The Segmentation Technique. One way to assess the attentional focus of the individual is through a behavior segmentation technique in which subjects are instructed to watch a film and indicate by pressing a button when a "meaningful event" occurs (Buck et al. 1982, 1980; Dickman, 1963; Newtson, 1976). Since the definition of what is meaningful is left to the subject, it allows an analysis of the subject's pattern of attention to the film.

For example, Goodman (1980) used a videotape of a person showing both instrumental actions (sitting down, picking up a magazine, lighting a cigarette, and the like) and emotional expressions (frowning, smiling, shaking the head, shrugging the shoulders, and so on). In one condition (Action Focus) subjects were instructed to press the button when the person on the videotape showed meaningful actions, in another (Emotion Focus) they were told to press when the person showed emotions, and in a third (No Focus) they were not specifically instructed to focus on either actions or emotions. Consensual points (CPs) were defined as intervals in which a higher-than-expected (one standard deviation above the mean) number of observers pressed the button (see Buck et al., 1982). In the Goodman (1980) study, the intervals were three seconds long.

Results indicated that the pattern of CPs in the Action Focus and Emotion Focus conditions were quite different. Analysis of the events occurring on the film at the CPs indicated that subjects in the Action Focus condition pressed to instrumental actions and those in the Emotion Focus condition pressed to emotional expressions. Interestingly, the pattern of CPs in the No Focus condition was quite similar to that of the Action Focus condition and dissimilar from the Emotion Focus condition, suggesting that under the circumstances of this study, these subjects attended to instrumental actions and at least consciously ignored the emotional expressions.

To determine the nature of the changes taking place at the CPs, three still photographs were taken over the three-second CP intervals. Ten "action-oriented CPs" from the Action Focus and No Focus conditions and ten "emotion-oriented CPs" from the Emotion Focus condition were so analyzed. Results indicated that, compared with Emotion CPs, Action CPs contained significantly more changes in interactions with environmental objects and in bodily position in space, and significantly fewer expressive changes in face or body. Facial expressions occurred at all of the emotion CPs. For two of them, expressive body changes—shrugging the shoulders and a slumping of the upper body—also occurred.

Goodman's study illustrates the point that people may, because of instructions, pay attention to different aspects of a nonverbal display. It is similarly possible that there are individual differences in these patterns of attention that are due to the process of the education of attention, that is, learning generally to attend to nonverbal cues or not.

CONCLUSIONS

The concepts of decoding rules and the education of attention have broad implications that go beyond the analysis of nonverbal receiving ability per se, in that they are relevant to the general analysis of person perception and attribution, including self-attribution. The ways people direct their attention to the multitude of cues in the environment, in other persons, and within themselves and their own bodies are critical in determining the kinds of information they extract from these sources (see Buck, 1981a). These may be based in part on innate factors as well as on learned decoding rules. I consider this further below. For the present, we shall consider two other complexities of nonverbal receiving ability that are not taken into account by recent tests.

RELATIONSHIP EFFECTS AND NONVERBAL RECEIVING ABILITY

SPECIFIC NONVERBAL RECEIVING ABILITY

"Specific nonverbal receiving ability" is the ability accurately to decode the nonverbal behavior of a person with whom one has a specific relationship. All of the measures of nonverbal receiving ability that we have considered assess sensitivity to persons that the receiver has never met and with whom he or she has no relationship. There is evidence that such sensitivity to the generalized other, or "general nonverbal receiving ability," is quite different from the sensitivity to the expressions of a person with whom one has an ongoing relationship (see Buck, 1979b; Buck and Lerman, 1979).

First, there is evidence that people often decode the expressions of persons who are known to them more accurately than they decode unknown persons. For example, mothers decode the expressions of their children more accurately than do undergraduates (Buck, 1975) and more accurately than they decode the expressions of other children (Zuckerman and Przewuzman, 1979). Children decode the expressions of their own mothers more accurately than those of unknown mothers (Abramovich, 1977) and the expressions of known peers more accurately than those of unfamiliar children (Abramovich and Daly, 1979).

There is also evidence that specific nonverbal receiving ability has relationships with relevant variables that are different from, and perhaps more meaningful than, those of general nonverbal receiving ability. Buck and Lerman (1979) found relationships between clinical training and the ability to decode the spontaneous expression of one's own client, while the relationships between clinical training and the ability to decode the clients of others, and ability on CARAT, were not significant. Also, Kahn (1970) and Gottman (1979) have found evidence that unique communication patterns ("private message systems") are more evident among happily married than non-happily married couples. Sabatelli et al. (1980, 1981a) studied specific receiving ability (ability to decode the partner) and general receiving ability (CARAT score) in dating and married couples, finding that neither specific nor general receiving ability was related to the length or reported quality of the relationship in dating couples. However, in married couples it was found that spouses were more accurate at decoding their partners' expressions than was a panel of undergraduate judges. Also, it was found that the wife's ability to decode her husband's expressions *on those trials in which the undergraduates could not* was positively and significantly related to both the wife's and husband's reported satisfaction with the relationship. In other words, the wife's ability to decode an overtly and obviously expressed message was not significantly related to marital satisfaction, but her sensitivity to expressions that others could not decode was. While this finding should be replicated, it is consistent with the Kahn (1970) and Gottman (1979) observations. Moreover, it suggests the possibility that global measures even of specific nonverbal receiving ability may not be sufficiently sensitive to the more subtle aspects of nonverbal communication (Sabatelli et al., 1981a).

This implies a significant limitation on attempts to develop general tests of nonverbal receiving ability, particularly when they are based on the nonverbal behavior of unknown persons. To the extent that nonverbal receiving ability is based on cues that are idiosyncratic and specific to a given sender, *any* measure of general receiving ability must produce findings that are incomplete and perhaps misleading. Clearly, more data on how nonverbal receiving ability varies across relationships would be most welcome.

RECEIVING ABILITY AND SENDING ACCURACY

An observation by Sabatelli et al. (1979) introduces still another complexity to the analysis of nonverbal receiving ability. This study investigated the relationship between nonverbal communication accuracy and cognitive style. It was generally expected that nonverbal receiving ability would be related to field dependence. This expectation was based on the description of field-dependent persons as more oriented toward external, social cues, and it was felt that such persons should be more experienced with and able to respond to nonverbal cues in others. It has been found that field-dependent persons spend more time looking at the faces of the persons with whom they are interacting (Konstadt and Forman, 1965; Nevill, 1974). However, Sabatelli et al.'s (1979) results indicated no significant relationships between cognitive style and receiving ability. Instead, field-dependent persons were found to be significantly better *senders* on the slide-viewing technique.

This finding suggests an interesting possibility: that the most controllable way of being a good receiver is to be a good sender. If a person actively sends information in the form of nonverbal expression (within limits), it is likely that others will reciprocate, in a way analogous to the reciprocity of self-disclosure that has been noted in the literature (see Cappella, 1981; Huston and Levinger, 1978; Rubin, 1975). Field-dependent persons have been found to be more verbally self-disclosing (Sousa-Poza et al., 1973), and the finding that they are better senders suggests that they may be more "nonverbally self-disclosing" as well. Beyond this, Sabatelli et al.'s research suggests the possibility of an *interactional* view of nonverbal receiving ability in which one determines the probability of encountering meaningful cues from others by providing meaningful cues to others. Such a possibility can only be evaluated in interactional settings in which both sending accuracy and receiving ability are assessed.

AN INTERACTIONAL VIEW OF RECEIVING ABILITY

The idea that one's level of receiving ability may be to some extent dependent on one's sending accuracy, in combination with the notion of

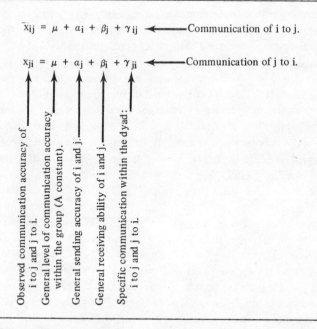

$$\bar{x}_{ij} = \mu + a_i + \beta_j + \gamma_{ij} \longleftarrow \text{Communication of i to j.}$$

$$x_{ji} = \mu + a_j + \beta_i + \gamma_{ji} \longleftarrow \text{Communication of j to i.}$$

Observed communication accuracy of i to j and j to i.

General level of communication accuracy within the group (A constant).

General sending accuracy of i and j.

General receiving ability of i and j.

Specific communication within the dyad: i to j and j to i.

FIGURE 7.1   The Kenny Model of Interaction Applied to Nonverbal Communication

specific receiving ability, suggests that a comprehensive analysis of non-verbal receiving ability must consider the phenomenon from an interactional point of view as well as the more common view that it is a trans-situational skill.

A way nonverbal receiving ability can be approached as an interactional concept associated with a specific dyadic relationship and a specific level of sending accuracy is seen in the model of interaction recently suggested by Kenny and his colleagues (Kenny and Nasby, 1980; Warner et al., 1979). This model is illustrated in Figure 7.1. In brief, Kenny argues that *any* measure of behavior taken during a dyadic interaction can be decomposed into four components: (1) the average level of the behavior across all dyads (μ); (b) the general tendency of one partner (i) to "send" that behavior to all partners (α); (c) the general tendency of the other partner (j) to "receive" that behavior from all partners (β); and (d) the specific level of that behavior within the ij dyad, after these general tendencies have been controlled (γ). The latter term represents a unique relationship effect.

In the terms of the nonverbal communication process between i and j, Xij represents the total communication accuracy score when i is sending to j; Xji represents the communication accuracy score when j is sending to i. Xij has four components in the model: (1) the general level of communication accuracy for all senders and receivers in the group in question (the grand mean μ); (2) i's general sending accuracy (αi); (3) j's general receiving ability (βj); and (4) the specific communication accuracy of i to j when these general factors are subtracted out (γij). The latter expression may be regarded as a formal definition of *specific communication accuracy*, that is, communication accuracy specific to a given dyad. Conversely, the communication accuracy when j is sending to i (Xji) involves the general sending accuracy of j, the general receiving ability of i, and the specific communication accuracy of j to i.

The analysis of these factors would obviously be useful in the analysis of nonverbal receiving ability; indeed, it could be argued that any conceptualization of receiving ability that does not consider these factors must be incomplete. Kenny and his colleagues have shown that simple dyadic designs, in which measures are obtained from only one dyad, are insufficient to obtain these estimates. In its stead, a "round-robin" design, in which measures are taken of two members of a dyad as they interact with others as well as with each other, is required (Warner et al., 1979). This allows the measurement of each person's general tendencies to "send" and "receive" the attribute in question as well as the contribution of the specific dyad. Kenny and Nasby (1980) have applied this analysis to the sending and receiving of liking within dyads, showing that strong reciprocity of liking can be demonstrated only when general tendencies to send and receive liking are removed from the analysis.

The application of the Kenny et al. analysis to the problem of nonverbal communication is straightforward, and it allows us to analyze the communication process in a new and more complete way.

NEW APPROACHES TO NONVERBAL
RECEIVING ABILITY

We have seen that the complexity of nonverbal receiving ability calls into question the usefulness of current measures as standardized tests of a trans-situational attribute. It should be noted, however, that these instruments have been useful as research tools, as in the alteration of the long form of PONS into short forms and instruments such as the NDT and MOVANS, and in the use of CARAT to compare and contrast with measures of specific nonverbal sensitivity. The segmentation of CARAT has also been of interest, as we shall see below. In a sense, the instruments have, by revealing their deficiencies, helped to point the way to new and, I hope, more useful approaches to nonverbal receiving ability.

In this section, I consider two potentially useful new approaches to nonverbal receiving ability: an "accuracy-in-process" approach that takes into account the notions of decoding rules and the education of attention, and an "interactional" approach that takes into account specific relationships and the importance of the assessment of certain aspects of nonverbal receiving ability in interactional settings.

AN ACCURACY-IN-PROCESS APPROACH
TO RECEIVING ABILITY

The Accuracy-versus-Process Controversy. At the time that studies of accuracy in person perception were under their strongest methodological criticism, Tagiuri and Petrullo (1958) suggested the abandonment of the accuracy approach to person perception entirely in favor of a process approach. They state that "attempts at studying correlates of accuracy have with very few exceptions produced negligible correlations and yielded very little insight into processes. . . . It is the process rather than its achievement that one must investigate if a broad understanding of the phenomenon is to be reached" (quoted by Cline, 1964: 239). On the other hand, Crow (1960) has pointed out that the process in question involves accuracy, that it is in fact a "process of functional achievement" (Cline, 1964: 239-240) and that therefore a focus on accuracy as well as process is necessary.

The notions of decoding rules and the education of attention are relevent to this controversy. The suggestion that the individual learns to attend to certain aspects of the complex nonverbal display and to ignore others and that such "decoding rules" differ from situation to situation implies that accuracy and process cannot be separated. The process by which the receiver scans and interprets the nonverbal display is critical in determining the information that she or he will extract from the display.

Segmentation and Accuracy. The segmentation technique allows a unique way to study this process, which also allows the analysis of accuracy. For example, Baron and I have applied the segmentation technique to the CARAT instrument in two studies (Buck et al., 1980, 1982). Both studies revealed differences in the sending behaviors of adult males versus females, the segmentation measures of the behavior of females being more highly related to their sending accuracy than was the case for males. These studies also investigated the relationships between the receivers' segmentation patterns and receiving ability as measured by the accuracy with which the receiver identifies the slide category, revealing that receiving ability on CARAT was negatively related to the number of button presses for female receivers (average $r = -.31$, $p > .01$) but not male receivers (average $r = -.01$). Thus, while viewing adults, accurate female receivers tended to segment less finely than did less accurate female receivers, while receiving ability was not related to fineness of segmentation in males. On the other hand, receiving ability and fineness of segmentation were positively correlated for both males and females when viewing the expressions of children (average $r = .23$, $p > .05$).

The Buck et al. (1982) study also assessed the quality of segmentation by determining the number of times a given receiver *hit* on CPs and *missed* CPs (pressed the button more than one second away from a CP). These proved to be significantly related to receiving ability only among female receivers, hits being positively correlated (average $r = .47$, $p > .05$) and misses negatively correlated (average $r = -.59$, $p > .005$) with receiving ability. The comparable figures for male receivers ($r = .22$ and $-.13$ respectively) were not significant.

Thus, as with sending accuracy, receiving ability is more related to segmentation measures in females than in males, suggesting the possibility that receiving ability is related to direct perceptual processing in females and a less direct, perhaps more cognitively mediated processing in males (Buck, 1981a, 1981b; Buck et al., 1980, 1982).

Another example of an application of the segmentation technique to the analysis of the quality of the process of person perception has been conducted by Brackett and Donnelly (1981). Judges indicated points at which they would intrude into a videotaped conversation between two persons. When both audio and video cues were available, significant consensus was demonstrated and CPs established. The videotapes, under different conditions of degradation—video only, video plus content-filtered voice, and nondegraded audio-video—were then shown to a group of judges. The new group showed a pattern of CPs similar to that of the first group in the nondegraded condition, but the other conditions, particularly the video-only condition, showed a significant drop in consensus and a lack of agreement with the first sample. The authors suggest that this inability to determine the proper points at which to enter a conversation with restricted audio cues is the basis of the difficulty with the conversational turn-taking process experienced by hearing-impaired persons.

AN INTERACTIONAL APPROACH TO RECEIVING ABILITY

We have analyzed two ways nonverbal receiving ability may be altered by relationship effects. First, the ability accurately to receive information from persons with whom one has a specific relationship history differs from general nonverbal receiving ability. Second, receiving ability may be dynamically influenced by the receiver's own sending accuracy in the context of an ongoing interaction.

These aspects of receiving ability must be assessed in settings in which persons with specified relationships with the receiver play the role of sender. The level of sensitivity to that person may then be compared with sensitivity to strangers in order to arrive at an estimate of specific nonverbal receiving ability. That was the procedure used in the Buck and Lerman (1979) and Sabatelli et al. (1979, 1980, 1981a, 1981b) studies. The Kenny model of interaction described previously provides an efficient technique for analyzing and organizing the data that result from such studies, partitioning the effects into variance due to general sending accuracy, general receiving ability, and specific relationship effects. Efforts are now under way to apply this analysis to data collected in the Sabatelli et al. studies.

Such data will not, however, address the issue of the dynamic relationship between sending accuracy and receiving ability in the context of an actual interaction. This would require the analysis of both sending accuracy and receiving ability in an actual interactional setting in which the receiver could influence the behavior of the other via the receiver's own expressiveness. Receivers in the Buck and Lerman and Sabatelli et al. studies viewed videotapes of the sender; there was no dynamic interchange. A measurement situation in which the receiver can directly influence the sender and in which simultaneous measures of sending accuracy and receiving ability can be taken has not yet been devised. A truly complete approach to nonverbal receiving ability, however, appears to require such an analysis.

THE NATURE OF NONVERBAL RECEIVING ABILITY

We have seen that there are at least four conceptually distinct factors that might account for an individual's level of nonverbal receiving ability in a given situation: (1) experience and skill in decoding nonverbal behavior in general, (2) attention to specific patterns of nonverbal behavior in others, (3) experience and skill in decoding the nonverbal behaviors of a specific person known to the receiver, and (4) the nonverbal expressiveness of the receiver in an interactional setting. The instruments designed to measure nonverbal receiving ability considered above are sensitive only to the first factor—the ability to decode a stranger when attention has been specifically directed to nonverbal cues (see Buck, 1980, 1981a, 1981b).

These instruments are interesting and have led to important advances, but a full understanding of nonverbal receiving ability will require much more, including at least the study of patterns of attention to complex nonverbal displays in circumstances in which the subject's attention is not specifically directed to the display, the expanded study of nonverbal receiving ability in the context of specific relationships, and the study of nonverbal receiving ability in interactional settings in which sending accuracy may be taken into account. In this final section I suggest a model of receiving ability and attempt to integrate this view with the present discussion.

INNATE FACTORS IN RECEIVING ABILITY

Darwin (1872) analyzed the evolution of emotion displays as follows: If the communication of a given emotion state is adaptive to a species, individuals showing evidence of this state in their visible behavior will tend to be favored. The more clearly the state is displayed, the more the individual is favored, so that over the generations, the display becomes "ritualized." However, although the tendencies to display have an innate basis, the nature of the actual display is also influenced by learned factors that are sensitive to the situation: the display rules.

The display would, however, be of little evolutionary value for the species if other animals failed to respond appropriately to it. It is rarely recognized that what is evolving must be not simply a display, but a communication system that involves a receiver as well as a sender. Thus, individuals who respond appropriately to the displays of others must also be favored, so that over the generations the attentional and perceptual systems of species members must become "preattuned" to the pickup of important displays.

The notion of innate systems underlying receiving ability has not been emphasized in most analyses of nonverbal receiving ability. Like most theorizing about the process of person perception in general, most researchers have assumed that the receiving process is largely learned. In other words, they assume that the sender's behavior has little or no meaning in itself as unelaborated stimulus input. The emphasis instead is on how the receiver learns through experience, imitation, or reinforcement to structure or process the raw data provided by the sender's behavior.

This kind of view has been challenged in recent years, particularly by the theory and research on perception generated by Gibson (1966, 1977), which emphasizes the importance of information present in the environment, suggesting that perception involves the direct "pickup" of this information with no need for its conversion, transformation, or processing. Gibson's view emphasizes the richness of the information given "as is" in the stimulus array. I shall present a brief account of Gibson's theory, which emphasizes the role of the evolution of perceptual systems, and shall consider the implications of this view for the analysis of person perception in general and nonverbal receiving ability in particular.

GIBSON'S ECOLOGICAL THEORY OF PERCEPTION

The Evolution of Perception. The notion of an evolution of receiving ability is consistent with Gibson's notion that perception must be determined by the nature of the ecological niche in which the species evolves. To Gibson, perception is made possible by compatibilities between the animal's qualities (the receptor apparatus and so on) and the environment. These compatibilities involve the evolved qualities of the organism, which may be "tuned" by experience. Gibson argues that the nature of the human animal—terrestrial, bipedal, social, possessing efficient binocular vision, and so on—has evolved hand in hand with a certain way of knowing the world. This is true of all species—each has evolved a way of knowing that is compatible with what it *must* know in order to survive in its environment. Thus, the organism is seen to be biologically prepared or "attuned" to properties of its environment that are objectively present and veridically perceived (Neisser, 1976: 19). In other words, our perceptual systems have evolved to "pick up" or extract certain information from the environment that is relevant to survival.

An interesting example of the evolution of communication, including the possible evolution of communication of emotion in an ecological context very different from our own, involves the dolphin. Dolphins have no sense of smell, and their sense of sight is of limited use in their undersea environment. It has been suggested, however, that they are capable of forming sonic "images" by sensing the echoes of the trains of high-frequency clicks they emit, which are focused by a "lens" of fat in the forehead. These sonic images may be highly refined; dolphins appear capable of making discriminations between degrees of hollowness in metal balls that equal the capabilities of human visual discrimination. It is clear that dolphins "can 'hear' the composition and texture of objects around them," and they may be able to "look *into* each other in eerie ways, inspecting the contours of internal air spaces" (K. S. Norris, in Linehan, 1979: 515-516). This sonic X-ray vision may provide the highly social dolphin with information about the emotional state of its fellows which is analogous to that obtained via spontaneous facial/gestural expression in primates such as ourselves, and which may serve a similar function: social coordination.

Affordances and Social Affordances. Gibson (1977) deals with the perception of meaning through the concept of *affordance.* Affordances involve conjunctions between the properties of the organism and the environment—all of the potential uses of objects constitute the activities they afford, and according to Gibson these are directly perceived (Baron and Buck, 1979; Neisser, 1976). Thus what makes an object afford "graspability" involves a conjunction between the physical properties of the object and the characteristics of the organism.

The adequacy of the affordance concept in dealing with the perception of meaning is the subject of controversy that is beyond the realm of the present discussion (see Neisser, 1976: 72-75; Heil, 1979). However, both Neisser and Gibson have suggested that affordances may involve the characteristics of other persons as well as physical objects in the environment. Thus, Gibson proposed that sexual behavior, nurturant behavior, cooperative behavior, and so on can be treated as affordances in which the sender provides possibilities for interaction that can be directly perceived by the receiver. It could be argued that the process of spontaneous nonverbal communication may be viewed in terms of such "social affordances."

There is some experimental evidence supporting the notion that perceptual systems are preattumed to nonverbal emotion displays important to the species. For example, infant rhesus monkeys who have been isolated from other monkeys since birth react with appropriate fearful behavior when confronted with a photograph of a large male monkey making a threat display (Sackett, 1966). Also, it has been demonstrated that human facial expressions of fear and anger are more readily associated with aversive events than are happy or neutral expressions in classical conditioning studies (Ohman and Dimberg, 1978; Lanzetta and Orr, 1980), and, as we saw earlier, human infants appear capable of discriminating certain facial expressions.

The Education of Attention. Gibson's viewpoint stresses the importance of the stimulus more than the processes going on within the receiver. If the stimulus is "veridically perceived," one should theoretically know what is perceived by describing the stimulus. However, it is clear that perceivers differ from one another in the information they extract from a given stimulus, and several authors have suggested that Gibson's theory is not entirely satisfactory in dealing with such differences (Heil, 1979). Neisser (1976) has suggested that Eleanor J. Gibson's work on cognitive development addresses some of these issues. She suggests that the difference between a skilled and naive perceiver lies in the former's ability to extract more information from the stimulus, detecting features and higher-order structures to which the naive receiver is not sensitive. Thus the perceiver's skill involves the ability to extract information efficiently rather than the ability to process information differently. An older child may learn to note information that a younger child ignors (Neisser, 1976).

The phrase "education of attention" was coined by Gibson (1966) to refer to the perceptual selection of good information. Gibson suggests that the perceptual organization of an event is an important aspect of observer skill, because it determines the information on which an observer may draw in making judgments and inferences. Thus, as suggested previously, a person skilled in nonverbal receiving ability may differ from a less skilled receiver not only in the ability to decode a nonverbal display once it is perceived, but also in the tendency to attend to nonverbal displays at all. A "poor receiver" may be a person who simply ignores the nonverbal displays of others, and such a person may be a successful decoder when attending to such displays.

LEARNING AND COGNITIVE FACTORS
IN RECEIVING ABILITY

Many who are essentially sympathetic with the Gibsonian view of "direct perception" have argued that it cannot be a complete account of the process (Heil, 1979). Neisser (1976), for example, argues that one must also understand how cognitive structures internal to the perceiver are modified by information in the environment. These cognitive structures, or schemata, to use Neisser's term, are involved in a perceptual cycle: They are modified by environmental information and in turn direct the process of perceptual exploration and attention, leading to the sampling of new environmental information. This is termed "mediated" as opposed to "direct" perception. Neisser's concept of perceptual cycles is similar to Piaget's (1971) process of equilibration through assimilation and accommodation and Elkind's (1971) cognitive growth cycles. All of these theories attempt to describe how the cognitive system "constructs its own structure" in the course of adaptation to the external world.

From our point of view, this implies that nonverbal receiving ability must involve more than a spontaneous and innately determined response to nonverbal displays. It must involve knowledge about what displays to attend to in what situations. This is the basis of the notion of decoding rules.

THE SOCIAL KNOWING CONTINUUM

Hochberg (1956) has suggested that the relationship between direct perception and mediated perception might best be represented as a con-

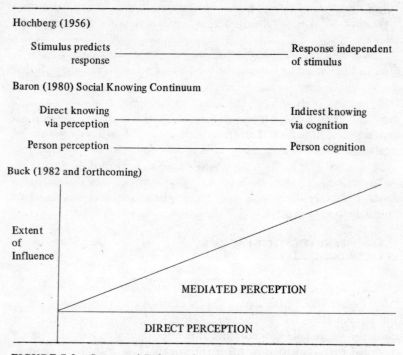

Hochberg (1956)

Stimulus predicts _____ Response independent
response   of stimulus

Baron (1980) Social Knowing Continuum

Direct knowing _____ Indirest knowing
via perception   via cognition

Person perception ——————————————— Person cognition

Buck (1982 and forthcoming)

Extent
of
Influence

MEDIATED PERCEPTION

DIRECT PERCEPTION

**FIGURE 7.2   Suggested Relationships Between Direct and Mediated
Perception**

tinuum, one extreme of which involves the case in which knowledge of the
stimulus is both necessary and sufficient to completely predict the
receiver's response and the other extreme of which involves the case in
which the receiver's response is independent of the stimulus, knowledge of
which is neither necessary nor sufficient for the prediction of the response.
Between these extremes lies a domain in which the stimulus accounts for
some but not all of the variance in the response. The upper part of Figure
7.2 illustrates this continuum.

Baron (1980; Baron and Buck, 1979; Baron and Harvey, 1980) has
suggested an analogous distinction that is relevent to this relationship. This
"social knowing continuum" is presented in the middle part of Figure 7.2.
At one extreme is perception-based knowing, where meaning is entirely
given by information in environmental events, requiring no additional
cognitive processing. At the other extreme is cognition-based knowing,
where meaning is purely a function of cognitive operations without regard
to the stimuli. When the object of knowledge is a person, Baron speaks of

person perception at one end of the continuum and *person cognition* at the other.

Both of these continua can be regarded as analogous to a continuum between "pure" direct perception and "pure" mediated perception. However, as I have suggested elsewhere, the relationship between direct and mediated perception may be too complex to describe as a continuum (Buck, forthcoming a). Instead, it may be useful to describe it in terms of a variant of the relationship shown in the lower part of Figure 7.2. This implies that mediated perception is always based on direct perception and cannot exist in "pure" form. The reverse is not, however, the case: Direct perception can exist without mediated perception. As detailed elsewhere, direct perception may be based on subcortical and paleocortical neural mechanisms, often integrated, perhaps, within the right cerebral hemisphere, while mediated perception may require neocortical mechanisms and left cerebral processing (Buck, 1982 and forthcoming).

CONCLUSIONS

I have presented a view of the nature of nonverbal receiving ability in which innate factors play a significant role. I proposed that the meaning of the nonverbal display is to some extent given directly to the receiver (assuming that the receiver attends to it), so that mediation by knowledge about that display is relatively unimportant. At the same time, it is clear that receiving is often mediated by such knowledge. Direct perception does not require knowledge or interpretation, only attention to the display. Direct perception is always present to some degree in the process of receiving nonverbal displays, and mediation by knowledge may or may not be present.

SUMMARY

In this chapter I have reviewed the status of nonverbal receiving ability as a trans-situational attribute, concluding that, unlike nonverbal sending accuracy, receiving ability is too complex to conceptualize usefully in such terms. Recent tests of nonverbal receiving ability were reviewed. It was noted that these different measures, supposedly of the same conceptual variable, relate to one another weakly or not at all, and that internal consistency has likewise proved to be a problem.

I then examined some of the factors that underlie the complexity of nonverbal receiving ability and concluded that learned patterns of attention to nonverbal cues (the outcome of the education of attention) could underlie decoding rules that would cause a person's nonverbal receiving ability to vary across different situations and different constellations of nonverbal cues. The fact that these "tests" of nonverbal receiving ability direct the attention of the subject specifically to nonverbal cues is seen as a particularly significant limitation in this regard. In addition, specific nonverbal receiving ability may differ in important respects from the ability to "read" strangers, which is assessed by these tests. Finally, I pointed out that the receiver may dynamically influence his or her ability to gain nonverbal information from others by supplying nonverbal information *to* others, who will then reciprocate. One's own expressiveness or sending accuracy, then, may be the most controllable way to ensure that others will be expressive and "decodable."

New approaches to nonverbal receiving ability were suggested based on these considerations, including the use of segmentation techniques to assess attentional patterns to nonverbal displays, and interactional approaches, in which the sending accuracy as well as the receiving ability of interactants is assessed and the unique variance due to the dyad is separated from general sending and receiving tendencies.

Finally, a new conceptualization of receiving ability was suggested which includes a much more important role for innate factors than has generally been the case. Gibson's theory of perception was cited as suggesting that the perceptual system must be "preattuned" by evolution to be sensitive to certain important features of the environment. The nonverbal displays of others certainly seem to qualify as important features of the environment, and it is suggested that, to an extent not yet understood, nonverbal receiving ability is based on innate "direct perception" as well as learned patterns of attention and decoding skills (mediated perception). The relationship between direct and mediated perception was discussed, and it was suggested that direct perception is always present in cases of receiving nonverbal cues, while mediated perception may not be present or may play a role of varying importance in the receiving process.

REFERENCES

Abramovich, R. Children's recognition of situational aspects of facial expressions. *Child Development,* 1977, *48,* 459-463.

Abramovich, R., and Daly, E. M. Inferring the attributes of a situation from the facial expressions of peers. *Child Development,* 1979, *50,* 486-589.

Alper, S. *Nonverbal receiving ability in preschool-age children.* Unpublished master's thesis, University of Connecticut, 1977.

Archer, D., and Akert, R. M. Words and everything else: Verbal and nonverbal cues in social interpretation. *Journal of Personality and Social Psychology,* 1977, *35,* 443-449.

Baron, R. M. Social knowing from an ecological event perspective: A consideration of the relative domains of power for cognitive and perceptual modes of knowing. In J. Harvey (Ed.), *Cognition, social behavior, and the environment.* Hillsdale, NJ: Lawrence Erlbaum, 1980.

Baron, R. M., and Buck, R. *A Gibsonian-event perception approach to the meaning of the nonverbal communication of emotion.* Paper presented at the American Psychological Association Symposium on the Meaning of Nonverbal Communication, New York, 1979.

Baron, R. and Harvey, J. H. Contrasting perspectives on social knowing: An overview. *Personality and Social Psychology Bulletin,* 1980, *6,* 502-506.

Blanck, P., and Rosenthal, R. *Measuring sensitivity to verbal and nonverbal discrepant and consistent multichannel messages: The MOVANS test.* Paper presented at the meeting of the Eastern Psychological Association, New York, 1981.

Blanck, P., and Rosenthal, R. Developing strategies for decoding "leaky" messages. In R. Feldman (Ed.), *The development of nonverbal behavior in children.* New York: Springer, 1982.

Blanck, P. D., Rosenthal, R., Snodgrass, S. E., DePaulo, B. M., and Zuckerman, M. Longitudinal and cross-sectional age effects in nonverbal decoding skill and style. *Developmental Psychology,* forthcoming. (a)

Blanck, P. D., Rosenthal, R., Snodgrass, S. E., DePaulo, B. M., and Zuckerman, M. Sex differences in eavesdropping on nonverbal cues: Developmental changes. *Journal of Personality and Social Psychology,* forthcoming. (b)

Blanck, P. D., Zuckerman, M., DePaulo, B. M., and Rosenthal, R. Sibling resemblances in nonverbal skill and style. *Journal of Nonverbal Behavior,* 1980, *4,* 219-226.

Block, J. A study of affective responsiveness in a lie detection situation. *Journal of Abnormal and Social Psychology,* 1957, *55,* 11-15.

Borke, H. The development of empathy in Chinese and American children between three and six years of age: A cross cultural study. *Developmental Psychology,* 1973, *3,* 102-108.

Brackett, D., and Donnelly, J. *Interruptions: The role of nonverbal, paralinguistic, and linguistic cues.* Paper presented at the convention of American Speech-Language-Hearing Association, Los Angeles, 1981.

Buck, R. Nonverbal communication of affect in children. *Journal of Personality and Social Psychology,* 1975, *31,* 644-653.

Buck, R. A test of nonverbal receiving ability: Preliminary studies. *Human Communication Research,* 1976, *2,* 162-171.

Buck, R. Nonverbal communication accuracy in preschool children: Relationships with personality and skin conductance. *Journal of Personality and Social Psychology,* 1977, *33,* 225-236.

Buck, R. The slide-viewing technique for measuring nonverbal sending accuracy: A guide for replication. *Catalog of Selected Documents in Psychology,* 1978, *8,* 63. (Abstract)

Buck, R. Individual differences in nonverbal sending accuracy and electrodermal responding: The externalizing-internalizing dimension. In R. Rosenthal (Ed.), *Skill in nonverbal communication: Individual differences.* Cambridge, MA: Oelgeschlager, Gunn & Hain, 1979. (a)

Buck, R. Measuring individual differences in the nonverbal communication of affect: The slide-viewing paradigm. *Human Communication Research,* 1979, *6,* 47-57. (b)

Buck, R. Nonverbal behavior and the theory of emotion: The facial feedback hypothesis. *Journal of Personality and Social Psychology,* 1980, *38,* 811-824.

Buck, R. The evolution and development of emotion expression and communication. In S. Brehm, S. Kassin, and F. Gibbons (Eds.), *Developmental social psychology.* New York: Oxford University Press, 1981. (a)

Buck, R. Sex differences in psychophysiological responding and subjective experience: A comment. *Psychophysiology,* 1981, *18,* 349-350. (b)

Buck, R. *Emotion and nonverbal behavior: The communication of affect.* New York: Guilford Press, forthcoming.

Buck, R. Emotion development and emotion education. In R. Plutchik and H. Kellerman (Eds.), *Emotions in early development.* New York: Academic Press, 1983.

Buck, R. Spontaneous and symbolic nonverbal behavior and the ontogeny of communication. In R. S. Feldman (Ed.), *The development of nonverbal behavior in children.* New York: Springer, 1982.

Buck, R., Baron, R., and Barrette, D. The temporal organization of spontaneous nonverbal expression: A segmentation analysis. *Journal of Personality and Social Psychology,* 1982, *42,* 506-517.

Buck, R., Baron, R., Goodman, N., and Shapiro, B. The unitization of spontaneous nonverbal behavior in the study of emotion communication. *Journal of Personality and Social Psychology,* 1980, *39,* 522-529.

Buck, R., and Carroll, J. *CARAT and PONS: Correlates of two tests of nonverbal sensitivity.* Unpublished manuscript, Carnegie-Mellon University, 1974.

Buck, R., and Duffy, R. Nonverbal communication of affect in brain-damaged patients. *Cortex,* 1980, *16,* 351-362.

Buck, R., and Lerman, J. General vs. specific nonverbal sensitivity and clinical training. *Human Communication,* 1979, Summer, 269-274.

Buck, R. W., and Miller, R. E. *A measure of sensitivity to facial expression.* Paper and videotape screening presented at the conference of the Anthropological and Documentary Film Conference, Temple University, Philadelphia, 1972.

Buck, R., Miller, R. E., and Caul, W. F. Sex, personality and physiological variables in the communication of emotion via facial expression. *Journal of Personality and Social Psychology,* 1974, *30,* 587-596.

Buck, R., Savin, V., Miller, R. E., and Caul, W. F. Nonverbal communication of affect in humans. *Journal of Personality and Social Psychology,* 1972, *23,* 362-371.

Campbell, R. J., Kagan, N., and Krathwohl, D. R. The development and validation of a scale to measure affective sensitivity (empathy). *Journal of Counseling Psychology,* 1971, *18,* 407-412.

Cappella, J. N. Mutual influence in expressive behavior: Adult-adult and infant-infant dyadic interaction. *Psychological Bulletin,* 1981, *89,* 101-132.

Cline, V. B. Interpersonal perception. In B. A. Maher (Ed.), *Progress in experimental personality research* (Vol. 1). New York: Academic Press, 1964.

Crow, W. J. *Process vs. achievement and generality over objects and judging tasks.* Presented at the American Psychological Association Symposium on New Frontiers in Person Perception Research, 1960.

Daly, E. M., Abramovich, R., and Pliner, P. The relationship between mothers' encoding and their children's decoding of facial expression of emotion. *Merrill-Palmer Quarterly,* 1980, *29,* 25-34.

Danish, S. J., and Kagan, N. Measurement of affective sensitivity: Toward a valid measure of interpersonal perception. *Journal of Counseling Psychology,* 1971, *18,* 51-54.

Darwin, C. *Expressions of the emotions in man and animals.* London: John Murray, 1872.

DePaulo, B. M., and Rosenthal, R. Ambivalence, discrepancy and deception in nonverbal communication. In R. Rosenthal (Ed.), *Skill in nonverbal communication.* Cambridge, MA: Oelgeschlager, Gunn & Hain, 1979. (a)

DePaulo, B. M., and Rosenthal, R. Age changes in nonverbal decoding skills: Evidence for increasing differentiation. *Merrill-Palmer Quarterly,* 1979, *25,* 145-150. (b)

DePaulo, B., Rosenthal, R., Eisenstat, R., Rogers, P., and Finkelstein, S. Decoding discrepant nonverbal cues. *Journal of Personality and Social Psychology,* 1978, *36,* 313-323.

Dickman, H. R. The perception of behavior units. In R. G. Barker (Ed.), *The stream of behavior.* New York: Appleton-Century-Crofts, 1963.

Duval, S., and Wicklund, R. A. *A theory of objective self-awareness.* New York: Academic Press, 1972.

Ehrlich, H. J., and Graeven, D. B. Reciprocal self-disclosure in a dyad. *Journal of Experimental Social Psychology,* 1971, *7,* 389-400.

Ekman, P., and Friesen, W. V. Nonverbal leakage and clues to deception. *Psychiatry,* 1969, *32,* 88-105.

Ekman, P., and Friesen, W. V. Constants across cultures in the face and emotion. *Journal of Personality and Social Psychology,* 1971, *17,* 124-129.

Ekman, P., and Friesen, W. V. Nonverbal behavior and psychopathology. In R. J. Friedman and H. M. Katz (Eds.), *The psychology of depression: Contemporary theory and research.* New York: John Wiley, 1974. (a)

Ekman, P., and Friesen, W. V. Detecting deception from the body or face. *Journal of Personality and Social Psychology,* 1974, *29,* 288-298. (b)

Ekman, P., and Friesen, W. V. *Unmasking the face.* Englewood Cliffs, NJ: Prentice-Hall, 1975.

Elkind, D. Cognitive growth cycles in mental development. In J. K. Cole (Ed.), *Nebraska Symposium on Motivation* (Vol. 19). Lincoln: University of Nebraska Press, 1971.

Eysenck, H. J. *The biological basis of personality.* Springfield, IL: Charles C Thomas, 1967.

Feshbach, N. D., and Roe, K. Empathy in six and seven year olds. *Child Development,* 1968, *39,* 135-145.

Field, T. M., and Walden, T. A. Perception and production of facial expressions in infancy and early childhood. In H. Reese and L. Lipsett (Eds.), *Advances in child development and behavior* (Vol. 16). New York: Academic Press, 1982.

Field, T., and Walden, T. Production and discrimination of facial expressions by preschool children. *Child Development,* forthcoming.

Fields, B., and O'Sullivan, M. *Convergent validation of five person perception measures.* Paper presented at the meeting of the Western Psychological Association, 1976.

Gibson, J. J. *The senses considered as perceptual systems.* Boston: Houghton-Mifflin, 1966.

Gibson, J. J. The theory of affordances. In R. E. Shaw and J. Bransford (Eds.), *Perceiving, acting and knowing: Toward an ecological psychology.* Hillsdale, NJ: Lawrence Erlbaum, 1977.

Gitter, G., Mostofsky, D., and Quincy, A. Race and sex differences in the child's perception of emotion. *Child Development,* 1971, *42,* 2071-2075.

Goodman, N. R. *Determinants of the perceptual organization of ongoing action and emotion behavior.* Unpublished doctoral dissertation, University of Connecticut, 1980.

Gottman, J. *Marital interaction: Experimental investigations.* New York: Academic Press, 1979.

Gray, J. A. The psychophysiological nature of introversion-extraversion: A modification of Eysencks' theory. In V. D. Nebylitsyn and J. A. Gray (Eds.), *Biological bases of individual behavior.* New York: Academic Press, 1972.

Hall, J. A. Gender effects in decoding nonverbal cues. *Psychological Bulletin,* 1978, *85,* 845-857.

Heil, J. What Gibson's missing. *Journal of the Theory of Social Behavior,* 1979, *9,* 265-269.

Hochberg, J. Perception: Toward the recovery of a definition. *Psychological Review,* 1956, *63,* 400-405.

Huston, T. L., and Levinger, G. Interpersonal attraction and relationships. *Annual Review of Psychology,* 1978, *29,* 119-156.

Izard, C. E. *Face of emotion.* New York: Appleton, 1971.

Jones, H. E. The study of patterns of emotional expression. In M. Reymert (Ed.), *Feelings and emotions.* New York: McGraw-Hill, 1950.

Jones, H. E. The longitudinal method in the study of personality. In I. Iscoe and H. W. Stevenson (Eds.), *Personality development in children.* Chicago: University of Chicago Press, 1960.

Jung, C. G. [*The integration of personality*] (S. M. Dell, trans.). New York: Farrar & Rinehart, 1939.

Kagan, N. I. *Affective sensitivity test: Validity and reliability.* Paper presented at the meeting of the American Psychological Association, San Francisco, 1977.

Kahn, M. Nonverbal communication and marital satisfaction. *Family Process,* 1970, *9,* 449-456.

Kalliopuska, M. Influence of children's position in the family on recognition of emotional impression. *Psychological Reports,* 1981, *49,* 1001-1002.

Kenny, D. A., and Nasby, W. Splitting the reciprocity correlation. *Journal of Personality and Social Psychology,* 1980, *38,* 249-256.

Kenny, D. A. Interpersonal perception: A multivariate round-robin analysis. In M. B. Brewer and B. E. Collins (Eds.), *Scientific inquiry and the social sciences.* San Francisco: Jossey-Bass, 1981.

Klaiman, S. *Selected perceptual, cognitive, personality, and socialization variables as predictors of nonverbal sensitivity.* Unpublished doctoral dissertation, University of Ottawa, 1979.

Konstadt, N., and Forman, E. Field dependence and external directness. *Journal of Personality and Social Psychology,* 1965, *1,* 490-493.

LaBarbera, J. D., Izard, C. E., Viteze, P., and Parisi, S. A. Four- and six-month-old infants' visual responses to joy, anger and neutral expressions. *Child Development,* 1976, *47,* 535-538.

Lanzetta, J. T., and Orr, S. P. Influence of facial expressions on the classical conditioning of fear. *Journal of Personality and Social Psychology,* 1980, *39,* 1081-1087.

Linehan, E. J. The trouble with dolphins. *National Geographic,* 1979, *155,* 506-541.

Neisser, U. *Cognition and reality.* San Francisco: W. H. Freeman, 1976.

Nelson, C. A., Morse, P. A., and Leavitt, L. A. Recognition of facial expressions by seven-month-old infants. *Child Development,* 1979, *50,* 1239-1242.

Nevill, D. Experimental manipulation of dependency motivation and its effects on eye contact and measures of field dependency. *Journal of Personality and Social Psychology,* 1974, *29,* 72-79.

Newtson, D. Foundations of attribution: The perception of ongoing behavior. In J. H. Harvey, W. J. Ickes, and R. F. Kidd (Eds.), *New directions in attribution research* (Vol. 1). New York: John Wiley, 1976.

Ohman, A., and Dimberg, U. Facial expressions as conditioned stimuli for electrodermal responses: A case of "preparedness"? *Journal of Personality and Social Psychology,* 1978, *36,* 1251-1258.

Olds, M. E., and Fobes, J. L. The central basis of motivation: Intracranial self-stimulation studies. *Annual Review of Psychology,* 1981, *32,* 523-576.

O'Sullivan, M., and Hagar, J. *Measuring person perception: New techniques, old problems.* Unpublished manuscript, San Francisco, 1980.

Pavlov, I. P. [*Conditioned reflexes*] (G. V. Anrep, trans.). Oxford: Clarendon Press, 1927.

Pendleton, K. L., and Snyder, S. S. Young children's perception of others. *Journal of Nonverbal Behavior,* forthcoming.

Piaget, J. Piaget's theory. In P. Mussen (Ed.) *Handbook of child development* (Vol. 1). New York: John Wiley, 1971.

Rosenthal, R., and DePaulo, B. Sex differences in accommodation in nonverbal communication. In R. Rosenthal (Ed.), *Skill in nonverbal communication.* Cambridge, MA: Oelgeshlager, Gunn & Hain, 1979.

Rosenthal, R., Hall, J. A., DiMatteo, M. R., Rogers, P. L., and Archer, C. *Sensitivity to nonverbal communication: The PONS test.* Baltimore: Johns Hopkins University Press, 1979.

Rubin, Z. Disclosing oneself to a stranger: Reciprocity and its limits. *Journal of Experimental Social Psychology,* 1975, *11,* 233-260.

Sarmi, C. Children's understanding of display rules for expressive behavior. *Developmental Psychology,* 1979, *15,* 424-429.

Sabatelli, R., Buck, R., and Dreyer, A. Communication via facial cues in intimate dyads. *Personality and Social Psychology Bulletin,* 1980, *6,* 242-247.

Sabatelli, R., Buck, R., and Dreyer, A. *Nonverbal communication accuracy in married couples: Relationships with marital complaints.* Manuscript submitted for publication, 1981. (a)

Sabatelli, R., Buck, R., and Dreyer, A. *Locus of control, interpersonal trust, and nonverbal communication accuracy.* Manuscript submitted for publication, 1981. (b)

Sabatelli, R., Dreyer, A., and Buck, R. Cognitive style and the sending and receiving of facial cues. *Perceptual and Motor Skills,* 1979, *49,* 203-212.

Sackett, G. P. Monkeys reared in isolation with pictures as visual input: Evidence for an innate releasing mechanism. *Science,* 1966, *154,* 1468-1473.

Sousa-Poza, J. F., Rohrberg, R., and Shulman, E. Field dependence and self-disclosure. *Perceptual and Motor Skills,* 1973, *36,* 735-738.

Snyder, M. Self monitoring of expressive behavior. *Journal of Personality and Social Psychology,* 1974, *30,* 526-537.

Snyder, M. Self monitoring processes. *Advances in Experimental Social Psychology,* 1979, *12,* 85-128.

Tagiuri, R., and Petrullo, L. (Eds.). *Person perception and interpersonal behavior.* Stanford, CA: Stanford University Press, 1958.

Tucker, D. M. Lateral brain function, emotion, and conceptualization. *Psychological Bulletin,* 1981, *89,* 19-46.

Warner, R. M., Kenny, D. A., and Stoto, M. A new round robin analysis of variance for social interaction data. *Journal of Personality and Social Psychology,* 1979, *38,* 1742-1757.

Young-Browne, G., Rosenfeld, H. M., and Horowitz, F. D. Infant discrimination of facial expressions. *Child Development*, 1977, *48*, 555-562.

Zuckerman, M., Blanck, P. D., DePaulo, B. M., and Rosenthal, R. Developmental changes in decoding discrepant and nondiscrepant nonverbal cues. *Developmental Psychology*, 1980, *16*, 220-228.

Zuckerman, M., and Przewuzman, S. Decoding and encoding facial expressions in preschool-age children. *Environmental Psychology and Nonverbal Behavior*, 1979, *3*, 147-163.

Chapter 8

MEASURING INDIVIDUAL DIFFERENCES

Maureen O'Sullivan

SOME FACE-TO-FACE encounters proceed with clarity and smoothness; others are confused and confusing. These differences in social interactions may reflect the interaction competence of the people involved. The term "interaction competence" is similar to what has previously been called social skill (Trower et al., 1978), social intelligence (Thorndike, 1920), behavioral intelligence (Guilford, 1967), empathy (Hogan, 1969), or inter-personal competence (Stricker, 1982). The research of these authors suggests that people differ in their social or interactional abilities and that these differences among individuals can be assessed.

In this chapter, "interaction competence" is used to refer to two conceptually different abilities: (1) the ability to understand the thoughts, feelings, and intentions of others as they are expressed in nonverbal cues (which has been called decoding ability), and (2) the ability to express or communicate one's own thoughts and feelings adequately and correctly to another person, either verbally or nonverbally (which has been called encoding ability).

The concept of interaction competence has a long history. This chapter provides an historical review of efforts in the domain, highlighting the need for construct validity. Then it presents and illustrates a model of construct validity by reviewing two recently developed interaction competence measures.

MEASURING INTERACTION DECODING
COMPETENCE, 1888-1982

Four different and largely nonoverlapping streams of research have addressed the problem of how to measure differences in interaction decoding competence: (1) the intellectual skills approach, (2) the post-diction paradigm, (3) the facial-expression recognition paradigm, and (4) the nonverbal cues approach.

THE INTELLECTUAL SKILLS APPROACH (1920-1975)

Although early investigators such as Rudolph (1903), Piderit (1888), and Feleky (1914) were interested in differences among people in their capacity to recognize facial expressions and body postures, Thorndike (1920) differentiated this ability theoretically from others. Thorndike suggested that there are three kinds of human intelligence: verbal intelligence, dealing with abstract ideas and words; mechanical intelligence, dealing with the capacity to work with three-dimensional, concrete objects, such as machinery and sculpture; and social intelligence, "the ability to understand and manage men and women, . . . to act wisely in human relations" (p. 124).

The George Washington Tests of Social Intelligence (Moss et al., 1927) were devised to measure Thorndike's hypothesized construct of social intelligence. These early tests included subtests of the ability to solve verbally stated social problems, to identify verbally described facial expressions, and to identify photographs of individuals from memory. To demonstrate that there was a separate social intelligence, it was necessary to show that these tests measured something other than verbal or abstract intelligence. Unfortunately, this evidence of discriminant validity was not forthcoming. Woodrow (1939) and Thorndike (1936) administered the George Washington Tests in a large battery of intelligence measures. Factor analyses indicated that the social intelligence tests were merely alternate forms of the general intelligence tests; they measured the same kinds of intellectual factors. This meant not only that the tests were invalid measures of the construct of social intelligence, but also that there was no evidence for a separate social intelligence. In failing to validate that the tests measured social intelligence, the construct of social intelligence itself was also undermined.

In this same period, Chapin (1942) suggested a measure of social insight. This was a longer and more sophisticated version of the social problems subtest of the George Washington series. In 1965, Gough resurrected this measure with new norm and validity data. Its verbal problem format, however, may contribute an unwanted amount of verbal ability variance.

The next research effort using an intellectual skills approach was that of Wedeck (1947). His innovation was to construct measures that used nonverbal stimuli, such as photographs and drawings, rather than primarily verbal stimuli. Wedeck was able to identify a separate factor that he termed "psychological ability." This was the first demonstration of a unique social skill. His work was published in England, however, at a time when interest in the question of social intelligence was not high; also, it used a method of factor analysis that was unfamiliar in the United States. Consequently, Wedeck's work has not been properly recognized.

In the early 1960s, O'Sullivan et al. (1965) started a series of studies of behavioral intelligence. His Structure of Intellect Model suggested that Thorndike's two-faceted social intelligence might be better understood as a domain of thirty independent kinds of behavioral intelligence. These factors of behavioral intelligence were subdivided into five different intellectual operations: cognition, evaluation, memory, convergent production, and divergent production. Each of these intellectual operations was performed on six kinds of intellectual products: units, classes, relations, systems, implications, and transformations. (Five operations times six products gives thirty intellectual abilities). Cognition of behavioral units means understanding behavioral units, such as discrete facial expressions and vocal intonations. Cognition of behavioral relations means understanding the social-emotional relationship between two people; cognition of behavioral systems means understanding social systems of three or more people.

Guilford and his students carried out two major test development and validation studies, one in the area of behavioral cognition (O'Sullivan et al., 1965) and the other in behavioral divergent production or social creativity (Hendricks et al., 1969). In the behavioral cognition study, twenty-three social intelligence tests were created (O'Sullivan and Guilford, 1975) and the six hypothesized factors were identified. For the behavioral creativity study, twenty-five tests were created and again the six hypothesized factors were identified. The behavioral cognition tests have been administered in other factor analytic studies in the United States (Hendricks et al., 1969; Tenopyr, 1967), as well as in Holland (Rombouts, 1978) and Germany (Jung, 1972). In all of these studies, the hypothesized factors were found, providing support for the validity of the Structure of Intellect constructs and their measures. Although the behavioral intelligence tests show promising factorial validity, their relationships with nonintellectual variables have not been adequately investigated.

THE POSTDICTION PARADIGM (1945-1972)

After World War II, interest in person perception, the ability to understand other people, was heightened by a popular postdiction technique (Dymond, 1949) in which judges completed a rating scale or personality inventory as they thought a stimulus person had completed it. This procedure had the merit of a built-in criterion for accuracy (Archer and Akert, 1977), since the actual scores of the stimulus persons were available. It was a small leap to the inference that people who identified a large percentage of the target person's answers were more empathic—more understanding of differences in other people—than judges who correctly identified a small percentage of such items.

Postdiction paradigms lost popularity when they were severely criticized for their susceptibility to response biases such as halo effects and assumed similarity (Gage and Cronbach, 1955; Campbell, 1955; Hastorf et al., 1955; Crow and Hammond, 1957). "Assumed similarity" refers to the common bias among judges to assume that other people are more or less similar to themselves. If a judge makes such an assumption and is correct (that is, the person being judged is indeed similar to the judge), he or she will receive a high person perception score. The high score, however, is not due to the judge's ability to differentiate among other people, but rather to the fortuitous action of a response bias. If the judge's assumption of similarity were incorrect (the target person was not similar in attitudes or values), a low person perception score would be obtained. In both cases, the postdiction paradigm, so susceptible to assumed similarity error, would not permit a valid assessment of differential accuracy.

Although several researchers (Hastorf et al., 1955) attempted to correct the postdiction paradigm statistically for assumed similarity bias, Cronbach (1955) sounded the death knell for this methodology. Using analysis of variance procedures, Cronbach demonstrated that scores from postdiction measures could be separated into two different sources of variance: one for differences between individuals (differential accuracy) and the other for differences among groups of individuals (stereotypic accuracy). "Differential accuracy" is the term used to identify the construct of interest, the ability to identify differences among other people in their beliefs, personality characteristics, feelings, and so on. "Stereotypic accuracy" denotes the ability to identify characteristics of groups accurately (for example, the usual behavior of young men or middle-aged women). If a target person is representative of the groups to which he or she belongs, a judge who is knowledgeable in this stereotypic sense will receive a high score. The score arises from an unwanted source, however: the capacity to assess stereotypic behavior accurately rather than differences among individuals. Recently, a measure intended to assess stereotypic accuracy was shown to be uncorrelated with a measure of the ability to recognize facial expressions of emotion (Weiss et al., 1981a).

A continuation of the postdiction paradigm is found in the work of Cline (1964). In his procedures, judges watch filmed interviews showing a variety of stimulus persons. Following each interview, judges complete a number of tests. One of these, the Behavior Postdiction Test, asks judges to predict the stimulus person's behavior in a variety of settings. The correct answers are determined not only by asking the stimulus person, but also by consulting five family members or friends. In addition to the Behavior Postdiction Test, the judges are given other measures, such as an adjective-checking task, a content memory task, and a visual memory task (Cline et al., 1972). Cline was one of the first researchers to use moving nonverbal stimuli as test materials (Cline and Richards, 1960).

IDENTIFYING FACIAL EXPRESSIONS
OF EMOTION (1888-1982)

In thinking about the components involved in understanding other people, scientists have long recognized the importance of understanding facial expressions of other people. As early as 1914, Feleky photographed herself posing a variety of facial expressions and examined how accurately people could identify the emotion she intended to express. Boring and Titchener (1923), two eminent early psychologists, studied reactions of students to a schematized drawing suggested by Piderit (1888). Buzby (1924) made an individual differences measure out of six of the Piderit faces and gathered norms on more than 700 students. Ruckmick (1921) developed a series of facial expression photographs to study differences in recognition ability. Langfeld (1918) used drawings from the Rudolph (1903) series to study individual differences in the ability to recognize facial expressions. In doing this, Langfeld explicitly related variations in the scores he obtained to personality differences in his subjects and possible differences in their social behavior.

A different approach was taken by Frois-Wittmann (1930), who photographed himself posing systematically varied facial expressions of emotion. He was far ahead of his time in recognizing the relationship between muscle actions and visible facial changes and in identifying different facial expressions in terms of the different muscle groups involved.

After this early work, interest in differences in the ability to recognize facial expressions of emotion waned. This decrease resulted in part from the experimental work of Landis (1929), which was interpreted to mean that facial expressions of emotion were idiosyncratic and therefore useless as stimuli in an individual differences measure. Excepting the work of Landis (Landis and Hunt, 1939), little research was done on facial expressions during the 1930s and 1940s.

In the 1950s, Woodworth and Schlosberg (1954) initiated a series of studies (Schlosberg, 1954; Engen et al., 1958; Abelson and Sermat, 1962) on the dimensions of emotion using faces as stimuli. These studies, however, were directed not at understanding variations in the ability to recognize facial expressions, but rather at determining the dimensions people used in describing emotional states.

In the 1960s, interest in individual differences in recognizing expressions of emotion was spearheaded by Silvan Tomkins (1962, 1963). He suggested that the face was central to the expression and experience of emotion, and his Primary Affect Measure (Tomkins and McCarter, 1964) provided a model of facial recognition testing, which has been imitated but not significantly improved by later researchers.

The Primary Affect Measure consists of 69 black and white photographs that show the posed expressions of children and adults of both sexes. The photos show neutral expressions as well as expressions of eight affects (fear, surprise, interest, anger, enjoyment, contempt, shame, and distress). The response alternatives are sets of four or five words. Each set reflects various aspects of the intended affect. For example, one set includes distressed, sad, lonely, and pained. Individual differences in the ability to recognize emotion were assessed using two different sets of error scores. One set provided decoding accuracy scores for each of the affects. The other set gave projection scores for each affect—the number of times a given affect was incorrectly used to describe the photos. Tomkins and McCarter suggested that the scores for each examinee be used to generate a profile they called the Affect Sensitivity Contour.

Izard (1971) suggested a similar test using 32 photographs, which he administered to subjects from nine different cultures. This test is less useful than Tomkins and McCarter's, despite its cross-cultural norms, because each of the affects is only represented by four photographs. Ekman and Friesen (1974) suggested another variation of Tomkin's measure called the Brief Affect Recognition Test (BART). This measure presented the stimuli tachistoscopically and used photographs that were superior in photographic quality and facial expression clarity to those used by Tomkins and McCarter or Izard. The BART technique was a first effort by Ekman and his colleagues to devise a test with clear stimuli but a task sufficiently difficult to provide adequate score variance. A more recent effort is the Affect Blend Test (Weiss et al., 1981b). This measure consists of fifty-six color photographs of adult men and women who were instructed to move facial muscles to express a variety of affect blends. A given photograph shows elements of more than one affect—both sadness and happiness, for example. Most of these facial expression recognition tests have been reviewed elsewhere (O'Sullivan, 1982) and will not be discussed further in this chapter. Rather, another, more recently developed test, Leathers and Emigh's (1980) Facial Meaning Sensitivity Test, will be used to represent this genre.

MEASURES USING NONVERBAL CUES
IN MOTION (1964-1982)

Each of the three preceding test traditions recognized, either implicitly or explicitly, the importance of nonverbal cues. All the facial recognition tests used photographic or drawn depictions of faces; early social intelligence tests used facial photographs for one test and verbal descriptions of facial expressions in another. The behavioral cognition tests used nonverbal stimuli, although these were mostly static. The postdiction paradigms used either actual people or videotaped or filmed presentations of them. All of these early measures were produced before audiovisual equipment was sufficiently economical to use in research.

In the 1960s, researchers became increasingly interested in nonverbal behavior per se, and a number of measures were proposed to assess interaction competence by researchers in the "new" field of nonverbal communication. Many of these measures are really continuations of the intellectual skills, the postdiction, or the facial expression research traditions. They can be grouped separately because they use new and different technologies, the nonverbal stimuli are moving, and many of the authors seem unaware of similar work that predates their own. These new nonverbal measures come from a variety of fields within the social sciences—communication, counseling, social psychology, and animal learning.

One of the earliest of these nonverbal researchers is Davitz (1964). He suggested a measure of the ability to recognize emotional states from vocal cues. Rothenberg (1970) also developed a nonverbal measure of vocal sensitivity intended for use with children. Kagan and his colleagues (Campbell et al., 1971; Danish and Kagan, 1971; Kagan et al., 1977) have been assessing differences in the ability to understand emotional communication in counseling and other interpersonal situations for more than ten years. Their measure, the Affective Sensitivity Scale, has multiple forms. The first three versions were black-and-white videotapes of actual client-therapist interactions. The two current versions are attractive 16mm color films of a variety of professional-client interactions: patient and physician, teacher and class, therapist and family, and the like. The Affective Sensitivity Scale is distinguished by its sampling from a variety of people, having a method for determining the accuracy of the criterion judgment and presenting visually attractive and realistic stimuli. Unfortunately, the early videotape versions of the Affective Sensitivity Scale and the later versions are not correlated, and most of the validity work of the Kagan group has been done with the early versions. Therefore, the validity of the current measures, despite their visual appeal, is unclear.

Another appealing nonverbal measure is the Social Interpretations Task (SIT), which was developed by Archer and Akert (1977). These authors were particularly concerned with the problem of determining the "correct" answer in social skills tests; their measure provides an ingenious solution to it. The drawback of SIT as an individual difference measure is its small number of items and the wide range of judgments it requires.

One of the most popular current measures of interaction competence is the Profile of Nonverbal Sensitivity (PONS) (Rosenthal et al., 1979). This measure consists of 220 items in which a single young woman simulates responses to twenty social situations, such as comforting a lost child, helping a customer, or talking about her divorce. Each item consists of one or more nonverbal channels and two verbally described social situations. The 220 nonverbal stimuli include 80 nonredundant ones (20 each for face, body, randomly spliced and content filtered speech) and 140 which are combinations of these same stimuli. The same face is shown alone, with the body, with randomly spliced speech, with a body and randomly spliced speech, and so on. Obviously, the 220 items are not independent samples of the skill being assessed. The basic stimuli of the PONS test have also been used to generate other measures with different names, such as the Nonverbal Discrepancy Test (DePaulo et al., 1978) and the MOVANS or Measure of Verbal and Nonverbal Sensitivity (Blanck and Rosenthal, 1982).

Another measure in the kinetic nonverbal domain is the Communication of Affect Receiving Ability Test (Buck, 1976a). This measure was selected for review since it is discussed in Buck's chapter in this volume and the contrasting points of view regarding it may be of interest.

PERSONALITY MEASURES OF INTERACTION COMPETENCE

All the preceding measures from the skills, postdiction, facial recognition, and nonverbal domain present a problem in interaction competence and ask subjects to solve it. Such measures assume that there is a right answer. Another approach is to assume that people who interact competently have distinctive personality traits, or belief systems, or sets of cognitive information. Researchers proceeding from this starting place have produced a number of "personality" measures that may or may not relate to interaction competence. These include Snyder's (1974) Self-Monitoring Scale, Mehrabian and Epstein's (1972) and Hogan's (1969) empathy measures, and Levenson and Gottman's (1978) social competence scale. (See also Buck's chapter in this volume.)

Since these measures are in the personality domain rather than directly in the area of competence, they are not reviewed in this chapter. It is likely, however, that personality variables may serve an important moderating function in interaction competence. Although some investigators report no consistent correlation between personality variables and interaction competence (Mehrota, 1971), such variables may make their contributions interactively. Shipe et al. (1973), for example, showed that neither need for affiliation nor behavioral cognition alone could predict peer popularity, but that both variables together could.

INTERACTION ENCODING COMPETENCE

Although the literature on interaction encoding competence is not as extensive as that on decoding, similar trends in research can be noted. Encoding usually refers to the nonverbal, expressive abilities of people. In this chapter, interaction encoding competence is defined to include both verbal and nonverbal competence.

THE INTELLECTUAL SKILLS APPROACH

With his definition of social intelligence, which included both understanding and managing other people, Thorndike (1920) initiated the research on both decoding and encoding abilities. Although most research on intellectual abilities emphasizes the decoding aspect, this is not always the case. Guilford (1967), in his Structure of Intellect Model, hypothesizes five factors of behavioral convergent production and five of behavioral divergent production. Behavioral convergent production means producing the one correct solution to a behavioral problem; behavioral divergent production means producing many different behavioral solutions. Although these terms define intellectual operations, they may also describe observable behaviors. For example, convergent production of behavioral units is the encoding of correct behavioral units, such as a facial expression, hand gesture, or vocal intonation. This is similar to what is usually meant by nonverbal encoding ability. In his work on behavioral divergent production, Guilford and his students (Hendricks et al., 1969) produced many different paper-and-pencil tests requiring written verbal responses, but also a few tests of the ability to generate posed facial expressions.

Another line of research in the skills area was initiated by Fredricksen et al. (1957), who suggested an in-basket test of managerial skill. Verbally described interpersonal problems in a business setting were presented to examinees, who responded as they might in a managerial situation.

A recent variation of the in-basket technique is Stricker's (1982) Interpersonal Competence Instrument, in which subjects watch filmed enactments of personnel problems. Subjects respond to the actor as they would in a real-life situation. These responses are audiotaped and scored in a variety of ways. This measure, like that of Fredricksen et al., uses business problems, but the responses require a broad interpersonal understanding as well as the ability to encode it verbally and nonverbally.

THE POSTDICTION PARADIGM

There has been little research on encoding skill within the postdiction paradigm. Cline et al. (1972) mentioned, parenthetically, the marked differences in expressive style among target persons and their effects on person perception. These comments were illustrative, however, and have not been investigated systematically.

THE FACIAL EXPRESSION PARADIGM

As with the postdiction paradigm, little empirical research has been done on facial encoding ability. Most of the early work tended to be anecdotal. Langfeld (1918), in studying the ability to decode facial expressions of emotion, noted that some judges obtained the right answer by imitating the posed expressions and reading these cues kinesthetically. He noted marked individual differences in this ability. Similarly, Landis (1929) reported differences not only in the ability to pose emotional expression, but also in the recognizability of facial expressions made spontaneously in response to various emotional stimuli.

A more recent and more systematized attempt to measure facial encoding ability is the Requested Facial Action Test (Ekman et al., 1980). This videotaped test first asks subjects to make certain verbally described facial movements and then to imitate a series of facial movements made by an actor on the TV screen. This test is a measure of the ability to make deliberate facial movements, not only emotional ones. It may not relate to other emotional or social encoding skills.

THE NONVERBAL PARADIGM

Most of the work in measuring nonverbal encoding skill was initiated by Buck's (1976a) slide-viewing paradigm. In this method, target persons view a series of slides intended to be emotionally arousing. As the target persons view the slides and describe how pleasant they find them, their heads and shoulders are being videotaped. Buck found that target persons differed considerably in how easy or difficult they were to decode. With some target persons, judges could tell how pleasant they said the slides were and what slide type they were viewing at an accuracy level greater than chance. With other target persons judges could not make these determinations at a better than a chance level. Buck, through his research, and especially by making this paradigm available to other researchers, stimulated interest in what the correlates of such encoding ability might be and how it relates to decoding ability. In Buck's research the relationship between encoding and decoding ability has tended to be negative.

Harper and his colleagues (1979) did a series of studies using Buck's paradigm with different slides and an improved design that established the actual affect-arousing capacity of the slides. Their research results did not agree with Buck's, for they found a slightly positive relationship between encoding and decoding ability. However, this relationship was moderated by the sex of the encoders.

Zuckerman and his colleagues (1975, 1976) also did a series of encoding-decoding studies. In some they used a Buck-like paradigm; in others they studied the ability to pose different emotional expressions. Although their results are inconsistent and relate to the format of the encoding task, the general trend suggests a slightly positive relationship between encoding and decoding. At present, the status of the relationship between encoding and decoding is unclear. It seems to be susceptible to the sex of the encoder as well as the particular kind of encoding task performed. Posing different facial expressions and reacting while watching slides do not yield the same results. (See Buck's chapter in this volume for an extensive discussion of this line of research.)

THE QUESTION OF VALIDITY

Although the process is less clear with the encoding measures, the history of the interaction decoding measures shows that the acceptance of a measure depends on its demonstrating its construct validity in some way. In the intellectual skills, postdiction, and facial expression paradigms, measures ceased to be investigated if sufficient evidence accumulated to undermine their construct validity. More recent efforts in the facial expression tradition and in the nonverbal areas have not been examined from this point of view (that is, whether or not they are construct valid). In order to address such an issue, the question of validity and how it is established for a measure needs to be answered. Several different kinds of validity may be distinguished: content validity, criterion validity (both predictive and concurrent), and construct validity.

A test is content valid if it samples the domain of interest adequately. For example, a measure intended to assess the ability to decode emotional expressions using only happy stimuli would not represent the whole domain of emotional expressiveness, but only a part of it. Such a test would not be content valid.

Criterion validity means the ability of a measure to predict or correlate with a criterion, either concurrently or sometime in the future. Predictive criterion validity is established before using high school grades to predict college grades, for example. Insofar as there is a significant positive correlation between high school and college grades, one "predicts" the other, because it precedes it in time.

Concurrent criterion validity means validating one measure against another at the same point in time. A frequent use of concurrent validation is to establish that a shorter measure is highly correlated with a longer one whose validity has already been established. A psychiatric symptom checklist might be validated against a more time-consuming psychiatric interview, for example. Both content and criterion validity are important, especially in solving practical problems. If the goal, however, is to understand what a test is measuring, then construct validity is needed.

Construct validity is based on a process by means of which an investigator demonstrates that a test actually reflects the construct or idea that it is supposed to measure. Merely calling a test a measure of interaction competence does not make it one. There must be evidence at various levels (1) that there is such a nonredundant concept or construct as "interaction competence," (2) that the construct can be operationalized into a measure, (3) that the proposed test actually measures the proposed construct, and (4) that the construct and the test function as theory dictates they should. For example, if one's understanding of interaction competence suggests that people high on this ability would be good therapists, then one way of partially demonstrating construct validity for a measure of interaction competence would be to show that good therapists score higher on the measure than poor therapists. Should good therapists not score higher on the interaction competence test, then several explanations present themselves: (1) The interaction competence test is not valid. (2) The determination of how good the therapists are is in error. (3) The hypothesis relating interaction competence to being a good therapist is incorrect. (4) Intervening variables are moderating the effect of the variables involved (for example, only good therapists in client-centered therapy need to be interactively competent; for behavior therapists, interaction competence is not correlated with their effectiveness).

It has become increasingly clear (Messick, 1975) that construct validity is the type of validity that underlies all others. Unless one knows what is being measured by a test (that is, unless the test's construct validity has been established), the source of its content or criterion validity remains unknown.

A well-known paradigm for exploring the construct validity of a measure is the multitrait, multimethod matrix suggested by Campbell and Fiske (1959), which stresses the importance of determining empirically whether a test measures something independent of its measuring method. In the Campbell and Fiske model, an investigator demonstrates that a construct, such as interaction competence, can be assessed by more than a single measure. Tests of the construct are then developed using at least two different methods. One test method might use verbal stimuli; the other might use audiovisual stimuli. If these two measures were significantly correlated, it would support the belief that the same or a similar construct was being measured by both tests. If two tests using the same method are highly correlated, it is unclear what determines the correlation—the similarity of the testing method or the similarity of the underlying construct. Correlation between two measures using different methods is partial confirmation of the inference that they are assessing the same construct. In the validity model to be presented, the multimethod aspect of the Campbell and Fiske model is renamed *reification validation.*

Another aspect of the Campbell and Fiske model is its multitrait strategy, in which it is demonstrated that the test being validated does not measure previously assessed traits or confounding traits that are not of interest. For example, two tests of interaction competence might be highly correlated because they are both measures of general intelligence. An investigator must establish empirically that his or her measure is unique and does not reflect some other construct that is logically related. The multimethod paradigm suggests what tests may be measuring; the multitrait paradigm suggests what tests may not be measuring. If an interaction competence measure cannot be differentiated from measures of other intellectual abilities (recall the early social intelligence tests), what does this say about the validity of the test—and the construct? Clearly, the test is invalid as a measure of interaction competence. The underlying construct, however, may or may not be invalid. If better measures of interaction competence are devised, the validity of the construct might be supported. Without demonstrating validity for the tests, however, validity for the underlying ideas cannot be assumed. In establishing a multitrait matrix, an investigator depends on his or her understanding of the domain in selecting variables that may be related to the construct of interest. In the test validity model to be described, the multitrait strategy is an important element of an aspect of validation called *elaboration validation.* In some sense, demonstrating construct validity is an unending process. In establishing reification and elaboration validation, an investigator is often limited by the inadequacy of existing measures. In validating a psychiatric symptom checklist, for example, reification validation suggests using an alternative measure, such as self-report of psychiatric symptoms. The validity and reliability of such a measure, however, may be so low that a failure of the measures to converge could easily be the fault of the self-report measure rather than the new symptom checklist.

A FOUR-STAGE VALIDATION MODEL

Many construct validity studies follow the method suggested by Campbell and Fiske. Although their paradigm suggests that clear definitions be drawn between the trait or construct of interest and other potentially confounding traits, this implied aspect of their model is often overlooked. An essential aspect of establishing and demonstrating construct validity is showing not only that the test is valid, but, even more important, that the idea or construct underlying the measure is also valid. To make this aspect of construct validation more obvious, a four-phase model of construct validation will be described and then used to evaluate two interaction decoding measures.

This model of construct validation has four aspects: two primarily conceptual ones, *Conceptualization* and *Operationalization,* and two primarily empirical ones, *Reification* and *Elaboration.* To date, most construct validity research has focused on the empirical stages. By and large, the underlying constructs have been incompletely and inadequately examined, if examined at all. Yet, as Petrinovich (1979: 385) has written, "The investigation of a test's construct validity is not essentially different from the general scientific procedures for developing and confirming theories."

STAGE I: CONCEPTUALIZATION
VALIDATION—DEFINING THE CONSTRUCT

In the first stage of construct validation, the construct of interest is defined and discussed at a logical level. Theory relevant to the construct is reviewed and the relationship of that preexisting theory or a new theory is made clear. Essentially, the test author says what he or she is trying to measure. At least four different approaches to assessing the decoding aspects of interaction competence have been differentiated (the intellectual skills, postdiction, facial expression, and nonverbal strategies). Others might be relevant as well. In proposing an interaction competence measure, an author needs either to relate the new test and its construct to a part of the existing literature or specifically to exclude it. The new construct needs to be embedded in, or contrasted with, existing constructs and measures at a theoretical level. Often this is not done.

A second aspect of clarifying one's construct is providing a clear and nonredundant terminology for it. As Wiemann and Backlund (1980: 186) have noted, "The orderly development of any new theory demands clear, generally acceptable definitions for the key words associated with that theory." At the beginning of this chapter, I indicated the plethora of terms in the field (social intelligence, person perception, interaction competence, and so on). These terms may refer to more or less the same thing, or they may not. When devising a test, however, exactly what one wishes to measure should be clear and should be reflected in a readily understood terminology.

The third aspect of conceptualization validation is determining at a logical level that there is congruence between the construct of interest and the task chosen to measure it. Often, difficulty in measuring what one really wishes to measure leads to measuring what one *can* measure. Unless what is actually being measured reflects the construct of interest, conceptualization validation is threatened. For example, facial photographs could be used as stimuli to assess a number of different abilities. A task requiring the use of simple words to label the emotions in the photographs might measure emotion recognition ability. A task to identify the social class of the photographed people might be assessing another kind of social skill. A task requiring recognition of the faces in the photographs at a later point in time is probably concerned with memory. It is unlikely that scores from these three tests would be highly correlated with one another. Even though the stimuli used are identical, the test tasks are sufficiently dissimilar that different psychological processes would probably be tapped by them. In the factor-analytic study of the behavioral cognition tests, a cartoon test of logical reasoning was used to show that the cartoon format of the behavioral cognition measures was not their major source of variance. Despite the cartoon format, the logical reasoning test loaded on verbal factors; the behavioral cognition tests did not. Thus, the construct validity of a measure is based on more than its appearance. The visual appeal of a test will affect its "face validity" (how valid the test looks to a user), but face validity is not psychometric validity and should not be confused with it. The kind of task a test requires is the major element in determining test scores.

STAGE II: OPERATIONALIZATION–SPECIFYING
ALTERNATIVE MEASURES

Specifying alternative ways to measure a construct is necessary in validating a construct. If only a single measure of a construct is conceived, it is unclear whether scores are specific to a single measuring technique or reflect a general construct that may be assessed through other kinds of observations. Ideally, the researcher conceives and produces several different methods or tests expected to measure the same construct. O'Sullivan et. al. (1965), for example, constructed three or four different tests for each of their six hypothesized behavioral cognition factors. Kagan and his colleagues (1977) produced five alternative forms of the Affective Sensitivity Scale, using two different test formats.

A second approach to specifying measures of the construct is to indicate the measures of other authors that should measure the same or a similar construct. Scores on the PONS, for example, have been correlated with scores on CARAT and CARAT-like tasks. The behavioral cognition tests have been correlated with PONS and other nonverbal and social skills tests (Fields and O'Sullivan, 1976).

A third approach to specifying alternative measures is to elicit different responses to the same stimulus set. For example, Buck (1976a) generated two decoding scores from a single set of stimuli. If these two scores are measures of the same construct, they should correlate with one another. If they are measures of different constructs, as Buck et al. (1972) suggest, validity must be established for each score separately in the same manner as for the whole test.

A fourth approach to specifying alternative measures concerns the items of a single test. When researchers suggest different items for a test, they are suggesting that each item is an alternative measure of the construct. Therefore, the items of a test measuring a single construct should be highly correlated with one another. This relationship among the items of a test is known as the measure's internal consistency. Although usually used to describe a measure's reliability, an internal consistency coefficient may also be regarded as validity evidence, because it reveals whether the items of a test are measuring the same construct. Although high internal consistency is neither a necessary nor a sufficient demonstration of validity, low internal consistency undermines the presumption that a single construct is being measured. If the same stimuli are used repeatedly in the same test, the usual internal consistency estimates may be spuriously high. Idiosyncratic responses to often repeated stimuli or response alternatives may erroneously inflate consistency over the whole test.

STAGE III: REIFICATION–RELATIONS
AMONG MEASURES IN THE DOMAIN

After clarifying the construct and specifying methods for measuring it, the next stage of construct validation is to demonstrate that different measures of the construct relate to one another. Reification validation has already been discussed as the multimethod aspect of the Campbell and Fiske model. Unless an investigator can measure a construct in several different ways, the validity of a construct remains unsubstantiated. Conversely, by demonstrating that tests hypothesized to correlate significantly do so, an investigator supports the validity not only of the construct, but also of its measures.

Constructing tests is a time-consuming and expensive process. Having successfully devised one test, many researchers fail to complete the process and produce a second or third. Until alternate measures are suggested, however, reification validation may not proceed. Many measures of interaction competence cannot be adequately validated because they lack alternative measures.

STAGE IV: ELABORATION–RELATIONS
WITH OTHER CONSTRUCTS

One aspect of elaboration validation, discriminant validity, is similar to the multitrait phase of the Campbell-Fiske model. In establishing discriminant validity, the investigator demonstrates that variables or constructs that are not theoretically related to the construct are not empirically related to it either. The discriminant validity established for the behavioral cognition tests and for PONS is the kind of multitrait demonstration that is required. With both these measures, it was possible to show that they did not measure a potentially confounding variable, namely general intelligence. The demonstration of this kind of discriminant validity opens the door to further investigation of these measures as indicators of a new kind of social, emotional, or intellectual skill. An important aspect of construct validation, then, is demonstrating what a test does *not* measure.

It is equally important to establish its convergent validity. In the Campbell-Fiske model, convergent validity refers to the convergence or significant correlation among different methods of measuring the same construct (what is called reification validation in this four-stage model). It is also important in validating constructs and tests to show convergence of one's measures with theoretically related constructs. Just as discriminant validity establishes the existence of a new construct, convergent validity enhances and refines its comprehension.

In pursuing convergent validation, a test author relates her measure to as many variables as possible. Preferably, the relationship of the measure to the network of variables with which convergent validity is sought is predicted beforehand. If the predicted relationships cannot be found, then the measure or its relationship with the other variables needs to be examined. The authors of PONS have done an exceptionally creative job in establishing convergent validity for their measure. They have demonstrated that scores on PONS are significantly related to popularity, being the mother of a preverbal child, being a successful foreign service officer, being an artist or musician, and numerous other behaviorally based criteria (Rosenthal et al., 1979). Their attempts to relate PONS to a wide array of personality measures have been less successful, but that may be due to the psychometric limitations of the personality measures rather than those of the PONS.

Demonstrating convergent validity in this way is an empirical endeavor. The numerical size and statistical significance of the correlation coefficients obtained is a matter of fact. Interpreting the meaning of a correlation matrix is a matter of perspective. With PONS, for example, Rosenthal and his colleagues interpret the correlations they have found as convergent validation of the PONS as a measure of nonverbal sensitivity (as its title suggests). O'Sullivan and Hager (1982), however, interpret the same findings as evidence that the PONS measures a social skill of some kind, but they reject the interpretation that this social skill is much related to nonverbal sensitivity. They base their alternative interpretation on the inadequate validation efforts with PONS at the Conceptualization, Operationalization, and Reification stages. Different interpretations of the same data highlight the importance of adequate theoretical underpinnings in empirical research. Although both reification and elaboration validation are essentially empirical endeavors, the interpretations made of the data obtained will organize and guide future research on the measures.

A CRITIQUE OF TWO MEASURES

The utility of the above model may be demonstrated by using it to evaluate two interaction competence measures: the Facial Meaning Sensitivity Test (FMST) and the Communication of Affect Receiving Ability Test (CARAT). Both of these measures are attempts to assess a particular aspect of interaction decoding competence, the ability to recognize facial expressions of emotion. As such, they represent only a small part of the domain of interaction competence, but the construct validity questions they raise are germane to all interaction competence measures. Although these tests are similar in attempting to measure facial expression recognition ability, they are different in their states of development. The FMST is a new test (Leathers and Emigh, 1980) whose lack of certain validation information may be due to its newness. CARAT, on the other hand, has been available for some time (1976a) and has been used in a number of research studies.

SIMPLE DECODING: FACIAL MEANING SENSITIVITY TEST (FMST)

The FMST (Leathers and Emigh, 1980) consists of forty photographs of the facial expressions of a single young woman; ten of the photographs are used in Part I, and thirty are used in Part II. In Part I, subjects choose one of ten broad affect labels (anger, happiness, bewilderment, fear, interest, sadness, contempt, disgust, determination, or surprise) to go with each of the ten photos. In Part II, subjects select sets of three photographs for each of the ten broad affect labels. After this selection, more specific affect labels are assigned within each set. Contempt, for example, is subdivided into disdain, arrogance, and superiority. The subject matches each of the contempt photos with one of three contempt labels (disdain, arrogance, or superiority). Reliability estimates for groups of decoders (computed using tests for homogeneity and intraclass correlations) are good. The reliability for individual scores, however, has not been reported. Since the ceiling on this test is quite low (most subjects obtain high scores on the test) the resulting restriction in score range might contribute to relatively low reliability.

Leathers and Emigh have done a good job at the conceptualization (Stage I) level of construct validation. They refer to most of the major researchers in the area of facial expressions of emotion and make it clear where they are agreeing with these authors and where they are disagreeing. They clearly state their purpose in developing the test: "to determine how specialized are the meanings that can be decoded from facial expressions . . . and . . . demonstrate how the instrument can be used to measure a receiver's current level of skill in decoding facial expression" (1980: 419). This clear statement of purpose, however, contains two different goals: the general theoretical one, of determining whether subjects can distinguish among relatively fine grades of emotional expression, and the individual differences one, of providing a measure of decoding skill. Although both purposes can be achieved by a single instrument, it usually takes more than a single research study to do so. Evidence is usually gathered from a number of studies in support of the general theoretical position, and then the results of such studies are used to produce an individual differences measure.

Another source of theoretical confusion with the FMST is whether it is intended as a measure of a general decoding ability in the facial expression domain or whether ten different emotional decoding scores are to result from it. Leathers and Emigh might not yet be ready to commit themselves on this issue. It should be addressed at the theoretical level, however, as a guide to interpreting future research.

The second aspect of conceptualization validation, providing a clear terminology, is less clearly achieved by the authors of the FMST. Although their term "facial meaning sensitivity" is nonredundant, it is also relatively nonspecific. Facial meaning could refer to static characteristics of the face, such as its attractiveness, its color, whether it looks intelligent, sexy, and so on. Since the FMST is intended as a measure of sensitivity to aspects of emotional expression, the term "meaning sensitivity" may be too broad.

In terms of task-construct congruence, the task of the FMST seems appropriate. The verbal labeling task seems relatively benign, although there may be some general intelligence variance involved in using the more unfamiliar labels, such as bewilderment, and in distinguishing, verbally, disgust from contempt.

Although the conceptualization validation of this instrument is good, there is relatively little construct validation evidence at the other three stages. In terms of operationalization validation, Leathers and Emigh have devised only a single test method and have represented each affect and affect "grade" with few items. A further threat to operationalization validation is the lack of stimulus sampling, since only a single young woman is portrayed in the FMST. In validating their test operations, the FMST authors used several methods of establishing the accuracy of their criterion: the poser's self-report, muscle-movement involvement, and judges' ratings. These three sources of evidence constituted a useful approach to specifying the characteristics of the stimuli, especially since they were all directed toward the appearance on the poser's face of affect cues.

Since no alternative test method for the FMST has been devised and no measures of other authors have been suggested as alternatives (as required by operationalization validation), reification validation cannot proceed. Without reification validation, elaboration validation evidence is difficult to interpret. In any case, there is no evidence that scores on the FMST relate to other variables in an interesting or predictable way. Although the FMST looks like a measure of the ability to recognize facial expressions of emotion (that is, it is face valid), this does not mean that it is one.

Demonstrating construct validity is a long and arduous process. The authors of the FMST have taken only the first step in demonstrating it for their measure.

COMPLEX DECODING: COMMUNICATION OF AFFECT RECEIVING ABILITY TEST (CARAT)

CARAT was designed to measure " 'nonverbal receiving ability' or the ability to accurately decode the affective state of another person based on . . . nonverbal behaviors" (Buck, 1976a: 162). The 32 stimuli in CARAT are 25 individuals viewing slides of four types: unusual, unpleasant, sexual, and scenic. The faces and shoulders of these individuals are videotaped as they view the slides and verbally report how pleasant or unpleasant they feel, using a nine-point rating scale. These videotapes are then shown without sound to observers, who rate how pleasant the stimulus person was feeling and choose which of the four slide types was being watched. The test yields two scores: (1) the correlation between the stimulus persons' self-ratings of pleasantness and each observer's ratings of their pleasantness, and (2) the number of correct slide category judgments.

The alpha reliability for an earlier version of CARAT was .52. The test-retest reliability for the pleasantness score has been variable, from very high to as low as −.18. Many of these reliability coefficients were determined on early versions of CARAT only, and further evidence on reliability of the current version is necessary.

Although there are many problems with CARAT, it offers a significant advantage over almost all available interaction decoding competence measures. The stimuli in CARAT occur naturally—are not posed like those in the FMST or widely used instruments like the PONS. Other aspects of CARAT are less impressive.

In terms of conceptualization validation, the status of CARAT remains unclear. Although Buck (1976b, 1980) is obviously knowledgeable about theories of emotion, the relationship of CARAT to a theory of emotion has never been explicated. Recall that CARAT offers two different scores: one based on accuracy of pleasantness ratings, the other on accuracy in choosing slide categories. The emotion domain has been variously described. It could be seen as a domain marked by bipolar dimensions of pleasantness-unpleasantness and attention-rejection. Alternatively, it could be defined as a set of categories of affects—such as fear, anger, or sadness—that are not necessarily reducible to bipolar dimensions. By using both kinds of scores for his measure and not describing why he does so, Buck leaves a major theoretical area unclarified. If it is unclear which construct is being measured or whether both are, the attempt to validate the measure and its construct(s) remains unguided.

In terms of definitional clarity, the same issue may be raised. What does "affect" mean in CARAT? Since affect is a widely used term in the social sciences, a unique term or a clearer explanation of the sense in which "affect" is being used is necessary. With respect to task-construct congruence, conceptualization validation is incomplete. In the CARAT paradigm, it is presumed that watching slides is a sufficient stimulus to arouse emotion. This has not been demonstrated by Buck. Using a similar methodology, Harper et al. (1979) had judges rate how emotionally aroused they felt while watching slides. This is one approach to the issue but not a complete solution. Even if judges rate a slide as emotionally arousing, this is not evidence that the emotion actually was aroused, or, if aroused, that it was shown on the face, or, if shown on the face, that it was a stimulus pattern that could reasonably be associated with an emotional state. In the CARAT paradigm, subjects talk about how they are feeling about the slides as they view them. This cognitive task may distort whatever emotion-arousing potential the slides have. For some subjects, talking about their emotional reactions may heighten them; for others, the cognitive organization involved in discussing their feelings may diminish or extinguish them. What the videotaped stimuli in CARAT represent, then, is problematic.

Buck et al. (1980) have undertaken to study the naturally occurring social units in these videotape materials using Newtson's unitization procedure. While the unitization procedure is a new approach to studying social psychological phenomena, it is unclear what relationship such a procedure has to verifying the presence in the materials of facial affective cues. Buck himself notes (see Buck's chapter) that an Action Focus and an Emotion Focus instruction in the unitization procedure give different results. Yet, he did not use an Emotion Focus in his own unitization research. Since a number of facial coding systems are now available (Ekman and Friesen, 1978), the use of one of them would seem to be a more salient method of examining the stimulus materials for affective cues. Another conceptual issue with CARAT is the extent to which its method is susceptible to the same limitations of halo effects and assumed similarity response bias of the early postdiction measures.

In terms of operationalization validation, the status of CARAT is unclear. The test produces two different scores: one for the pleasantness ratings and the other for the accuracy of the category judgments. Early in his research program, Buck et al. (1972) seemed to suggest that these reflected two different abilities. Later, Buck (1976) suggested that a significant correlation ($r = .31$) between these two scores indicated a general decoding ability. If the scores are intended to be different measures of the same construct, then this is acceptable operationalization validation. If they are intended as measures of two different abilities, then their significant correlation undermines that presumption.

Buck himself has reported little reification validation evidence. What has been reported (see Buck's chapter) is not promising. Rosenthal and his colleagues (1979), in validating the PONS, have reported both significant and insignificant correlations between PONS and CARAT. Further work needs to be done with CARAT at this level of construct validation.

In terms of elaboration validation, Buck has reported a number of interesting findings, such as the relationship between encoding scores on CARAT and physiological measures such as heart rate and GSR. (He finds an inverse relationship. People who are good encoders show less physiological arousal.) Buck has also examined the relationship between decoding strangers (as in CARAT) and decoding someone well known, like a dating partner (Sabatelli et al., 1980). A children's version of CARAT has also been developed for use in developmental research. Although these kinds of elaboration validation studies provide exactly the kind of evidence that should be gathered in establishing the construct validity of a measure, the interpretation of them is unclear, since what CARAT actually measures has not been adequately examined.

At a logical level, a question can be raised about whether the stimulus persons in CARAT are either experiencing or expressing emotion. They are obviously behaving in different ways, but in what ways is unclear. Had CARAT been shown to relate to other measures that more obviously assess the ability to recognize facial expressions of emotion, its construct validity would be more convincing. Without demonstrating that CARAT is a measure of the ability to "receive affect," experiments using it as a measure cannot be interpreted as evidence of how such ability functions.

CONCLUSION

The very concreteness of psychological tests and their scores is both the basis of their appeal and the source of their scientific weakness. It is easy to assume that a test with an adequate score distribution, which relates in an interesting way to other variables, must measure something of value. The history of attempts to measure interaction competence clearly suggests that this is not so. Four different research traditions involved in measuring interaction competence were outlined. In each of them, the inability to demonstrate the construct validity of the underlying ideas, as well as that of their measures, led to the eventual discrediting of that research effort. In recent years, a number of investigators have attempted to measure interaction competence using nonverbal cues. Many of these newer techniques share the shortcomings of earlier tests: inadequate construct definition; few, if any, alternative measures; uncontrolled response biases; and instrument unreliability.

I suggest a four-stage construct validation model that extends the multimethod, multitrait model of Campbell and Fiske. In validating tests, the ideas on which they are based are also verified or disproved. Although empirical relations with other tests and other variables are central to the process of construct validation, a more basic and overriding task is an adequate explanation of the theory and construct the test is intended to measure. The four-stage validation model explicates the need for adequate conceptualization and operationalization in establishing construct validity.

Most test constructors are aware of the necessity for empirical evidence about their measure. Many, however, neglect the theoretical work that supports the evidence obtained later, at the reification and elaboration stages of construct validation. The model has been used both to show the work that needs to be done in proceeding to validate a new test, the Facial Meaning Sensitivity Test, and to improve the previous validation efforts with an older measure, the Communication of Affect Receiving Ability Test.

Given what we know about nonverbal variables, it appears likely that communication researchers will devote increasing attention to the development of nonverbal instruments. This has great potential. But unless we attend to the lessons of the past, we may be condemned to the same failures that frustrated earlier investigators.

REFERENCES

Abelson, R. P., and Sermat, V. Multidimensional scaling of facial expressions. *Journal of Experimental Psychology,* 1962, *63,* 546-554.

Archer, D., and Akert, R. M. Words and everything else: Verbal and nonverbal cues in social interpretation. *Journal of Personality and Social Psychology,* 1977, *35,* 443-449.

Blanck, P. D., and Rosenthal, R. Developing strategies for decoding "leaky" messages: On learning how and when to decode discrepant and consistent social communications. In R. S. Feldman (Ed.), *The development of nonverbal behavior in children.* New York: Springer, 1982.

Boring, E. G., and Titchener, E. B. A model for the demonstration of facial expressions. *American Journal of Psychology,* 1923, *34,* 471-485.

Buck, R., Savin, V. J., Miller, R. E., and Caul, W. F. Communication of affect through facial expressions in humans. *Journal of Personality and Social Psychology,* 1972, *23,* 362-371.

Buck, R. A test of nonverbal receiving ability: Preliminary studies. *Human Communication Research,* 1976, *2,* 162-171. (a)

Buck, R. *Human motivation and emotion.* New York: John Wiley, 1976. (b)

Buck, R. Nonverbal behavior and the theory of emotion: The facial feedback hypothesis. *Journal of Personality and Social Psychology*, 1980, *38*, 811-824.

Buck, R., Baron, R., Goodman, N., and Shapiro, B. Unitization of spontaneous nonverbal behavior in the study of emotion communication. *Journal of Personality and Social Psychology*, 1980, *39*, 522-529.

Buzby, D. E. The interpretation of facial expression. *American Journal of Psychology*, 1924, *35*, 602-604.

Campbell, D. T. An error in some demonstrations of the superior social perceptiveness of leaders. *Journal of Abnormal and Social Psychology*, 1955, *51*, 694-695.

Campbell, D. T., and Fiske, D. W. Convergent and discriminant validation by the multitrait-multimethod matrix. *Psychological Bulletin*, 1959, *56*, 81-105.

Campbell, R. J., Kagan, N., and Krathwohl, D. R. The development of a scale to measure affective sensitivity (empathy). *Journal of Counseling Psychology*, 1971, *18*, 407-412.

Chapin, F. S. Preliminary standardization of a social insight scale. *American Sociological Review*, 1942, *7*, 214-228.

Cline, V. B. Interpersonal perception. In B. A. Maher (Ed.), *Progress in experimental personality research* (Vol. 1). New York: Academic Press, 1964.

Cline, V. B., Atzet, J., and Holmes, E. Assessing the validity of verbal and nonverbal cues in accurately judging others. *Comparative Group Studies*, 1972, *3*, 383-394.

Cline, V. B., and Richards, J. M. Accuracy of interpersonal perception–A general trait? *Journal of Abnormal and Social Psychology*, 1960, *60*, 1-7.

Cronbach, L. J. Processes affecting scores on "understanding of others" and "assumed similarity." *Psychological Bulletin*, 1955, *52*, 177-193.

Crow, W. J., and Hammond, K. R. The generality of accuracy and response sets in interpersonal perception. *Journal of Abnormal and Social Psychology*, 1957, *54*, 385-390.

Danish, S. J., and Kagan, N. Measurement of affective sensitivity: Toward a valid measure of interpersonal perception. *Journal of Counseling Psychology*, 1971, *18*, 51-54.

Davitz, J. R. (Ed.). *The communication of emotional meaning*. New York: McGraw-Hill, 1964.

DePaulo, B. M., Rosenthal, R., Eisenstat, R. A., Finkelstein, S., and Rogers, P. Decoding discrepant nonverbal cues. *Journal of Personality and Social Psychology*, 1978, *36*, 313-323.

Dymond, R. F. A scale for the measurement of empathetic ability. *Journal of Consulting Psychology*, 1949, *13*, 127-133.

Ekman, P., and Friesen, W. V. Nonverbal behavior and psychopathology. In R. J. Friedman and M. M. Katz (Eds.), *The psychology of depression: Contemporary theory and research*. Washington, DC: Winston & Sons, 1974.

Ekman, P., and Friesen, W. V. *The facial action coding system*. Palo Alto, CA: Consulting Psychologists Press, 1978.

Ekman, P., Roper, G., and Hager, J. C. Deliberate facial movement. *Child Development*, 1980, *51*, 886-891.

Engen, T., Levy, N., and Schlosberg, H. The dimensional analysis of a new series of facial expressions. *Journal of Experimental Psychology*, 1958, *55*, 454-458.

Feleky, A. M. The expression of the emotions. *Psychological Review*, 1914, *21*, 33-46.

Fields, B., and O'Sullivan, M. *Convergent validation of five person perception measures*. Paper presented at the meeting of the Western Psychological Association, Los Angeles, April 1976.

Fredericksen, N., Saunders, D. R., and Ward, B. The in-basket test. *Psychological Monographs*, 1957, Whole No. 438.

Frois-Wittmann, J. F. The judgment of facial expression. *Journal of Experimental Psychology*, 1930, *13*, 113-151.

Gage, N. L., and Cronbach, L. J. Conceptual and methodological problems in interpersonal research. *Psychological Review*, 1955, *62*, 411-422.

Gough, H. C. A validational study of the Chapin Social Insight Test. *Psychological Reports*, 1965, *17*, 355-368.

Guilford, J. P. *The nature of human intelligence.* New York: McGraw-Hill, 1967.

Harper, R. G., Weins, A. N., and Matarazzo, J. D. The relationship between encoding-decoding of visual nonverbal emotional cues. *Semiotica*, 1979, *8*, 171-192.

Hastorf, A. H., Bender, I. E., and Weintraub, D. J. The influence of response patterns on the "refined empathy score." *Journal of Abnormal and Social Psychology*, 1955, *51*, 341-343.

Hendricks, M., Guilford, J. P. and Hoepfner, R. Measuring creative social intelligence. *Reports from the Psychological Laboratory*, 1969, No. 42. (Los Angeles: University of Southern California).

Hogan, R. Development of an empathy scale. *Journal of Consulting and Clinical Psychology*, 1969, *33*, 307-316.

Izard, C. E. *The face of emotion.* New York: Appleton-Century-Crofts, 1971.

Jung, P. *Beiziehungen zwischen Tests der socialen Intelligenz zu verbaler Test-intelligenz und soziometrischen Variableo.* Unpublished Diplomarbeit, Universität des Saarlandes, Saarbrucken, 1972.

Kagan, N., Warner, D., and Schneider, J. *The Affective Sensitivity Scale.* Paper presented at the American Psychological Association Symposium on Measuring Individual Differences in Emotion Recognition and Expression, San Francisco, 1977.

Landis, C. The interpretation of facial expression in emotion. *Journal of General Psychology*, 1929, *2*, 59-72.

Landis, C., and Hunt, W. A. *The startle pattern.* New York: Farrar, Straus & Giroux, 1939.

Langfeld, H. S. Judgments of facial expression and suggestion. *Psychological Review*, 1918, *25*, 488-494.

Leathers, D. G. and Emigh, T. H. Decoding facial expressions: A new test with decoding norms. *Quarterly Journal of Speech*, 1980, *66*, 418-436.

Levenson, R. W., and Gottman, J. M. Toward the assessment of social competence. *Journal of Consulting and Clinical Psychology*, 1978, *46*, 453-462.

Mehrota, C. Behavioral cognition as related to interpersonal perception and some personality traits of college students. *Educational and Psychological Measurement*, 1971, *31*, 145-153.

Mehrabian, A., and Epstein, N. A measure of emotional empathy. *Journal of Personality*, 1972, *40*, 525-543.

Messick, S. The standard problem: Meaning and values in measurement and evaluation. *American Psychologist*, 1975, *30*, 955-966.

Moss, F. A., Hunt, T., Omwake, K. T., and Bonning, M. M. *Social intelligence test.* Washington, DC: Center for Psychological Services, 1927.

O'Sullivan, M. Measuring the ability to recognize facial expressions of emotion. In P. Ekman (Ed.), *Emotion in the human face* (2nd ed.). New York: Cambridge University Press, 1982.

O'Sullivan, M., and Guilford, J. P. Six factors of behavioral cognition: Understanding other people. *Journal of Educational Measurement*, 1975, *12*, 255-271.

O'Sullivan, M., Guilford, J. P., and DeMille, R. The measurement of social intelligence. *Reports from the Psychological Laboratory*, 1965, No. 34. (Los Angeles: University of Southern California).

O'Sullivan, M., and Hager, J. C. *Measuring person perception: New techniques, old problems.* Unpublished manuscript, University of San Francisco, 1982.

Petrinovich, L. Probabilistic functionalism: A conception of research method. *American Psychologist*, 1979, *34*, 373-390.

Piderit, T. [*La mimique et la physiognomonie*] (A. Girot, trans.). Paris: Ancienne Librairie Germer Bailliere et Cie, 1888.

Rombouts, H. *Sociale intelligentie.* Unpublished doctoral dissertation, University of Amsterdam, 1978.

Rosenthal, R., Hall, J. A., DiMatteo, M. R., Rogers, P. L., and Archer, D. *Sensitivity to nonverbal communication: The PONS Test.* Baltimore: Johns Hopkins University Press, 1979.

Rothenberg, B. B. Children's social sensitivity and the relationship to interpersonal competence, intrapersonal comfort, and intellectual level. *Developmental Psychology*, 1970, *2*, 335-350.

Ruckmick, C. A. A preliminary study of the emotions. *Psychological Monographs*, 1921, *30*, 30-35.

Rudolph, H. *Der Ausdruck der Gemutshewegungen des Meoscheo.* Dresden: Verlag von Gerhard Kuhtmann, 1903.

Sabatelli, R. M., Buck, R., and Dreyer, A. Communication via facial cues in intimate dyads. *Personality and Social Psychology Bulletin*, 1980, *6*, 242-247.

Schlosberg, H. Three dimensions of emotion. *Psychological Review*, 1954, *61*, 81-88.

Shipe, D., Rosser, M., and Sidhu, R. *Social intelligence, affiliation motivation, and interpersonal effectiveness in non-academic youth.* Paper presented at the meeting of the American Psychological Association, Montreal, September 1973.

Snyder, M. The self-monitoring of expressive behavior. *Journal of Personality and Social Psychology*, 1974, *30*, 526-537.

Stricker, L. Interpersonal Competence instrument: development and preliminary findings. *Applied Psychological Measurement*, 1982, *6*, 69-81.

Tenopyr, M. Social intelligence and academic success. *Educational and Psychological Measurement*, 1967, *27*, 961-965.

Thorndike, E. L. Intelligence and its uses. *Harper's Magazine*, 1920, *140*, 227-235.

Thorndike, R. L. Factor analysis of social and abstract intelligence. *Journal of Educational Psychology*, 1936, *27*, 231-233.

Tomkins, S. S. *Affect, imagery, consciousness. Vol. 1. The positive affects.* New York: Springer, 1962.

Tomkins, S. S. *Affect, imagery, consciousness, Vol. II. The negative affects.* New York: Springer, 1963.

Tomkins, S. S., and McCarter, R. What and where are the primary affects? Some evidence for a theory. *Perceptual and Motor Skills*, 1964, *18*, 119-158.

Trower, P., Bryant, B., and Argyle, M. *Social skills and mental health.* Pittsburgh: University of Pittsburgh Press, 1978.

Wedeck, J. The relationship between personality and "psychological ability." *British Journal of Psychology*, 1947, *37*, 133-151.

Weiss, A., Weiss, F., and O'Sullivan, M. *The Average American Test: A measure of stereotypic accuracy.* Paper presented at the meeting of the California State Psychological Association, Sacramento, January 1981. (a)

Weiss, F., Weiss, A., and O'Sullivan, M. *The Affect Blend Test.* Paper presented at the meeting of the California State Psychological Association. Sacramento, January 1981. (b)

Wiemann, J. M., and Backlund, P. Current theory and research in communicative competence. *Review of Educational Research,* 1980, *50,* 185-199.

Woodrow, H. The common factors in fifty-two mental tests. *Psychometrika,* 1939, *4,* 100-107.

Woodworth, R. S., and Schlosberg, H. *Experimental psychology.* New York: Holt, 1954.

Zuckerman, M., Hall, J. A., DeFrank, R. S., and Rosenthal, R. Encoding and decoding of spontaneous and posed facial expressions. *Journal of Personality and Social Psychology,* 1976, *34,* 966-977.

Zuckerman, M., Lipets, M. S., Koivumaki, J., and Rosenthal, R. Encoding and decoding nonverbal cues of emotion. *Journal of Personality and Social Psychology,* 1975, *32,* 1068-1076.

Chapter 9

THE NONVERBAL DOMAIN
Implications for Theory, Research, and Practice

Randall P. Harrison and John M. Wiemann

THIS VOLUME has surveyed a number of current trends in nonverbal communication research. From this review, a number of important issues are apparent on the horizon. These issues have implications for theory, research, and practice, both in the field of communication generally and in the specific domain of nonverbal communication.

In this final chapter, we provide a brief historical perspective, the context from which this book emerged. We note a few of the nonverbal issues that are *not* addressed in this volume, and we recap briefly some of the concerns raised by our authors. We then peer into the future, asking about the next chapter in nonverbal research.

HOW WE GOT HERE

Scholarly interest in nonverbal communication goes back at least to the age of Aristotle in the West and Confucius in the East. Aristotle, for example, commented on animal behavior and on human passions. But his intellectual legacy was not particularly conducive to an exploration of the nonverbal domain. He started with a static universe, which could be analyzed with two-valued logic. From this sprang a model for rational discourse that still permeates much communication scholarship today.

To this intellectual heritage, Descartes added a dichotomy between mind and body that further focused attention on the rational and the verbal. The rise of science and industry in the West gave spur to an interest in literacy—to communication that was orderly, rational, linear, verbal, and numerical.

In the past century, however, a number of Western thinkers advanced theories that called attention to nonverbal issues. Darwin proposed his theory of evolution, suggesting that human emotional expression has its roots in animal survival. Freud examined the human unconscious and suggested that verbal statements may be rational—or rationalizations. Marx advanced his theory of class struggle, cal' ng attention to structural forces in human society. Einstein proposed theories that are still reshaping our images of time, space, matter, energy, and information. It is no longer easy to believe, with Aristotle, that we live in a simple, static universe composed of only four major elements: earth, water, air, and fire.

At a very practical level, the past century has seen a major shift in the human ecology, a change that has focused attention on the crucial importance of communication. During most of human history, the typical individual lived in a small community where everyone knew everyone else, from birth to death. Everyone knew everything—or at least knew who did know and if it was known. In the last hundred years, this has changed radically. While much of the world population still lives in a traditional information environment, the Western industrial world has experienced a revolution. Knowledge has exploded. Specialization is essential. And crucial interactions take place daily with people we have *not* known all our lives.

As scholars began to take a closer look at communication, they began to note events that were not easily explained by attending only to words. At the same time, new technology was having its impact. In the rise of television, for example, we saw a major communication medium with a robust nonverbal component. In turn, the availability of film in the laboratory meant that researchers could now carefully examine aspects of interaction that were previously unavailable for study. Easy and inexpensive access to videotape has made records of nonverbal behavior commonplace.

The phrase "nonverbal communication" first appeared as a book title in the mid-1950s (Ruesch and Kees, 1956). Many scholars, including some of the pioneers in the field, do not like the label "nonverbal" nor the phrase "nonverbal communication" (Sebeok, 1976; Kendon, 1978). "Nonverbal" sounds like a residual category; it smacks of the same two-valued logic, the same mind-body dichotomy, that many scholars are trying to jettison. And "nonverbal communication" appears to beg the question about how certain non-language events relate to human interaction. Captionless cartoons may be "nonverbal communication," but most researchers are interested in what might properly be called verbal nonverbal communication: the integrated use of word, gesture, expression, and artifact in time and space.

In spite of the objections, however, "nonverbal communication" has seemed a label preferable to "body language," "kinesics," "coenetics," and other denominations (for more on this, see Knapp, 1978). For better or for worse, "nonverbal communication" has become the familiar tag for non-word events of informational value.

By 1980, Frye was able to publish a book-length bibliography with more than 4,000 references to nonverbal research. Other bibliographies, using different criteria, add even more citations (Key, 1977; Davis and Skupien, 1981). Today nonverbal research appears to be expanding at an exponential rate.

THE NONVERBAL DOMAIN

Our modern English word *communication* springs from the Latin root *communis,* or common. Other English words from the same family tree include *communion* and *community.* In a broad sense, communication is a process through which we come to share—to hold in common—thoughts, feelings, and actions. An additional proviso is that this sharing is done through the exchange of messages. These messages, of course, may be verbal or nonverbal or—perhaps most frequently—a combination of verbal and nonverbal.

While the domain of the verbal message is complex, it is fairly easy to specify. A key element is the word, in spoken or written form. Verbal communication uses the vocal-auditory channel for speech and the ortho-graphic-visual channel for print.

The domain of the nonverbal message appears to be more far-flung. Almost any perceivable event can be turned into a code, just as Paul Revere did with lanterns: "one if by land, two if by sea." The full range of sensory channels may be called into play: seeing, hearing, tasting, smelling, touching.

NONVERBAL MESSAGES

The human repertoire appears to include four broad categories of nonverbal messages. First are messages of the body, produced by the appearance or movement of the human form. These have been called "performance codes" (Harrison, 1974) or "somatic messages" (Poyotas, in preparation).

Second are messages of artifact, produced by creating, arranging, or displaying objects ranging from personal dress to public monuments. These have been called "artifactual codes" or "object language" (Ruesch and Kees, 1956).

Third are messages of space and time. All communication takes place *in* space and time. But these dimensions can emerge from the background to provide their own commentary. Important events are scheduled for prime time, and they are given respectful duration. Important people and significant objects are assigned prominent positions and generous allotments of space. Thus dictates the "spatio-temporal codes" of our culture.

Fourth are messages of the media, such as art and music and the special effects of visual or sound recording. The same nonverbal event can be presented in close-up or long-shot, in slow motion or instant replay, with musical background or special sound. These are examples of the "mediatory codes."

The researcher has asked how these four classes of nonverbal messages interrelate at four levels of analysis: the intrapersonal, the personal, the interpersonal, and the impersonal, or institutional.

LEVELS OF ANALYSIS

Increasing attention has gone toward understanding the way nonverbal events are organized and processed *within* the individual. Investigators have explored the internal relationship between verbal and nonverbal, between thought and image, the relationship of affect, cognition, and behavior, the relationship of right brain to left brain, and of new brain to old brain. Kendon, in Chapter 1, points toward a basic question: How are speech and gesticulation organized and managed at the intrapersonal level? Other researchers have argued that the division of functions between the right and left hemispheres provides the fundamental way to define nonverbal and verbal communication (Andersen et al., 1981).

At the personal level, we find questions about the presentation of self, person perception, and decoding and encoding skills, addressed by Buck (Chapter 7) and O'Sullivan (Chapter 8).

Concerns at the intrapersonal and personal levels feed into the main focus of this volume: the interaction sphere. How is interaction structured—from the seemingly simple taking of turns, discussed by Duncan (Chapter 5), on up? How does a nonverbal message like touch relate to intrapersonal feelings, to personal perceptions, and to interpersonal relationships (Heslin and Alper, Chapter 2)? What other nonverbal events contribute to interpersonal dimensions, such as involvement (Cappella, Chapter 4), expectations (Burgoon, Chapter 3), or the development and decay of relationships (Knapp, Chapter 6)?

Finally, nonverbal messages operate at the impersonal or institutional level, a range we have not scaled in this volume. But interesting questions can be asked about the role of nonverbal symbols in mass media or in intercultural understanding. And interesting questions are being asked about the ways messages of the media may shape nonverbal processes at the interpersonal, personal, and intrapersonal levels (Salomon, 1979).

In sum, out of the total nonverbal domain, this collection has focused primarily on messages of body and space, of people in interaction with others. A chief concern has been how a long list of nonverbal variables influences human relationships within the interaction sphere.

LOOKING FORWARD

In recent years, the growing literature on nonverbal communication has been reviewed a number of times (Duncan, 1969; Harrison et al., 1972; Harrison, 1973; Knapp, 1978; Burgoon, 1980; Crouch, 1980). The first, obvious trend, of course, is the sheer growth of data. It has become increasingly difficult for a single article to cover the field. Authors have begun to delimit their scope by examining a specific time frame or by following a particular discipline (for example, Burgoon, 1980). Even book-length reviews of nonverbal data have grown to impressive size (Knapp, 1978; Harper et al., 1978). A single nonverbal variable, such as facial expression, plus a single dependent variable, such as emotion, can lead to lengthy reviews (Ekman and Oster, 1979; Ekman, 1982).

While the reader struggling with this literature may feel awash in data, there are several encouraging trends. First is a growing sophistication about the use of theory, an understanding of the presuppositions and priorities that have led to certain traditions. Second is a growing sophistication about the use of methodology. Advances have been made, not only in methods of observation, in instrumentation, and in statistical analysis, but also in the growing awareness of methodological alternatives. Third is a growing sophistication in the application of findings. The first wave of popularized "body language" literature is receding, and a more thoughtful and complex analysis is emerging. These three trends feed into a number of predictions about the future. But first, let's take a closer look at the advances in theory, research, and practice.

ADVANCES IN THEORY

The nonverbal domain has drawn researchers from a number of parent disciplines. While this has led to spirited exploration, it has also led to tumult and confusion. Often, researchers from competing areas talk past each other, unaware of their own jargon or presuppositions.

Historically, two main colonial powers have mined the nonverbal domain. One is psychology. It traces its roots to founding fathers, such as Wilhelm Wundt (1911/1973). Along the way, it has enlisted the interest of other leaders in the field, such as Allport and Vernon (1933).

The other major tradition is anthropological. It similarly has a venerable history, but it became particularly strong in America, where anthropologists and linguists joined forces to study American Indian languages.

The psychological tradition tends to focus on the individual and specific nonverbal variables. It then asks about the antecedent conditions of these variables. For example, what personal states or traits lead to a nonverbal variable such as a smile? The nonverbal variable might be explored for consequences. How is a smile interpreted? What impact does it have on interaction?

Along the way, the psychological tradition got increasingly complex, especially as it moved toward social psychology. But it also picked up allies in quite different areas, such as ethology (Von Cranach et al., 1979). In particular, the rediscovery of Darwin led to a rich vein of exploration (Ekman, 1973).

The anthropological tradition, meanwhile, focused less on the individual and the isolated nonverbal variable. Rather, it looked at structure, within culture and interaction, and within the codes that individuals use. Early work included the classic study of Efron (1941/1972) and contributions from leaders like Bateson and Mead (1942).

Along the way, the anthropological tradition also recruited allies, not only from structural linguistics, but also from social psychiatry, information theory, and cybernetics. (This rich tradition has recently received an excellent review by Kendon, 1982, and we will not try to recapitulate his work in this brief space.)

Today, second- and third-generation researchers in the nonverbal territory move more freely across the boundaries that once divided the psychological approach from the anthropological perspective. But there still tends to be a preference for either starting with the individual and moving up to interaction, or starting with social structure and moving down to interaction. These differing orientations lead to somewhat different conceptualizations of "interaction." They also lead to differing views about the nature of "nonverbal codes."

THEORIES IN COMMUNICATION

Communication researchers have become increasingly sophisticated about the theories they employ. This seems particularly important in areas such as nonverbal communication, where disciplines with quite different theoretical presuppositions have converged on a single target and where data gathering has far outstripped theory construction.

For the study of human communication generally, three alternative perspectives have been debated recently: the covering law model (Berger, 1977), the systems approach (Monge, 1977), and the rules/action theory approach (Cushman, 1977). The covering law approach is familiar in experimental psychology. The systems approach has been used widely in the study of organizational communication (Redding, 1979). The rules tradition is strong in areas such as linguistic anthropology (Hymes, 1980).

While it is impossible to review here the advantages and disadvantages of each approach, we note that each perspective has been applied to the area of nonverbal communication. Each has particular strengths, depending on the research concern of the investigator. The human organism, for example, is a concrete, living system, and at a basic biological and psychological level, covering law models work well. Language, and perhaps some nonverbal codes, are, on the other hand, abstract systems. They become "living" only when used by a live communicator. Here the rules perspective may prove particularly fruitful. Finally, interaction involves mixed systems—live humans using an abstract code system to create a communication system that may be analyzed at various levels. At the interpersonal level, the rules perspective seems particularly productive, as exemplified by the research programs of Burgoon and Duncan.

GOALS OF RESEARCH

In competing paradigms, confusion often exists about goals and about what will be accepted as evidence. Here, too, however, we see a growing sophistication.

The primary goals of research typically involve discovery, proof, and illustration. For researchers in the empirical, experimental tradition, these three are usually seen as a sequence. Discovery is first, and it may come in various ways—through insight, observation, or theoretical deduction.

The second stage is proof. Here the empirical researcher has well-established canons, including careful description, the creation of categories and coding systems with known reliability, the measurement of frequency and rate, systematic sampling, and the application of appropriate statistical analysis. Finally, illustration may be important, depending on how the findings are to be disseminated.

In nonexperimental traditions, the discovery of rules or patterns may be the chief goal. In structural linguistics, for example, methodology focuses on *how* discoveries are to be made. Once elaborated and illustrated, these discoveries seem so obvious that there is little perceived need for statistical proof.

When the experimental and nonexperimental traditions converge on the study of nonverbal communication, disagreement arises about both priorities and evidence. The experimenter wants to nail down measurable variables that can be manipulated to provide statistical proof. To the nonexperimental investigator, this often seems premature: the grabbing of variables before the investigator understands the whole picture and what may be important. In turn, the finding the nonempirical researcher offers may be viewed by the experimentalist as merely an interesting hypothesis or anecdotal illustration, a claim yet needing proof. Increasingly, however, researchers appear to recognize that each—discovery, proof, and illustration—is important, and the investigator has an array of methodologies to pursue each goal (Scherer and Ekman, 1982).

ADVANCES IN METHODOLOGY

Since the time of Darwin (1872/1965), three major methodologies have been used to gather data about nonverbal phenomena: the judge study, in which subjects are asked to respond to a nonverbal variable; the experiment, in which nonverbal variables are manipulated and controlled; and field observation, in which nonverbal variables are observed in natural settings, with or without manipulation (see Heslin and Alper's chapter for illustrations of each).

Over the years, each of these methodologies has been elaborated and refined. The finding that experimenters may communicate to subjects, unconsciously and nonverbally, was itself a major discovery (Rosenthal, 1966). It brought about a significant refinement in experimental technique for all behavioral science.

For the immediate future, the definitive work on research techniques will be the *Handbook of Methods in Nonverbal Behavior Research* (Scherer and Ekman, 1982). The handbook complements and expands the methodological discussions in several essays in this volume, such as the chapters by Duncan, O'Sullivan, and Buck. For the serious nonverbal researcher, it covers in depth, and in one place, many methodological issues and alternatives.

ADVANCES IN APPLICATION

When nonverbal communication first trickled out of the laboratory, it ignited a spate of popular books. Readers were given dictionaries of nonverbal tricks with which they could seduce lovers or best their business competitors. Koivumaki (1975) scored these early attempts to apply knowledge about nonverbal communication; she called them little more than "psychopornography" (see also Harrison, 1975).

Popular articles still appear, but both popularizers and audiences have become more discerning. Meanwhile, a number of serious researchers have investigated how best to analyze and improve nonverbal skills (Argyle, 1979; Gross, 1973; Rosenthal, 1979). The spectrum of application extends to the so-called body therapies (Diamond, 1979; Schutzenberger and Geffroy, 1979), to "visualization" (Samuels and Samuels, 1977; Simonton and Matthews-Simonton, 1978), and to nonverbal skills such as drawing (Edwards, 1979). Some of the applications of nonverbal research, such as "neuro-linguistic programming," are quite powerful, if proponents are to be believed (Cameron-Bandler, 1978; Grinder and Bandler, 1976; Pucelik, 1981).

ETHICAL CONCERNS

The area of nonverbal research shares the ethical concerns of all scientific investigation. But it seems at times to hold a unique opportunity for mischief.

Modern researchers tend to be more sensitive than some of their early predecessors, who, for example, hypnotized subjects and then told them their families had been killed so that researchers could watch the expressions of grief. Even today, however, the nonverbal researcher wrestles with problems of invasion of privacy, the need for deception, the possibility of causing embarrassment or even psychological damage, and the need to maintain strict confidentiality. In addition, scientists have become increasingly aware of the problems involved in the dissemination and use of their findings. Problems range from exaggerated claims to misrepresentations in the media to misapplications to applications with inappropriate audiences.

There are no easy answers to any of these questions. It is possible that the "ethics of nonverbal research" will itself be one of the next major areas of study.

EMERGING ISSUES

The research paths charted by the contributors to this volume have not been easy. Some are on the cutting edge of what appear to be major new directions. Some are mopping up what are admittedly difficult, and sometimes messy, research areas. In general, it appears that the easy findings in nonverbal communication have been skimmed off by early explorers. What lies ahead is a difficult and often tedious task.

Progress will come through increased attention to theory, through refinements and innovations in research methods and through the successful application of significant findings.

Three basic conceptual problems, however, continue to confront the researcher: (1) how to construe the individual as a communicator, (2) how to construe interaction, and (3) how to construe nonverbal cues, codes, and messages.

On the first issue, there is a growing recognition that the human being is, simultaneously, a biological, psychological, social, and cultural creature. There is an awareness of the importance of emotion as well as cognition (Rorty, 1980). But it is difficult to bring all these facets into simultaneous focus in research.

The construal of the individual as communicator thus varies. The human, for example, can be viewed as a separate information-processing system who decodes, processes, stores, and encodes messages. In the tradition of Mead (1934), the self can be viewed as a dynamic entity that emerges in the process of interaction with others. Similarly, interaction can be construed as a minimal chain—A responds to B and B responds back—or as a complex, multilevel, multidimensional process. Finally, nonverbal variables may be construed singly, or as packages that operate interchangeably to perform identifiable functions, or as code systems of varying complexity, with ranges of communication potential.

However researchers resolve these issues for themselves, it appears that the field will see complementary movement, as some investigators dig deeper and some explorations broaden our horizons. In any event, future research must take into account the complexity of the communication system—the interrelationships of language and movement and of the various movement modalities.

AN EXAMPLE: THE SMILE

To ground this abstract discussion in a concrete example, we take a seemingly simple nonverbal variable, the smile. One of the first questions researchers asked was: Is the smile innate and universal? or is it learned and cultural? The answer appears to be "yes."

The inner physiological state of joy brings a smile to the lips. But the smile can also be produced on demand, and we have "display rules" that may modify the smile even when it is felt (Ekman and Friesen, 1975; Harrison, 1976).

The smile appears to be one of the more obvious nonverbal variables; coders easily detect "smile" or "no-smile." And it seems that smiling should relate to a number of interesting interpersonal questions.

One straightforward question might be: Do people smile more or less while lying? Researchers who have explored that question tend to find no difference in the frequency of smiling between liars and non-liars, or between truth-telling and lying (Hemsley, 1977; Hocking and Leathers, 1980; Knapp et al., 1974; Krauss et al., 1976; Kraut, 1978; Kraut and Poe, 1980; McClintock and Hunt, 1975; Mehrabian, 1971; O'Hair et al., 1981).

But several possibilities remain. The structuralists would argue that frequency or rate of smiling may not be important; it is *when* the individual smiles that may be significant (Kendon, 1982).

Another possibility is that there are different kinds of smiling. What appears to be one nonverbal variable may, in fact, be several. This, indeed, is the argument advanced by Ekman (Ekman and Friesen, 1982; Ekman, in preparation). He identified nineteen different smiles and argues that previous investigators have failed to find significant differences because they did not distinguish among "felt," "false," and "miserable" smiles.

To discover nineteen kinds of smiles, Ekman and his associates first had to develop an intricate coding system, a monumental task that took some six years of full-time effort (Harrison, 1980). The coding scheme analyzes more than forty different "muscle action units" which occur in the face (Ekman and Friesen, 1978). The technique is now available to other researchers. But it is not an approach the casual investigator will rush to adopt. It requires about 150 hours to train each coder, and each minute of videotaped expression requires hours of analysis by trained coders.

Similar investments of time and effort have gone into the study of interaction, by researchers who start from a structural perspective (Birdwhistell, 1970; Byers, 1979; Davis, 1982; Goodwin, 1981; Hall, 1974; McQuown, n.d.). It is not uncommon to spend thirty or forty hours analyzing one minute of film or videotape.

In sum, the nonverbal domain is a rich new territory for exploration. But the next generation of discoveries is likely to be hard-won.

IMPLICATIONS FOR COMMUNICATION

Finally, we note that studies in the nonverbal domain have generated new insights about the total process of communication. Many early models of communication, for example, tended to be verbal and linear. This provided a powerful first cut. But it also proved to be only part of the picture. Instead of focusing on only verbal messages and cognition, contemporary research spotlights a more complete scene, including nonverbal messages and the full range of affect, cognition, and behavior.

Similarly, early models tended to see a linear sequence of thought-feeling-action. The communicator, thinking in words, then articulated the thoughts in speech or writing. The receiver comprehended this verbal message. Then feelings fell into place—that is, attitude change occurred. Then appropriate action took place. Modern models, however, open the possibility that the sequence may be feeling-action-thought, or action-feeling-thought, or that all three occur simultaneously, richly interlaced with verbal and nonverbal feedback.

It seems likely that nonverbal research will continue to enrich and illuminate our understanding of human communication. The effort will be great. But it will be worth the investment.

REFERENCES

Allport, G. W., and Vernon, P. E. *Studies in expressive movement.* New York: Macmillan, 1933.

Andersen, P. A., Garrison, J. D., and Andersen, J. F. Implications of a neurophysiological approach to the study of nonverbal communication. In G. C. Wilhoit and H. de Bock (Eds.) *Mass Communication Review Yearbook* (Vol. 2). Beverly Hills, CA: Sage, 1981.

Argyle, M. New developments in the analysis of social skills. In A. Wolfgang (Ed.), *Nonverbal behavior: Applications and cultural implications.* New York: Academic Press, 1979.

Bateson, G., and Mead, M. *Balinese character: A photographic analysis.* New York: New York Academy of Sciences, 1942.

Berger, C. R. The covering law perspective as a theoretical basis for the study of human communication. *Communication Quarterly,* 1977, *25,* 7-18.

Birdwhistell, R. L. *Kinesics and context.* Philadelphia: University of Pennsylvania Press, 1970.

Burgoon, J. Nonverbal communication research in the 1970s: An overview. In D. Nimmo (Ed.), *Communication Yearbook 4.* New Brunswick, NJ: Transaction, 1980.

Byers, P. Biological rhythms as information channels in interpersonal communication behavior. In S. Weitz (Ed.), *Nonverbal communication: Readings with commentary* (2nd ed.). New York: Oxford University Press, 1979.

Cameron-Bandler, L. *They lived happily ever after.* Cupertino, CA: Meta Publications, 1978.

Crouch, W. The nonverbal communication literature: A book review. *Australian SCAN: Journal of Human Communication,* 1980, *8,* 1-11.

Cushman, D. P. The rules perspective as a theoretical basis for the study of human communication. *Communication Quarterly,* 1977, *25,* 30-45.

Darwin, C. *The expression of the emotions in man and animals.* Chicago: University of Chicago Press, 1965. (Originally published in London, 1872)

Davis, M. (Ed.). *Interaction rhythms: Periodicity in communicative behavior.* New York: Human Sciences Press, 1982.

Davis, M., and Skupien, J. (Eds.). *The nonverbal communication literature 1971-1980.* New York: Arno Press, 1981.

Diamond, J. *Your body doesn't lie.* New York: Warner Books, 1979.

Duncan, S. D. Nonverbal communication. *Psychological Bulletin,* 1969, *72,* 118-137.

Edwards, B. *Drawing on the right side of the brain.* Los Angeles: J. P. Tarcher, 1979.

Efron, D. *Gesture, race, and culture.* The Hague: Mouton, 1972. (Originally published, 1941)

Ekman, P. (Ed.). *Darwin and facial expression : A century of research in review.* New York: Academic Press, 1973.

Ekman, P. (Ed.). *Emotion in the human face* (2nd ed.). Cambridge: Cambridge University Press, 1982.

Ekman, P. *Liars and lie catchers.* Manuscript in preparation.

Ekman, P., and Friesen, W. V. *Unmasking the face.* Englewood Cliffs, NJ: Prentice-Hall, 1975.

Ekman, P., and Friesen, W. V. *Facial action coding system.* Palo Alto, CA: Consulting Psychologists Press, 1978.

Ekman, P., and Friesen, W. V. Felt, false, and miserable smiles. *Journal of Nonverbal Behavior,* 1982, *6,* 238-252.

Ekman, P., and Oster, H. Facial expressions of emotion. *Annual Review of Psychology,* 1979, *30,* 527-554.

Frye, J. K. *FIND : Frye's index to nonverbal data.* Duluth: University of Minnesota, 1980.

Goodwin, C. *Conversational organization.* New York: Academic Press, 1981.

Grinder, J., and Bandler, R. *The structure of magic. Vol. 2. Nonverbal communication.* Palo Alto, CA: Science and Behavior Books, 1976.

Gross, L. Modes of communication and the acquisition of symbolic competencies. In G. Gerbner, L. Gross, and W. Melody (Eds.), *Communication technology and social policy.* New York: John Wiley, 1973.

Hall, E. T. *Handbook for proxemic research.* Washington, DC: Society for the Anthropology of Visual Communication, 1974.

Harper, R. G., Wiens, A. N., and Matarazzo, J. D. *Nonverbal communication: The state of the art.* New York: John Wiley, 1978.

Harrison, R. P. Nonverbal communication. In I. de Sola Pool, W. Schramm, N. Maccoby, F. Frey, E. Parker, and J. L. Fein (Eds.), *Handbook of communication.* Chicago: Rand-McNally, 1973.

Harrison, R. P. *Beyond words: An introduction to nonverbal communication.* Englewood Cliffs, NJ: Prentice-Hall, 1974.

Harrison, R. P. Body language revisited. *Journal of Communication,* 1975, *25,* 223-224.

Harrison, R. P. The face in face-to-face interaction. In G. R. Miller (Ed.), *Explorations in interpersonal communication.* Beverly Hills, CA: Sage, 1976.

Harrison, R. P. Profile: Paul Ekman. *The Kinesis Report,* 1980, *3,* 1-15.

Harrison, R. P., Cohen, A. A., Crouch, W. W., Genova, B.K.L., and Steinberg, M.L. The nonverbal communication literature. *Journal of Communication,* 1972, *22,* 460-476.

Hemsley, G. D. *Experimental studies in the behavioral indicants of deception.* Unpublished doctoral dissertation, University of Toronto, 1977.

Hocking, J. E., and Leathers, D. G. Nonverbal indicators of deception: A new theoretical perspective. *Communication Monographs,* 1980, *47,* 119-131.

Hymes, D. Foreword. In S. B. Shiminoff, *Communication rules: Theory and research.* Beverly Hills, CA: Sage, 1980.

Kendon, A. Review of *Nonverbal communication: A research guide and bibliography,* by M. R. Key. *Ars Semeiotica: International Journal of American Semiotica,* 1978, *2,* 90-92.

Kendon, A. The organization of behavior in face-to-face interaction: Observations on the development of a methodology. In K. R. Scherer and P. Ekman (Eds.), *Handbook of methods in nonverbal behavior research.* Cambridge: Cambridge University Press, 1982.

Key, M. R. *Nonverbal communication: A research guide and bibliography.* Metucheun, NJ: Scarecrow Press, 1977.

Knapp, M. L. *Nonverbal communication in human interaction* (2nd ed.). New York: Holt, Rinehart & Winston, 1978.

Knapp, M. L., Hart, R. P., and Dennis, H. S. An exploration of deception as a communication construct. *Human Communication Research,* 1974, *1,* 15-29.

Knapp, M. L., Wiemann, J. M., and Daly, J. A. Nonverbal communication: Issues and appraisal. *Human Communication Research,* 1978, *4,* 271-280.

Koivumaki, J. H. Body language taught here. *Journal of Communication,* 1975, *25,* 26-30.

Krauss, R. M., Geller, V. and Olson, C. *Modalities and cues in the detection of deception.* Paper presented at the American Psychological Association, Washington, D.C., 1976.

Kraut, R. E. Verbal and nonverbal cues in the perception of lying. *Journal of Personality and Social Psychology,* 1978, *36,* 380-391.

Kraut, R. E. and Poe, D. On the line: The deception judgments of customs inspectors and laymen. *Journal of Personality and Social Psychology,* 1980, *39,* 784-798.

McQuown, N. (Ed.). *The natural history of an interview.* Microfilm collection of manuscripts on cultural anthropology, 15th series, University of Chicago, Joseph Regenstein Library, Department of Photoduplication, n.d.

McClintock, C. C., and Hunt, R. G. Nonverbal indicators of affect and deception in an interview setting. *Journal of Applied Social Psychology,* 1975, *5,* 54-67.

Mead, G. H. *Mind, self and society.* Chicago: University of Chicago Press, 1934.

Mehrabian, A. Nonverbal betrayal of feelings. *Journal of Experimental Research in Personality* 1971, *5,* 64-73.

Monge, P. R. The systems perspective as a theoretical basis for the study of human communication. *Communication Quarterly,* 1977, *25,* 19-29.

O'Hair, H. D., Cody, M. J. and McLaughlin, M. L. Prepared lies, spontaneous lies, Machiavellianism and nonverbal communication. *Human Communication Research,* 1981, *7,* 325-339.

Poyotas, F. New perspectives for an integrative research of nonverbal systems. In M. R. Key and D. Preziosi (Eds.), *Nonverbal communication today: Current research,* in preparation.

Pucelik, F. *META introductory handbook.* Norman, OK: META International, 1981.

Redding, W. C. Organizational communication theory and ideology: An overview. In D. Nimmo (Ed.), *Communication Yearbook 3.* New Brunswick, NJ: Transaction, 1979.

Rorty, A. O. (Ed.). *Explaining emotions.* Berkeley: University of California Press, 1980.

Rosenthal, R. *Experimenter effects in behavioral research.* New York: Appleton-Century-Crofts, 1966.

Rosenthal, R. (Ed.). *Skill in nonverbal communication: Individual differences.* Cambridge, MA: Oelgeschlager, Gunn & Hain, 1979.

Ruesch, J., and Kees, W. *Nonverbal communication.* Berkeley: University of California Press, 1956.

Salomon, G. *Interaction of media, cognition and learning.* San Francisco: Jossey-Bass, 1979.

Samuels, M., and Samuels, N. *Seeing with the mind's eye.* New York: Random House, 1977.

Scherer, K. R., and Ekman, P. (Eds.). *Handbook of methods in nonverbal behavior research.* Cambridge: Cambridge University Press, 1982.

Schutzenberger, A. A., and Geffroy, Y. The body and the group: The new body therapies. In S. Weitz (Ed.), *Nonverbal communication: Readings with commentary* (2nd ed.). New York: Oxford University Press, 1979.

Sebeok, T. A. The semiotic web: A chronical of prejudices. In T. A. Sebeok, *Contributions to the doctrine of signs.* Lisse, Holland: Peter De Ridder Press, 1976.

Simonton, O. C., and Matthews-Simonton, S. *Getting well again.* Los Angeles: J. P. Tarcher, 1978.

Von Cranach, M., Foppa, K., Lepenies, W., and Ploog, D. (Eds.). *Human ethology.* Cambridge: Cambridge University Press, 1979.

Wundt, W. *The language of gestures.* The Hague: Mouton, 1973. (Originally published in *Volkerpsychologie,* 1911)

Complet Works
Swami Vivecanende
1999

Sully Outlines Psychology

ABOUT THE CONTRIBUTORS

TARI ALPER received her B.S. in psychology from Purdue University and is currently a Ph.D. candidate in administrative sciences in Purdue's Krannert School of Business Administration. Her research interests include nonverbal communication and application of Loevinger's theory of ego development to interpersonal relations.

ROSS BUCK, Ph.D., is Professor in the departments of Communication Sciences and Psychology at the University of Connecticut. He is author of *Human Motivation and Emotion* and a forthcoming book, *Emotion and Nonverbal Behavior: The Communication of Affect.* Current research interests include the role of cerebral lateralization in emotional expression, the relationship of emotional expression and bodily stress, and the analysis of individual and cultural differences in emotion communication.

JUDEE K. BURGOON, who received her doctorate in communication and educational psychology from West Virginia University, is Associate Professor of Communication at Michigan State University. Her major research interests include nonverbal communication, relational communication, and print media. She has published four textbooks and many articles in journals of communication, psychology, and journalism.

JOSEPH N. CAPPELLA, who received his Ph.D. from Michigan State University, is Associate Professor in the Department of Communication Arts at the University of Wisconsin–Madison. His research interests include the study and modeling of social interaction, cognitive processes in social interaction, and the physiological effects of verbal and nonverbal behaviors.

STARKEY DUNCAN, Jr., is Professor on the Committee on Cognition and Communication at the University of Chicago. He is the author (with Donald Fiske) of *Face-to-Face Interaction.*

RANDALL P. HARRISON is a Research Psychologist at the University of California, San Francisco, and the author of *Beyond Words: An Introduction to Nonverbal Communication, The Cartoon: Communication to the Quick,* and a forthcoming book, *The Nonverbal Dimension.*

RICHARD HESLIN, who received his A M. from Harvard University and his Ph.D. from the University of Colorado at Boulder, is Associate Professor of Psychology at Purdue University. His research interests deal with the aspects of nonverbal behavior that involve intimacy and invasion of privacy. He is co-author (with Miles Patterson) of *Nonverbal Behavior and Social Psychology,* and during 1982-1983 Visiting Professor of Management at Indiana State University.

ADAM KENDON, who received his D.Phil. from Oxford University, has taught at Cornell University, was for some years associated with Bronx State Hospital in New York, and has been a Senior Research Fellow in Anthropology at Australian National University in Canberra. He will be a Visiting Professor of Anthropology at Connecticut College, New London, until 1983. His main interests are in the behavioral organization of face-to-face interaction and gesture and its relationship to spoken language. His current research is concerned with an Australian Aboriginal sign language.

MARK L. KNAPP, who received his Ph.D. from Pennsylvania State University, is Professor of Speech Communication at the State University of New York at New Paltz. His research interests are in interpersonal and nonverbal communication. He is a former president of the International Communication Association, author of *Nonverbal Communication in Human Interaction,* and currently the editor of *Human Communication Research.*

MAUREEN O'SULLIVAN is Professor and Chair, Department of Psychology at the University of San Francisco, and Clinical Professor, University of California, San Francisco (Department of Psychiatry).

JOHN M. WIEMANN, who received his Ph.D. from Purdue University, is Assistant Professor of Communication Studies at the University of California, Santa Barbara. His research interests include communicative competence and nonverbal communication.